BlackBerry® Bold™ FOR DUMMIES®

by Dante Sarigumba
and Robert Kao

WILEY

Wiley Publishing, Inc.

BlackBerry® Bold™ For Dummies®

Published by
Wiley Publishing, Inc.
111 River Street
Hoboken, NJ 07030-5774

www.wiley.com

WILEY

About the Authors

Dante Sarigumba is a long-time user of BlackBerry and a gizmo enthusiast. He is a co-host of the Mobile Computing Authority biweekly podcast. He works for a major investment bank in New York as a software developer and lives in South Brunswick, New Jersey, with his wife, Rosemarie, and two sons, Dean and Drew.

Robert Kao is one well-rounded professional. His ability to translate his technical knowledge and communicate with users of all types led him to co-write *BlackBerry For Dummies* and *BlackBerry Pearl For Dummies.* He started out as a BlackBerry developer for various financial firms in New York City, that truly global city. A graduate of Columbia University, with a Computer Engineering degree, he currently lives in South Brunswick, New Jersey.

Dedication

To Yosma, Dean, and Drew: My greatest treasures. Thank you for your thoughts, understanding, and support.

— Dante Sarigumba

I would like to thank my father (MHK) and mother (SYT) for everything they've done for me. I wouldn't be here without their kindness and support. I would also like to thank my lovely wife, Marie-Claude, and little Jade for all their support.

— Robert Kao

Acknowledgments

Collectively, we want to give a big thanks to Greg Croy for the opportunities to work with the *For Dummies* brand and congratulate him on his retirement! Enjoy it, Greg.

In addition, we'd like to thank the following people:

- ✔ Katie Mohr, our acquisitions editor.
- ✔ Carol McClendon, our agent, for presenting our proposal to the right people.
- ✔ Our editors, for making us look good.

In addition, we thank the rest of the Wiley staff. Without you all, this book would not have been possible.

— Dante & Rob

Publisher's Acknowledgments

We're proud of this book; please send us your comments at www.dummies.custhelp.com. For other comments, please contact our Customer Care Department within the U.S. at 877-762-2974, outside the U.S. at 317-683-3993, or fax 371-572-4002.

Some of the people who helped bring this book to market include the following:

Acquisitions, Editorial, and Media Development

Project Editor: Pat O'Brien

Acquisitions Editors: Katie Mohr, Tiffany Ma

Senior Copy Editor: Teresa Artman

Technical Reviewer: Kevin Michaluk

Editorial Manager: Kevin Kirschner

Editorial Assistant: Amanda Graham

Senior Editorial Assistant: Cherie Case

Cartoons: Rich Tennant
(www.the5thwave.com)

Composition Services

Project Coordinator: Katherine Crocker

Layout and Graphics: Samantha K.Cherolis, Joyce Haughey, Ronald Terry

Proofreaders: Debbye Butler, John Greenough

Indexer: Steve Rath

Publishing and Editorial for Technology Dummies

    Richard Swadley, Vice President and Executive Group Publisher

    Andy Cummings, Vice President and Publisher

    Mary Bednarek, Executive Acquisitions Director

    Mary C. Corder, Editorial Director

Publishing for Consumer Dummies

    Diane Graves Steele, Vice President and Publisher

Composition Services

    Debbie Stailey, Director of Composition Services

Contents at a Glance

Table of Contents

Introduction

*H*i there, and welcome to *BlackBerry Bold For Dummies*. If you already have a BlackBerry Bold, this is a great book to have around when you want to discover new features or need something to slap open and use as a quick reference. If you don't have a Bold yet and have some basic questions (such as "What is a BlackBerry Bold?" or "How can a BlackBerry Bold help me be more productive?"), you can benefit by reading this book cover to cover. No matter what your current BlackBerry user status — BUS, for short — this book helps you get the most out of your BlackBerry Bold.

Right off the bat, BlackBerry Bold isn't a fruit you find at the supermarket but rather is an always-connected handheld device that has e-mail capabilities and a built-in Internet browser. With your BlackBerry Bold, you're in the privileged position of always being able to receive e-mail and browse the Web.

On top of that, a BlackBerry Bold has all the features you expect from a personal organizer, including a calendar, to-do lists, and memos. Oh, and did we mention that a BlackBerry Bold also has a built-in mobile phone? Talk about multitasking! Imagine being stuck on a commuter train: With your BlackBerry Bold by your side, you can compose e-mail while conducting a conference call — all from the comfort of your seat.

That's not all. BlackBerry Bold goes a step further to make it more fun for you to own this device. You can snap a picture with its camera, record a funny video, listen to your music collection, and enjoy watching that video on YouTube.

In this book, you'll find all the basics as well as the extra mile by highlighting some of the lesser-known (but still handy) features of the BlackBerry Bold. Your Bold can work hard for you when you need it to and can play hard when you want it to.

About This Book

BlackBerry Bold For Dummies is a comprehensive user guide as well as a quick user reference. This book is designed so that you can read it cover to cover if you want, but you don't need to read one chapter after the other. Feel free to jump around while you explore the different functionalities of your BlackBerry Bold.

We cover basic and advanced topics, but we'll stick to the most practical and frequently used. If you use or want to use a certain function of your BlackBerry Bold, it's likely covered here.

Who Are You?

In this book, we try to be considerate of your needs. But because I've never met you, my image of you is as follows. If some of these idea are true about you, this may just be the book for you:

- You have a BlackBerry Bold and want to find out how to get the most from it.

- You don't have a BlackBerry Bold yet, and you're wondering what one could do for you.

- You're looking for a book that doesn't assume that you know all the jargon and tech terms used in the PDA industry. (*PDA* stands for *personal digital assistant,* by the way. Take that, you jargon, you!)

- You want a reference that shows you, step by step, how to do useful and cool things with a BlackBerry Bold without bogging you down with unnecessary background or theory.

- You're tired of hauling your ten-pound laptop with you on trips, and you're wondering how to turn your BlackBerry Bold into a miniature traveling office.

- You no longer want to be tied to your desktop system for the critical activities in your life, such as sending and receiving e-mail, checking your calendar for appointments, and surfing the Web.

- You like to have some fun, play games, and be entertained from a device, but don't want to carry an extra game gadget on your bag.

What's in This Book

BlackBerry Bold For Dummies consists of six parts, and each part consists of different chapters related to that part's theme.

Part I: Getting Started with BlackBerry Bold

Part I starts with the basics of your Bold. You know — what it is, what you can do with it, and what the parts are. We describe how you navigate using the QWERTY keyboard. We also show you how to personalize and express yourself through your BlackBerry Bold. This part wraps up with must-knows about security and where to go for help when you get into trouble with your BlackBerry Bold.

Part II: Organizing with Bold

Part II deals with the fact that your BlackBerry Bold is also a full-fledged PDA. We show you how to get your Bold to keep your contacts in Contacts as well as how to manage your appointments and meetings in Calendar. We also show you how to take notes and manage your to-do's using your Bold. And finally, as you'll see, most BlackBerry applications interconnect, working hard for you.

Part III: Getting Online with Your Bold

Part III shows you what made BlackBerry what it is today — always-connected e-mail. We also get into the other strengths of the BlackBerry — Web surfing functionality — but it doesn't stop there. We point out how you can use other forms of messages like text and instant messaging. And while on it, you'll also find unique form of messages on the BlackBerry that you may not have known about, such as PIN-to-PIN messages and BlackBerry Messenger. And rest assured that your BlackBerry will be a good companion when you're traveling; read how to use its GPS capabilities.

Part IV: Music, Pictures, and Movies on Your Bold

You find the fun stuff in Part IV. Rock your world and use your Bold to play music, watch videos, and take pictures. You also get the scoop on how to record videos and sample ring tones. Plus, you get timesaving shortcuts on the Media applications as you go along.

Part V: Working with Desktop Manager and PocketMac

In Part V, you find details about BlackBerry Desktop Manager (BDM) and some of the paces you can put it through with your BlackBerry Bold, including making backups and installing BlackBerry applications from your PC to your Bold. You also find out how to port data from your older devices (BlackBerry or not) to your new Bold. And I didn't forget to cover important stuff, such as data-syncing your appointments and contacts with desktop applications like Outlook. And for Mac users, there's a dedicated chapter that walks you through PocketMac, which you can use for data synchronization between your Mac and Bold.

Part VI: The Part of Tens

All *For Dummies* books include The Part of Tens, and this book is no different. Here, we show you sites where you can get cool BlackBerry Bold accessories and great applications.

Icons in This Book

If a paragraph sports this icon, we're talking about BlackBerry devices provided by your employer.

This icon highlights an important point that you don't want to forget because it just might come up again. We'd never be so cruel as to spring a pop quiz on you, but paying attention to these details can definitely help you.

This book rarely delves into the geeky, technical details, but when it does, this icon warns you. Read on if you want to get under the hood a little, or just skip ahead if you aren't interested in the gory details.

Here's where you find not-so-obvious tricks that can make you a BlackBerry Bold power-user in no time. Pay special attention to the paragraphs with this icon to get the most out of your Bold.

Look out! This icon tells you how to avoid trouble before it starts. Especially trouble that's hard to fix, difficult to change back, really expensive, or totally embarrassing.

BlackBerry Bold devices can use two operating system versions: 4.6 and 5.0. In some cases, the instructions for your Bold depend on your OS. If your Bold uses OS 4.6, follow the instructions in this book with the 4.6 icon and ignore the instructions with the 5.0 icon. (Some features are available only with OS 5.0, so there may not be a matching 4.6 icon.)

Are you an OS 5.0 user? Step this way for red-carpet service, Valued Friend and Customer. You have your own OS 5.0 instructions in the book, and this nifty 5.0 icon to go with them. When you see a 4.6 icon, ignore that information. (Sometimes, you won't even see a similar 4.6 icon because there isn't a similar feature.)

Where to Go from Here

If you want to find out more about the book or have a question or comment, please visit the following:

- ✔ www.BlackBerryForDummies.com
- ✔ www.BlackBerryGoodies.com, where we answer your questions

Now you can dive in! Give Chapter 1 a quick look to get an idea of where this book takes you, and then feel free to head straight to your chapter of choice.

Part I

Getting Started with BlackBerry Bold

The 5th Wave   By Rich Tennant

"I can be reached at home on my cell phone, I can be reached on the road with my pager and PDA. Soon I'll be reachable on a plane with e-mail. I'm beginning to think identity theft wouldn't be such a bad idea for a while."

In this part . . .

The road to a happy and collaborative relationship with your BlackBerry starts here. Chapter 1 covers all the nuts and bolts: how the BlackBerry Bold works, its look and feel, and its connectivity. Chapter 2 describes how to navigate the Bold using the QWERTY keyboard. Chapter 3 discusses customizing your Bold and also offers timesaving shortcuts.

Chapter 1

Your BlackBerry Isn't an Edible Fruit

*B*ecause you're reading this book, you probably have a BlackBerry Bold (and we're pretty sure that you aren't eating it). We're curious, though — what actually convinced you to buy this particular handheld mobile device? Was it the always-connected e-mail, the multimedia player to replace your iPod or iPhone, or a really good sales pitch? The list could go on and on — and we might never hit on the exact reason you got yours. For whatever reason you bought your BlackBerry Bold, congratulations; you made an intelligent choice.

The same smarts that made you buy your BlackBerry Bold are clearly at it again. This time, your intelligence led you to pick up this book, perhaps because your intuition told you there's more to your BlackBerry Bold than meets the eye.

Your hunch is right. Your BlackBerry Bold *can* help you do more than you thought. For example, your BlackBerry Bold is a whiz at making phone calls, but it's also a computer that can check your e-mail and surf the Web. We're talking *World Wide* Web here, so the sky's the limit. Help is always at your fingertips instead of sitting on some desk at home or at the office:

- ✔ Need to check out the reviews of that restaurant on the corner?

- ✔ Need to know — right now — what's showing in your local movie theaters, or what the weather will be like tonight, or what's the best place to shop the sales?

- ✔ Need to know your current location and get directions to that cozy bed-and-breakfast, or retrieve news headlines, or check stock quotes?
- ✔ Want to do some online chatting or view some pictures online?
- ✔ Hankering to network with your old classmates?

You can do all these things (and more) with your BlackBerry Bold.

BlackBerry Bold is also a full-fledged *personal digital assistant (PDA)*. Out of the box, it provides you with the organizational tools you need to set up to-do lists, manage your appointments, take care of your address books, and more.

Being armed with a device that's a phone, an Internet connection, a PDA, a GPS device, and a full-on media player all built into one makes you a powerful person. With your BlackBerry Bold (along with this resourceful book), you really can increase your productivity and become better organized. Watch out, world! BlackBerry Bold-wielding powerhouse coming through!

If you stick with us, you find out all you need to get the most out of your device or maybe even save a troubled relationship. (Well, the last one is a bit of an exaggeration, but we got your attention, right?)

How It All Works: The Schematic Approach

If you always ask, "How do they do that?" you don't have to go far. The following sections are just for you.

The role of the network service provider

Along with wondering how your BlackBerry Bold actually works, you might also be wondering why you didn't get your BlackBerry Bold from RIM (Research In Motion) rather than from a network service provider such as AT&T or Rogers. Why did you need to go through a middle person? After all, RIM makes the BlackBerry Bold.

That's an excellent question, and here's the quick-and-dirty answer: RIM needs a delivery system — a communication medium, as it were — for its technology to work. Not in a position to come up with such a delivery system all by its lonesome, RIM partnered (and built alliances across the globe) with what developed into its network service providers — the big cellphone companies. These middlemen support the wireless network for your BlackBerry

Bold so that you can connect to the BlackBerry Bold Internet service and get all those wonderful e-mails (and spend so much valuable time surfing the Internet). See Figure 1-1 for an overview of this process.

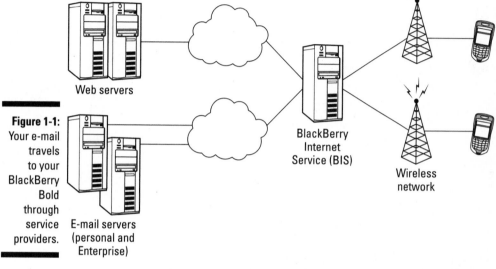

Web servers

Figure 1-1:
Your e-mail
travels
to your
BlackBerry
Bold
through
service
providers.

E-mail servers
(personal and
Enterprise)

BlackBerry
Internet
Service (BIS)

Wireless
network

Network service providers don't build alliances for nothing, right? In return, RIM gave them the right to customize the BlackBerry Bold Firmware and add their carrier version of the Application Center.

Connecting to your computer

Nowadays, a personal computer is a household necessity. You probably spend a lot of time using them, and they hold information you need. No surprise that BlackBerry works hand in hand with your PC. The USB cable that comes with your BlackBerry Bold does more than just charge your device.

Part V helps you use your PC connection with the help of BlackBerry Desktop Manager (BDM) and all the utilities that come with it. For instance, in Chapter 15, you find how to sync your device with the personal information manager (PIM) data that you keep in your PC. You can also read Chapter 17 for directions about switching from another device (even a non–BlackBerry device) to a new BlackBerry Bold. For example, you find out how to import your contact list into your new BlackBerry Bold. Chapter 18 tells you how to protect your data. Last, Chapter 19 talks about installing new applications to your BlackBerry Bold with the help of your PC.

If you have a Mac instead of a PC, you can still sync with the PocketMac Sync on your Mac. RIM doesn't actually support the application but does provide the software for free. Read more in Chapter 16.

Be bold in the world with your BlackBerry Bold

If you got your BlackBerry Bold from AT&T, chances are that your BlackBerry Bold will continue to work when you travel to, say, London or Beijing. All you need to worry about is remembering to turn on your BlackBerry Bold (and maybe the extra roaming charges).

Because your BlackBerry Bold is quad band, it works in more than 90 countries. What is *quad band?* Basically, different cellphone networks in different countries operate on different frequencies. For example, the United States and Canada operate on 850 and 1900 MHz, and Europe and Asia Pacific operate on 900 and 1800 MHz.

Your quad-band BlackBerry Bold is designed to work on 850 MHz, 900 MHz, 1800 MHz, and 1900 MHz, so you're covered almost wherever you go. Check with your network service provider to see whether your BlackBerry Bold will work at your destination before you hop on a plane, just to be sure.

Nothing stands still in this world, and this saying is proven by the fact that Global System for Mobile Communication (GSM) has spawned *High Speed Downlink Packet Access (HSDPA),* which are technologies that have been growing because they work on the same GSM phone infrastructure. This HSDPA is now available in the United States through most major network service providers. HSDPA competes in the marketplace against Code Division Multiple Access's (CDMA) EvDo.

What's all this alphabet soup mean to you? CDMA and GSM aren't compatible. Your phone works on only one technology. When you travel outside North America, you face the burning question: CDMA or GSM? (Read: Will my BlackBerry Bold work on this country's network?)

Your BlackBerry Bold runs on GSM, so you should be okay to travel outside the United States. Most non–North American countries are on GSM networks. If you're a CDMA kind of person, you might have some "issues," as they say. When in doubt, talk to your network service provider.

Know your BlackBerry history

Your BlackBerry Bold is truly a wondrous thing, boasting many features beyond your ordinary mobile phone. And its "sudden" popularity didn't happen overnight. Like any other good product, BlackBerry has come a long way from its (relatively humble) beginnings.

In the days when the PalmPilot ruled the PDA world, RIM was busy in its lab, ignoring the then-popular graffiti input method, and designing a device with a QWERTY keyboard (the kind of keyboard people were already used to from working on their computers). RIM didn't stop there, however. It added an always-connected e-mail capability, making this device a must-have among government officials as well as finance and health professionals.

To meet the needs of government officials and industry professionals, RIM made reliability, security, and durability the priorities when manufacturing its devices. Today, the BlackBerry Bold comes from the same line of RIM family products, inheriting all the good genes while boosting usability and adding more functions to its core BlackBerry applications. As a result, BlackBerry is popular among both _prosumers_ (professional customers) and consumers. Starting with BlackBerry Pearl, RIM has been targeting the mainstream consumer market. Clearly, with BlackBerry Bold, RIM is winning the hearts of consumers while maintaining its hold on the enterprise market.

Oh, the Things You Can Do!

In the BlackBerry world, always-connected e-mail used to be the primary factor that made BlackBerry Bold very attractive and was likely first in the long list of reasons you got yours. And, if you need to go global, you can use your BlackBerry Bold in more than 100 countries. Just hop off your flight, turn on your BlackBerry Bold, and voilà: You can receive and send e-mails whether you're in Hong Kong, London, or Paris. Your significant other can get in touch with you wherever you are — just to say hi or to remind you that you promised Aunt Edna a bottle of Chanel No. 5.

Make sure that your network service provider has the technology to go global. See the preceding section for more info. Generally, you can receive and send e-mails just like you do when you're at home. Whether you have AT&T in the U.S. or Rogers in Canada, your BlackBerry Bold will work if you have a full data and voice plan. Check with your carrier before you start your trip.

Although e-mail and communication is your BlackBerry Bold's strength, that isn't the only thing it can do. The following sections go beyond e-mail to point out some of the device's other major benefits.

All-in-one multimedia center

Previously, many people hesitated to buy a BlackBerry because of the lack of multimedia functions. They wanted a camera and audio and full video play-back. BlackBerry has changed all that and has more features than you may expect. Not only does BlackBerry Bold have a high-resolution 2.0 megapixel camera (see Chapter 12) — but it also has a memory slot for a microSD chip (see Chapter 2). What does that mean?

Well, it means your BlackBerry Bold can function as the following:

- A music player
- A video player and recorder
- A digital camera
- A portable flash drive
- Your personal photo collection

Internet and social networking at your fingertips

Yup, with the new BlackBerry Bold on a 3G network, you can surf the 'Net nearly as smoothly as you do on a desktop computer. You'll get an alert when your stock is tanking. True, that isn't fun, but you want this information as quickly as possible. With your BlackBerry Bold, you can continue chatting with your friends through all types of instant message applications, just as if you never left your desktop PC, and your friends will thank you for persuad-ing them away from buying that losing stock.

Intrigued? Read how BlackBerry Bold can take full advantage of the Web in Chapter 10.

On-the-go GPS

Your BlackBerry Bold comes with an onboard GPS that allows you to pinpoint your location with the BlackBerry Map application and other third-party applications such as Google Maps and TeleNav.

Read more about BlackBerry Bold's built-in GPS in Chapter 11.

Me and my great personal assistant

You might be saying, "But I'm really a busy person, and I don't have time to browse the Web. What I *do* need is an assistant to help me better organize my day-to-day tasks." If you can afford one, by all means go ahead and hire a personal assistant. The next best thing is a personal *digital* assistant (PDA). Just like people come in many flavors, so do many PDAs.

Whip out that BlackBerry Bold of yours and take a closer look. That's right; your BlackBerry Bold is also a full-fledged PDA, helping you do all this and much more:

- ✔ Remember all your acquaintances (Chapter 4).
- ✔ Manage your appointments (Chapter 5).
- ✔ Keep a to-do list (Chapter 6).

A computer in the palm of your hand

Remarkable communication device? Check.

Full-fledged PDA? Check.

Full-featured media player? Check.

These capabilities are just the tip of the iceberg. Don't underestimate the device because of its size: Your BlackBerry Bold is also a powerful computer.

Need convincing? Here goes. Out of the box, with no fiddling, it comes with a great set of organizational and productivity tools. Software developers besides RIM are taking advantage of this growing market, which means that hundreds of applications are out there for you. For example, you can download graphics-intensive games or a mortgage calculator.

Download? Absolutely! BlackBerry Bold supports the downloading of applications through BlackBerry Bold Browser. And of course, downloading the application can be done both wired and wireless (or over the air; OTA). In April 2009, RIM rolled out BlackBerry App World, the company's response to the popular iPhone App Store, which allows BlackBerry owners to easily browse for BlackBerry applications on their device and download them directly. Other third-party BlackBerry application stores are tremendously popular in the BlackBerry community, such as the CrackBerry.com App Store powered by MobiHand. (For more information on downloading third-party applications, see Chapter 19.)

What's the difference between BlackBerry App World and BlackBerry Application Center?

- ✔ BlackBerry Application Center most likely came with your BlackBerry Bold.

  Application Center contains only applications that your network service provider want you to see.

- ✔ App World needs to be manually downloaded by you from RIM's Web site.

  App World has an unfiltered list of BlackBerry applications for you

Look, Dad! No hands!

Your BlackBerry Bold is equipped with a sleek stereo headset that doubles as a mic for hands-free talking. This accessory is your doctor's prescription for preventing the stiff neck that comes from wedging your BlackBerry Bold against your ear with your shoulder. At the minimum, it helps free your hands so that you can eat Chinese takeout. Some places require you by law to use an earphone while driving (but only when you're talking on a cellphone, of course).

Avoid using your cellphone while driving, hands-free or not.

But RIM didn't stop with just your standard wired earphones. BlackBerry Bold also supports cool wireless earphones based on Bluetooth technology. How could a bizarrely colored tooth help you here? *Bluetooth* is the name for a (very) short-distance wireless technology that connects devices. See Chapter 7 for how to connect your BlackBerry Bold to a Bluetooth headset.

Putting a sentry on duty

The virtual world isn't exempt from general human nastiness; in fact, every day a battle is fought between those trying to attack a system and those trying to protect it.

A computer connected to the Internet faces an extra risk of being cracked by a hacker or infected by a virus. (Viruses try to replicate themselves and generally bug you.)

Saving power

Anyone with previous BlackBerry experience knows typically, BlackBerry is a highly efficient power consumer. With the older BlackBerry, you can go for five days on a single charge.

The addition of a color, high-resolution screen, GPS, and Bluetooth support has weakened the power efficiency. Power requirements have increased so much that you need to recharge roughly every two days. But hey, now you have a GPS on deck!

Fortunately, security is a BlackBerry strong point. Viruses often come as e-mail attachments. However, BlackBerry supports very few file types out of the box (mostly images and documents). You won't face threats from e-mails with these attachments. And in an enterprise environment, the data that you send to or get from the PDA is *encrypted* (coded) to prevent snooping.

RIM also has a Signature process for application developers that forces developers to identify themselves and their programs if they're developing any applications for the BlackBerry that need to integrate with either BlackBerry core applications or the OS.

Remember the *I love you* and *Anna Kournikova* viruses? These are virtual evils transmitted through e-mail, scripts, or sets of instructions in the e-mail body or attachment that can be executed either by the host e-mail program — or, in the case of an attachment, by the program associated with the attached file. Fortunately, BlackBerry's Messages doesn't support scripting languages. BlackBerry's viewer for such files doesn't support scripting either, so you won't be facing threats from e-mails having these attachments.

The security measures that RIM implemented on the BlackBerry platform have gained the trust of the U.S. government as well as many of the Forbes Top 500 enterprises in the financial and health industries.

Chapter 2

Navigating the BlackBerry Bold

*R*egardless of whether you previously owned a BlackBerry, you might have heard that the new BlackBerry Bold is totally different. You might be wondering how you spot a new BlackBerry Bold. Looks aren't deceiving in this case. From the outside, the new BlackBerry Bold is a lot slimmer than older BlackBerry handhelds. The new design has a brighter and higher-resolution screen. Bear with us and you will be master of your BlackBerry Bold in no time.

Anatomy 101: The Body and Features of Your BlackBerry Bold

In this and the following sections, we show you all the keys and features on your BlackBerry Bold. Figure 2-1 shows the primary ones.

First, the major features:

- ✔ **Display screen:** The graphical user interface (GUI) on your BlackBerry Bold.
- ✔ **QWERTY keyboard:** The input for your BlackBerry Bold — very straightforward.
- ✔ **Escape key:** Use this key to cancel a selection or return to a previous page within an application. If you hold this key down, it returns you to the Home screen from any program.
- ✔ **Menu key:** Use this key to display the full menu of the application you're using.

Mute

End/Power

Volume Keys

Figure 2-1:
Main
features
on a
BlackBerry
Bold.

Left Convenience key

Alt

Send

Menu

Trackball

Escape

Symbols

Shift

Enter

Speakerphone

✔ **Trackball:** Navigate the display screen with the trackball. It allows you four directional movements. When you press the trackball, the short menu of the application you're using appears.

✔ **Convenience keys:** With BlackBerry Bold, you have one or two convenience keys. By default, the convenience keys are preprogrammed to open an application.

In Chapter 3, we show you how to reprogram the convenience keys so that they display the programs you use the most.

✔ **microSD slot:** The BlackBerry Bold has a microSD slot opening next to the left convenience key.

✔ **Send key:** Because your BlackBerry Bold can also function as a cellular phone, this key allows you to go straight to the Phone application, regardless of which application you are currently using. When you are already in the Phone application, the Send key starts dialing the number you entered.

✔ **End key:** While on a phone call, use this key to end your call. If not on a phone call, this key allows you to jump straight back to the Home screen from wherever you are.

✔ **Power key:** Press and hold the Power key to turn your BlackBerry Bold on or off.

✔ **Mute key:** Mutes a call when on a call.

Two types of contextual menus can appear on your BlackBerry Bold, as shown in Figure 2-2.

✔ **Full menu:** Lists all the options and features you can perform. The full menu is accessed by pressing the Menu key.

✔ **Short menu:** An abbreviated list of the full menu (Figure 2-2). The short menu is accessed by pressing the trackball when you aren't prompted by a dialog box.

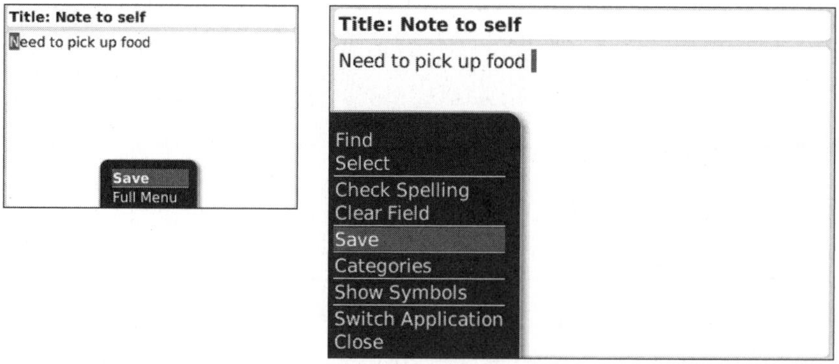

Figure 2-2:
Examples
of a short
menu and
full menu in
the Memo
application.

Title: Note to self

Need to pick up food

Save
Full Menu

Title: Note to self

Need to pick up food

Find
Select
Check Spelling
Clear Field
Save
Categories
Show Symbols
Switch Application
Close

Display screen

When you first turn on your BlackBerry Bold, the display screen displays the *Home screen,* which is your introduction to the interface of your BlackBerry Bold. The different icons represent the different applications found in your BlackBerry Bold. See Figure 2-3 for an example of what your Home screen might look like.

Figure 2-3: Your BlackBerry Bold might come with a Home screen like this.

(36) Messages

Depending on the theme you're using, you might see your applications listed in text form rather than as icons. Remember that how your GUI looks depends on how you want it to look because the font and theme are customizable. For more on personalizing your BlackBerry Bold, see Chapter 3.

QWERTY keyboard

Unlike some PDA manufacturers — and they know who they are — RIM (Research In Motion) chose the same QWERTY keyboard you know and love from your personal computer as the BlackBerry Bold input method. That was a great decision because it means that you don't have to master some new way of writing — graffiti or whatever — to get data into your BlackBerry Bold. All you have to do is type on a familiar keyboard — and you already know how to do that.

Whether you use your pinky or your index finger, how you type on your BlackBerry Bold is up to you. However, most people find that typing with two thumbs is the most efficient method.

Escape key

Simple yet useful, the Escape key allows you to return to a previous screen or cancel a selection. The Escape key is the arrow key to the right of the trackball.

Trackball

You can perform two functions with the trackball: scrolling and pressing. When you scroll with your trackball, you can navigate the display screen in four directions. In a text-filled screen, such as the body of an e-mail, you can usually navigate through the text in four directions.

Depending on where you are on the BlackBerry Bold's screen, different situations determine what happens when you press the trackball, also called the *trackball click:*

- ✔ **Display a drop-down list.** When you're in a choice field, pressing the trackball displays a drop-down list of choices for that field.

- ✔ **Confirm a choice.** The trackball can also function as a confirmation key. For example, when you need to select a choice in a drop-down list, you can press the trackball to confirm the highlighted choice.

- ✔ **Display a short menu.** When you're in a text-filled screen (e-mail body or Web page), pressing the trackball displays a short menu (refer to Figure 2-2, right), which is just an abbreviated version of the full menu. You get the full menu by pressing the Menu key.

Menu key

The Menu key brings up the full menu for the application you're using. When on the Home screen, pressing the Menu key displays a list of applications installed on your BlackBerry Bold. If you want to change the order of the applications in the list, see Chapter 3.

When on the Home screen, the behavior of the Menu key depends upon the BlackBerry Bold theme. The behavior just described is based on the default theme. See Chapter 3 for more on changing themes.

The microSD slot

Your BlackBerry Bold comes with 1GB of internal memory. If you're a music or video fan, you know that 1GB can't keep you entertained for a long commute. But no need to worry. The folks at RIM incorporated a microSD slot into your BlackBerry Bold so that you can add extended memory and store all the media files you want.

You can purchase a microSD card separately for a relatively low price these days. At the time of this writing, a 4GB microSD card costs about $10 to $15.

Your BlackBerry's microSD compatibility depends on its operating system:

- ✔ OS 4.6 supports up to 16GB of microSD capacity.
- ✔ OS 5.0 supports up to 32GB of microSD capacity.

General Navigation Guidelines

In this section, we go over general shortcuts and navigation guidelines. On a Web page or an e-mail full of text, you can perform the tasks listed in Table 2-1.

Table 2-1	Bold Keyboard Shortcuts
Press This . . .	**To Do This . . .**
T	Move to top of page.
B	Move to bottom of page.
Space key	Move to top of next page.
Press and hold the Shift key, and scroll the trackball horizontally.	Select a line.
Press and hold the Shift key, and scroll the trackball vertically.	Select multiple lines.
Press and hold the Shift key, and press the trackball.	Copy selected text.
Press and hold the Shift key, and press the Delete key.	Cut selected text.
Press and hold the Shift key, and press the trackball.	Paste text.
A letter key, and scroll the trackball	Insert accented character.
Sym key and press the letter below the symbol.	Insert symbol.
Alt and right Shift key	Caps lock
Alt and left Shift key	Num lock

Switching applications

When you're navigating in an application, an option called Switch Application appears when you press the Menu key. Switch Application (similar to Alt+Tab in Windows) lets you multitask between applications (see Figure 2-4).

If you have OS 5.0 on your Bold, the quickest way to get to Switch Application is by pressing and holding the Menu key for 2 seconds.

Figure 2-4:
Switch
Application
menu.

If you're using OS 4.6, switch applications by pressing the Alt and Escape keys. (The Alt key is located to the left of the Z key, and the Escape key is the arrow key to the right of the trackball.)

If you always use a particular application, such as Tasks, you can program the convenience key so that you can get to your favorite application even more quickly than by using the Switch Application function.

Changing options

Throughout this book, you see examples of an options field being changed to a different value. The easiest way to change the value in a field is to first use the trackball to scroll to the field. Then press the trackball to display a drop-down list of choices (see Figure 2-5), and finally press the trackball again on your choice.

Figure 2-5:
An example
of an option
field's drop-
down list.

General Keyboard Shortcuts

In many instances in this book, when you're asked to go to a BlackBerry Bold application (Profile, for example), you have to first scroll to it from the Home screen, and then click the trackball. You may be thinking, "Hey, there must be a shortcut for this," and you're right. This section and the ones that follow cover such general keyboard shortcuts, all in the name of making your life easier. (Shortcuts that are more application-specific are covered in the chapter dealing with the particular application.)

Before you get all excited about shortcuts, you need to take care of one bit of housekeeping. To use some of these general keyboard shortcuts, you first have to make sure that the Dial from Home Screen setting — buried deep within the Phone application — is turned off.

Inquiring minds want to know, so we'll tell you. The Dial from Home Screen option is designed for users who make frequent BlackBerry Bold phone calls. If you aren't a frequent phone user and want to access all applications with a press of a button, get ready to ditch Dial from Home Screen.

Here's how to turn off the Dial from Home Screen setting:

1. **From the BlackBerry Bold Home screen, highlight the Phone application, and then press the trackball.**

2. **Press the Menu key, and then select the Options icon.**

    A screen that lists a range of options appears.

3. **Select General Options.**

    The General Options screen appears.

4. **Highlight the Dial from Home Screen field, and then select No.**

    Doing so shuts down the Dial from Home Screen option, enabling you to use Home screen shortcuts.

5. **To confirm your changes, press the trackball, and then select Save from the menu that appears.**

If you're a frequent phone user on your BlackBerry Bold, as opposed to an e-mail or Internet user, you may not want to turn off the Dial from Home Screen feature.

Using Home screen shortcuts

When you disable the Dial from Home Screen feature, you are free to use any Home screen shortcut. (The name for these shortcuts is actually a pretty good fit because you can use these shortcuts only while you are on the Home screen.)

Okay, here goes. To call up the application listed in the first column of Table 2-2, press the key listed in the table's second column.

Table 2-2	Home Screen Shortcuts
Application	*Shortcut Key*
Messages	M
Saved Messages	V
Compose	C
Search	S
Contacts	A
Tasks	T
Profile	F
Browser	B
Calendar	L
Calculator	U
MemoPad	D
Keyboard Lock	K
Phone	P

Other (non-Home screen) shortcuts

The following shortcuts can be used at any time, regardless of which screen you're in — or whether you have Dial from Home Screen enabled, for that matter:

- **Soft Device Reset (also known as the *3-Button Salute*):** Pressing Alt+ Shift+Del forces a manual soft reset, which is just what you need when your BlackBerry Bold crashes or when you install an application and it needs a manual reset. A hard reset can be done by pulling out the battery from the back of the BlackBerry Bold. Without getting into the technical jargon, from a BlackBerry Bold user's perspective, a hard reset takes longer and is usually the last resort to solve any issues before contacting the help desk.

- **HelpME:** In the BlackBerry Bold world, SOS is actually spelled Alt+Shift+H. Use it when you're on the phone with technical support. (It gives support personnel info such as your BlackBerry Bold PIN, memory space, and version number so that they have information about your BlackBerry Bold when they try to troubleshoot your problems.)

Your BlackBerry PIN isn't a security password; rather, it is a unique number that identifies your BlackBerry Bold, sort of like a serial number. But unlike a serial number, you can message another BlackBerry by using PIN-to-PIN messages (please see Chapter 9).

Chapter 3

Turning On Your BlackBerry Bold — And Keeping It Happy

. . . .

In This Chapter

▶ Putting your stamp on your BlackBerry Bold

▶ Watching your BlackBerry Bold's back

▶ Blocking spam e-mail and unwanted SMS messages

. . . .

*R*egardless of how long you've had your BlackBerry Bold — one week, one month, one year, or five years — you'll want to have it around for as long as you possibly can. (Or, at least until you have the bucks for that way-cool new model that's surely coming down the pike.) And, for the duration that you *do* have your device, you'll want to trick it out so that your BlackBerry Bold doesn't feel and sound exactly like the millions of other BlackBerry Bold devices out there. (C'mon, admit it — your BlackBerry Bold is definitely a fashion statement, so you better feel comfortable with what that statement is saying.)

In addition to customizing your BlackBerry Bold so that it expresses the inner you, you want to make sure that you keep your BlackBerry Bold in tip-top shape by watching out for such things as its battery life and information security. Luckily for you, this chapter puts any and all such worries to rest by filling you in on all you need to know to keep your BlackBerry Bold a finely tuned (and yet quirkily personal) little smartphone.

Your wish is our command. Follow the tips and techniques outlined in the following sections and you, too, can have your very own personalized BlackBerry Bold.

Making Your BlackBerry Bold Yours

BlackBerry smartphones are increasingly popular, so much so that close to 30 million BlackBerry smartphones are out there serving the needs of people like you. Because of this fact, we're certain that finding ways to distinguish your BlackBerry Bold from your colleagues' is high on your list of priorities.

BlackBerry OS by the numbers

At the time of publication, there are two different BlackBerry OS versions that can run on the BlackBerry Bold:

✓ BlackBerry OS 4.6

✓ BlackBerry OS 5.0

To find the BlackBerry OS version you're running, select the BlackBerry Options tool icon, and then select About. In the About screen, you see the number of the BlackBerry OS version that you are running:

✓ v4.6.x.xxx

✓ v5.0.x.xxx

Many of the screens and features for OS 4.6 and OS 5.0 are the same. Where there are differences in this book, you see an icon for OS 4.6 or OS 5.0. Use the instructions for your operating system, and skip the instructions for the other system.

Branding your BlackBerry Bold

Like any number of other electronic gadgets that you could possibly own, your BlackBerry Bold comes to you off the shelf fitted with a collection of white-bread factory settings. This section helps you put your name on your BlackBerry Bold, figuratively and literally. You can start by branding your name on your BlackBerry Bold. Follow these steps:

1. **Press the Menu key, scroll to the Options icon, and then press the trackball.**

2. **Scroll through the list of options until you find the Owner setting; then press the trackball.**

   You see places to enter your owner information.

3. **Enter your name in the Name field and your contact information in the Information field.**

   The idea here is to phrase a message (like the one shown in Figure 3-1) that would make sense to any possible Good Samaritan who might find your lost BlackBerry Bold and want to get it back to you.

   If you lock or don't use your BlackBerry Bold for a while, the standby screen comes on, displaying the owner information that you entered. Read how to lock your BlackBerry Bold, either manually or by using an auto setting, in the later section "Keeping Your BlackBerry Bold Safe."

4. **Confirm your changes by pressing the trackball and then choosing Save from the menu that appears.**

Owner
Name: Robert Kao
Information:
If found, please contact rob@robkao.com

Thank you.

Figure 3-1:
List your
owner info
here.

Choose a language, any language

Branding your BlackBerry Bold with your own John Hancock is a good start, but setting the language to your native tongue so that you don't need to hire a translator to use your BlackBerry Bold is equally important — and equally easy. You can also set your input method of choice here, which can affect whether AutoText shows up. Don't worry. We explain what that means in the next section.

Here's how you choose a language:

1. **Press the Menu key, scroll to the Options (wrench) icon, and then press the trackball.**

2. **Scroll through the list of options until you find the Language setting, and then press the trackball.**

   Here you can choose the language and input method of your choice.

3. **Select the Language field, and then scroll the drop-down menu to select your native tongue.**

   Depending on your network provider, as well as what region (North America, Europe, and so on) you're in, the language choices you have can vary. Most handhelds sold in North America default to English or English (United States).

   If your network provider supports it, you can install more languages into your BlackBerry Bold by using Application Loader in BlackBerry Bold Desktop Manager (BDM). For more information on Application Loader, see Chapter 19.

4. **Confirm your changes by pressing the trackball, and then choosing Save.**

   Isn't it great when you can actually read what's onscreen? But don't think that you're finished quite yet. You still have some personalizing to do.

Typing with ease using AutoText

Even the most devoted BlackBerry Bold user has to admit that typing on a full keyboard is easier than thumb-typing on a BlackBerry Bold. In an attempt to even the score a bit, your BlackBerry Bold comes equipped with an AutoText feature, which is a kind of shorthand that can cut down on how much you have to type.

AutoText basically works with a pool of abbreviations that you set up. You then just type an abbreviation to get the word you associated with that abbreviation. For example, after setting up *b/c* as an AutoText word for *because,* anytime you type **b/c**, you automatically get *because* onscreen.

Your BlackBerry Bold comes with a few default AutoText entries. Here are some useful ones:

  ✔ **mypin:** Displays your BlackBerry PIN

  ✔ **mynumber:** Displays your BlackBerry phone number

  ✔ **myver:** Displays your BlackBerry model number and OS version

The whole AutoText thing works best if you set up your own personal code, mapping your abbreviations to their meanings. (This is why we discuss AutoText as part of personalization.)

To set up your own code, do the following:

1. **From the Home screen, press the Menu key, scroll to the Options icon, and then press the trackball.**

2. **Scroll to the AutoText option, and then press the trackball.**

   Here, you can choose to see (or search for) existing AutoText words or create new ones.

3. **Press the Menu key, scroll to New, and then press the trackball.**

   The AutoText screen appears, as shown in Figure 3-2.

4. **In the Replace field, enter the characters that you want to replace (in this example, *b/c*). In the With field, type what replaces your characters (in this example, *because*).**

5. **In the Using field, choose between the SmartCase and Specified Case options.**

   • *SmartCase* capitalizes the first letter when the context calls for that, such as the first word in a sentence.

   • *Specified Case* replaces your AutoText with the exact text found in the With field.

For example, say you have the AutoText *bbg* set up for the term *black-berryGoodies.com* and you want it to appear as is, in terms of letter cases (the first *b* isn't capitalized). If you were to choose SmartCase for this particular AutoText, it would be capitalized as the first word in a sentence, which isn't what you want. On the other hand, if you use Specified Case, your AutoText always appears as *blackberryGoodies.com* no matter where it is in the sentence.

6. **Scroll to the Language field, and then select All Locales from the list of options.**

   Our preference for this setting for any self-created AutoText is All Locales. What this means is that regardless of the language input method (for example, English U.K., English U.S., or French), any self-created AutoText is available for you to use. So, in the case of the AutoText *bbg* (BlackBerryGoodies.com), whether you are typing in French or Chinese, you can use this AutoText. On the other hand, if you select only the French input method for *bbg* as the Language field, you would be able to use this only if your input method is set to French in the Language option.

   You can choose the input method in the Language options. We go over choosing a language input method next.

7. **Confirm your changes by pressing the trackball, and then choosing Save.**

If you specify a language input method other than All Locales, your input method setting in the Language option must match the Language field in AutoText to use your newly created AutoText. Follow these steps:

1. **Press the Menu key, scroll to the Options icon, and then press the trackball.**

2. **Scroll through the list of options until you find the Language setting; then press the trackball.**

   Here you can choose the language and input method.

3. **Select the Input Method field, and then select the input method you need from the list.**

   For your new AutoText setting to work (assuming that you didn't choose All Locales as the language for your AutoText), this option needs to match the input method set in your Language option.

4. **Confirm your changes by pressing the trackball, and then choosing Save.**

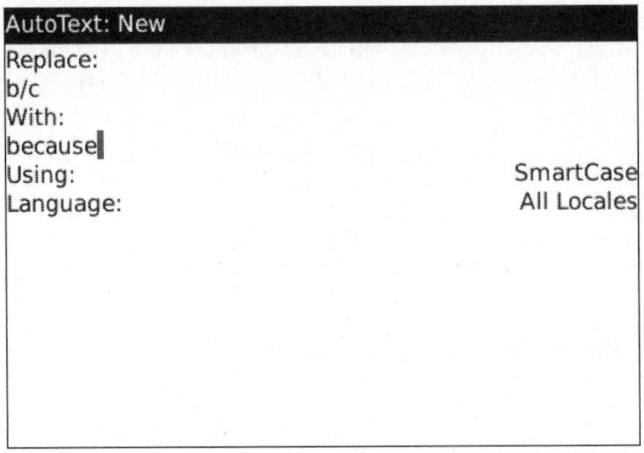

```
AutoText: New
Replace:
b/c
With:
because
Using:                                    SmartCase
Language:                                 All Locales
```

Figure 3-2:
Create
AutoText
here.

Getting your dates and times lined up

Having the correct date, time, and time zone is important when it comes to your BlackBerry Bold for, we hope, obvious reasons. Many of the fine features that make up the BlackBerry Bold core experience, as it were, depend on the time, date, and time zone being accurate.

Need an example? How about your BlackBerry Bold calendar events? Imagine, if you will, that you have a make-or-break meeting set for 9 a.m. (in your time zone) with a client in Paris, France, who is in who-knows-what time zone. You definitely want to be on time for that appointment, but you probably won't be if you're planning on having your BlackBerry Bold remind you — that is, if you haven't set up the appropriate date, time, and time zone. Follow these steps to do that:

1. **Press the Menu key, scroll to the Options icon, and then press the trackball.**

2. **Scroll to the Date/Time setting, and then press the trackball.**

   The Date/Time screen appears.

3. **Scroll to your time zone, and then press the trackball.**

   The Date/Time screen confirms the time zone that you chose.

4. **Scroll to the Time field and use the trackball to adjust the proper hour and minutes.**

5. **Scroll to the Date field and use the trackball to adjust the date appropriately.**

6. Scroll to the Date/Time Source field, and then press the trackball.

This sets your date and time source to your service provider's server time. See Figure 3-3.

7. To confirm your changes, press the Menu key, and then select Save.

Doing so saves your date and time settings in perpetuity — a really long time, in other words.

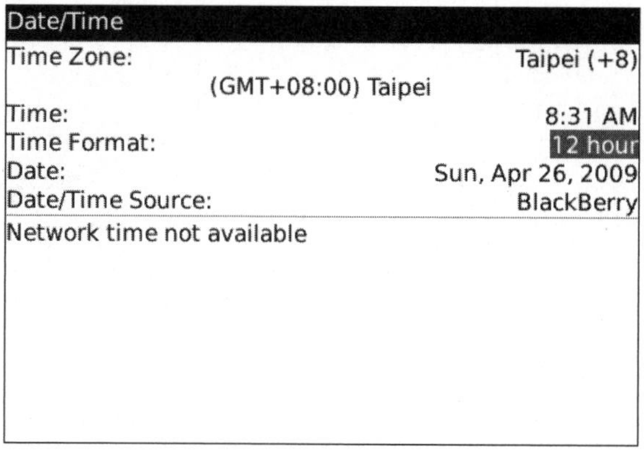

Date/Time	
Time Zone:	Taipei (+8)
(GMT+08:00) Taipei	
Time:	8:31 AM
Time Format:	12 hour
Date:	Sun, Apr 26, 2009
Date/Time Source:	BlackBerry
Network time not available	

Figure 3-3:
Set the date and time of your BlackBerry Bold.

Customizing your screen's look and feel

Right up there with making sure that your date and time settings are accurate is getting the display font, font size, and screen contrast to your liking. Now we know that some of you don't give a hoot if your fonts are Batang or Bookman as long as you can read the text, but we also know that some of you won't stop configuring the fonts until you get them absolutely right. For all you tweakers out there, here's how you play around with your BlackBerry Bold's fonts:

1. Press the Menu key, scroll to the Options icon, and then press the trackball.

2. Scroll to the Screen/Keyboard setting, and then press the trackball.

The Screen/Keyboard screen appears with various customizable fields, as shown in Figure 3-4.

3. Highlight the Font Family field, and then select a font from the drop-down list.

You can choose from three to ten fonts, depending upon your provider.

```
Screen/Keyboard
Font Family:                              BBAlpha Sans
Font Size:                                          7
Font Style:                                     Plain
The quick brown fox jumps over the lazy dog.
Backlight Brightness:                             100
Backlight Timeout:                            30 Sec.
Automatically Dim Backlight:                       On
LED Coverage Indicator:                            On
Key Tone:                                         Off
Key Rate:                                      Normal
Currency Key:                                       $
Right Side Convenience Key Opens:    Default (Camera)
Left Side Convenience Key Opens:              Nothing
Trackball
```

Figure 3-4:
The Screen/
Keyboard
screen,
waiting for
personaliza-
tion.

4. **Continuing down the Screen/Keyboard screen, highlight the Font Size field, and then select a font size.**

   One thing to keep in mind is that the smaller the font size, the more you can see onscreen; however, a smallish font is harder on the eyes.

   Note: As you scroll up and down the list of fonts and font sizes, notice that the text The quick brown fox jumps over the lazy dog in the background takes on the look of the selected font and size so that you can preview what the particular text looks like. (In case you were wondering, this sentence uses every letter in the alphabet.)

5. **Confirm your changes by pressing the Menu key, and then selecting Save.**

Similar to setting Font Size, you can also play with Font Style to set it to Bold, Italic, or Plain.

With fonts out of the way, it's time to change the brightness of your screen as well as a few other viewing options, including how to program the Convenience key to exactly what is convenient to you:

1. **Press the Menu key, scroll to the Options icon, and then press the trackball.**

2. **Scroll to the Screen/Keyboard setting and then press the trackball.**

   The Screen/Keyboard screen appears with its various customizable fields. (Refer to Figure 3-4.)

3. **Highlight the Backlight Brightness field, and then select the desired brightness from the drop-down list.**

   You can choose from 0 to 100, where 0 is the darkest and 100 is the brightest.

4. **Highlight the Left Side Convenience Key Opens field, and then select what you want your left-side key to open when you press it.**

   Your BlackBerry Bold comes with left and right Convenience keys; you can perform Step 4 for both the left- and right-side Convenience keys.

5. **Select the Backlight Timeout field, press the trackball, and choose the amount of time for the backlight timeout.**

   You can choose from ten seconds up to two minutes. The lower this setting, the less time you'll have backlighting (after you press each key). However, a low setting helps you conserve battery life.

When you're outdoors with a bright sun on your BlackBerry Bold, you'll probably have difficulty reading your BlackBerry Bold screen. With your BlackBerry Bold, you can have "Automatically Dim Backlight" features turned on so that it autoadjusts the backlight to be bright enough for you to read your BlackBerry Bold while outdoors. This feature is on by default.

6. **Highlight the Trackball Horizontal Sensitivity field, and then select how sensitive you want the trackball to be horizontally.**

   You can choose from 20 to 100, where 20 is the least sensitive and 100 is the most sensitive.

7. **Highlight the Trackball Vertical Sensitivity field, and then select how sensitive you want the trackball to be vertically.**

   Again, 20 is the least sensitive, and 100 is the most sensitive. Keep in mind that if your trackball is too sensitive, it will be hard to control.

8. **To confirm your changes, press the Menu key and select Save.**

Choosing themes for your BlackBerry Bold

Your BlackBerry Bold is preloaded with different *themes,* which are predefined sets of looks (wallpaper, fonts, menu layout). You can download themes from BlackBerry Bold's mobile Web site.

Follow these steps to change your theme:

1. **Press the Menu key, and then select the Options icon.**

2. **Select the Theme setting.**

   You see a list of available themes.

3. **Scroll to and select the theme you want.**

   You see a preview of the theme you selected. See Figure 3-5.

4. **Press the Menu key, and then select Activate.**

   You should be able to see the change immediately.

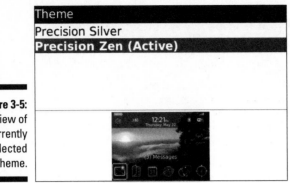

Figure 3-5: Preview of currently selected theme.

You can download other themes. Just remember that you have to use your BlackBerry Bold, not your PC, to access the following URL:

▮ ✔ http://mobile.blackberry.com

Wallpaper for your BlackBerry Bold

Like your desktop PC, you can customize the BlackBerry Bold Home screen with personalized wallpaper. You set an image to be your BlackBerry Bold Home screen background by using the BlackBerry Bold Media application. Follow these steps:

1. **From the Home screen, press the Menu key, and then select the Media application.**

   In Media are these categories: Music, Video, Ring Tones, and Pictures.

2. **Scroll to and select the Picture category.**

   Doing so brings up two folders: The Preloaded Media folder stores pictures that came with your BlackBerry Bold, and the Device Memory folder stores pictures that you took with your camera.

3. **Scroll to and select one of the folders.**

   This lists all the pictures in the folder.

4. **Select the picture you want to use for your Home screen background.**

   The selected picture appears in full-screen view.

5. **Press the Menu key, and then select Set as Home Screen Image.**

   The picture is now your new Home screen wallpaper.

6. **Press and hold the Escape key (to the right of the trackball) to return to the Home screen and see the result.**

You can download free wallpapers from the following Web sites (as long as you use your BlackBerry Bold, not your PC, to access the URLs):

✔ http://mobile.blackberry.com

✔ www.blackberrywallpapers.com

✔ www.crackberry.com/free-wallpapers

After you have your BlackBerry Bold's look and feel just the way you want, there's just one thing left to do before you can move on. You need to get your BlackBerry Bold to sound how you want it to.

Let freedom ring

The whole appeal of the BlackBerry Bold phenomenon is the idea that this little electronic device can make your life easier. One of the ways it accomplishes this is by acting as your personal reminder service — letting you know when an appointment is coming up, a phone call is coming in, an e-mail has arrived, and so on. Basically, your BlackBerry Bold is set to bark at you if it knows something it thinks you should know, too. Figure 3-6 lists the kinds of things your BlackBerry Bold considers bark-worthy, ranging from browser alerts to tasks deadlines.

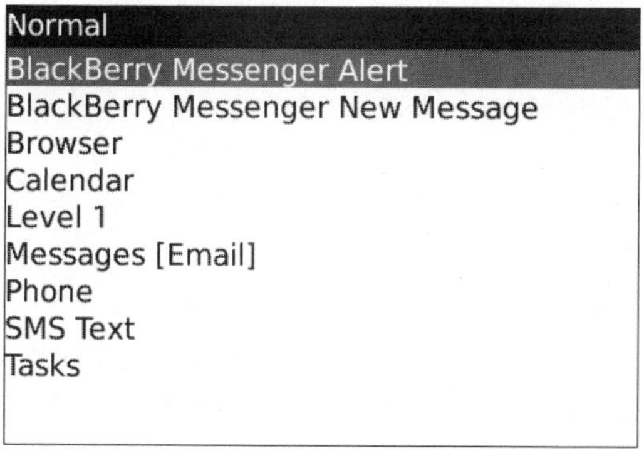

Figure 3-6: Set attention-needy applications here in OS 4.6 (left) and OS 5.0 (right).

Normal
BlackBerry Messenger Alert
BlackBerry Messenger New Message
Browser
Calendar
Level 1
Messages [Email]
Phone
SMS Text
Tasks

Different people react differently to different sounds. Some BlackBerry Bold barks would be greatly appreciated by certain segments of the population, whereas other segments might react to the same sound by pitching their BlackBerry Bold under the nearest bus. The folks at Research In Motion are well aware of this and have devised a great way for you to customize how you want your BlackBerry Bold to bark at you — they call it your *profile*.

You can jump right into things by using a predefined profile, or you can create your own profile. The upcoming sections take a look at both approaches.

Whether you create your own profile or customize a predefined profile, each profile is divided into several categories that represent the application for which you can define alerts.

In BlackBerry OS 4.6, the application to set your profiles is named Profiles and includes the following categorizations:

- ✔ **BlackBerry Messenger Alert:** Alerts you when BlackBerry Messenger has something to notify you regarding new contact notification.

- ✔ **BlackBerry Messenger New Message:** Alerts you when BlackBerry Messenger has a new message from a BlackBerry Messenger contact.

- ✔ **Browser:** Alerts you when you receive a new *channel push,* which is just a Web page sent to your BlackBerry Bold.

- ✔ **Calendar:** Alerts you when you have upcoming appointments.

- ✔ **Level 1 (urgent e-mail messages):** Alerts you with a special tone when you have an urgent e-mail: urgent, as defined by your sender. Also, a BlackBerry PIN-to-PIN message can be considered urgent. For more on PIN-to-PIN, see Chapter 9.

- ✔ **Messages [Email]:** Alerts you when a new e-mail message is in your inbox.

- ✔ **Phone:** Alerts you if you have an incoming call or a new voice mail.

- ✔ **SMS Text:** Alerts you when you have an SMS message.

- ✔ **Tasks:** Alerts you of an upcoming to-do deadline.

In BlackBerry OS 5.0, profiles can be found in the Sounds application, and Sound items are organized into the following categories:

- ✔ **Phone:** Alerts you if you have an incoming call or voice mail.

- ✔ **Messages:** Alerts you if you have an incoming e-mail, SMS, MMS, or BlackBerry PIN messages. Also, you can set different alerts for each individual e-mail account.

- ✔ **Instant Messages:** Alerts you if you have any BlackBerry Messenger Alerts; if you have third-party instant message installed (such as Google Talk), you can set the alerts here as well.

- ✔ **Reminders:** Alerts you if you have set up calendar reminders, tasks reminders, or e-mail Follow Up Flags (see Chapter 8).

- ✔ **Other:** Alerts you when there is a new browser channel message or other third-party applications. See Chapter 10.

You can personalize all the listed applications (such as Sound, in Figure 3-7) according to how you want to be alerted. Because how you customize them is similar, we use one application, Messages, as an example in the text that follows.

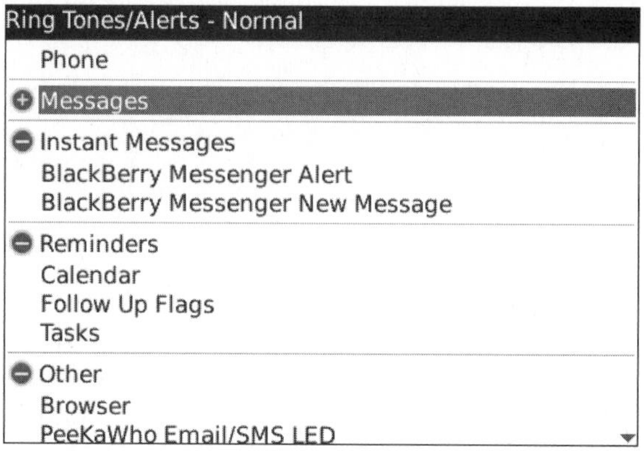

Ring Tones/Alerts - Normal

Phone

⊕ Messages

⊖ Instant Messages
   BlackBerry Messenger Alert
   BlackBerry Messenger New Message

⊖ Reminders
   Calendar
   Follow Up Flags
   Tasks

⊖ Other
   Browser
   PeeKaWho Email/SMS LED

Figure 3-7: Custom ring tones and alerts in the Sound application in OS 5.0.

After this, we go over creating a profile from scratch. You may be wondering why you need to create a profile if you can personalize the predefined ones. If you like to keep the predefined settings the way they are, creating a profile is the way to go.

Using factory settings

If you're okay with customizing a predefined, factory-loaded profile, just do the following if you have OS 4.6:

OS 4.6

1. **From the BlackBerry Bold Home screen, select the Profile application.**

   A pop-up screen appears, listing different profiles (Quiet, Vibrate, Normal).

2. **Scroll to the end of the list and select Advanced.**

   A screen appears listing different profiles.

3. **Scroll to the Normal profile in the list, press the Menu key, and then select Edit.**

   The Normal screen appears, listing the applications with alert capabilities mentioned in the preceding section. (Refer to Figure 3-6.)

4. **Select the Messages [Email] application.**

   You're faced with the Messages for Normal profile, which is divided into an Out of Holster section and an In Holster section, as shown in Figure 3-8. A *holster* (in this context) is simply the belt clip or case that houses your BlackBerry Bold while you aren't using it. BlackBerry Bold is smart enough to know when it is in a holster. With RIM's BlackBerry holster, a magnet built into the holster will autoswitch you to the in-holster mode within the selected profile.

   You can choose another application and follow the next steps to personalize the other applications listed in each profile.

Messages [Email] in Normal
Out of Holster:	Vibrate+Tone
Ring Tone:	BBPro_Sanguine
Volume:	Mute
Number of Beeps:	1
Repeat Notification:	LED Flashing
Number of Vibrations:	2
In Holster:	Vibrate
Ring Tone:	BBPro_Sanguine
Volume:	Mute
Number of Beeps:	1
Repeat Notification:	LED Flashing

Figure 3-8: Choose a tone to alert you when your BlackBerry Bold is out of its holster.

5. **Highlight the Out of Holster field, and then select a tone from the drop-down list of alert options.**

Doing so enables sound in the Out of Holster mode.

6. **Highlight the Ring Tone field, and then select the tune you like from the drop-down list.**

As you scroll through the tunes and pause, your BlackBerry Bold plays the tune so that you know what it sounds like before you change it.

7. **Press the Menu key, and then select Save.**

As you may have guessed from how Messages in the Normal profile is divided, your BlackBerry Bold can notify you in different ways based on whether your BlackBerry Bold is in plain view (Out of Holster) or tucked away next to your belt (In Holster). To set up a different sound for In Holster mode, just put the necessary info in the fields for the In Holster section — and be sure to choose a different tune this time. (Choosing the same tune kind of defeats the purpose, doesn't it?)

If you're like us and get more than 200 e-mails daily, you probably don't want your BlackBerry Bold sounding off 200 times a day. You can set up your BlackBerry Bold so that it notifies you only if an e-mail has been marked as urgent, requiring your immediate attention. You can do this by setting the notification for your Messages application to None for both In Holster and Out of Holster. Then in the Level 1 option (refer to Figure 3-6), you can set your desired notification for both In Holster and Out of Holster. That way, you conveniently filter out any unnecessary e-mail notifications, leaving just the urgent stuff to sound off to you.

For BlackBerry OS 5.0, follow these steps to customize alerts for BlackBerry Messenger:

1. **From the BlackBerry Bold Home screen, select the Sounds application.**

   A pop-up screen appears, listing different profiles (Silent, Vibrate, Normal, Loud, Medium, Phone Calls Only, All Alerts Off).

2. **Scroll to the end of the list and select Edit Profiles.**

   A screen appears listing different profiles.

3. **Scroll to the Normal profile in the list, press the Menu key, and then select Edit.**

   The Normal screen appears, listing the applications with alert capabilities mentioned in the preceding section. (Refer to Figure 3-6.)

4. **Expand Messages and select any of the e-mail accounts you have.**

   A screen appears with options to set ring tone, LED, and vibration. See Figure 3-9 for OS 5.0.

   For Ring Tone, here are the following options you can set:

   - *Ring Tone:* You can specify the ring tone sound you want.

   - *Volume:* Here you specify how loud you want the ring tone to be. It ranges from Silent to 10, 10 being the loudest.

   - *Count:* Number of times the ring tone repeats, ranges from 1 to 3.

   - *Play Sound:* Here you can specify whether the ring tone will play while your BlackBerry Bold is in or out of holster or always play.

   For LED, you can set it to be On or Off.

   For vibration, you can set it to be On, Off, or Custom. If you choose Custom, the following Options present themselves:

   - *Length:* You can set how long each vibration lasts: Short, Medium, or Long.

   - *Count:* Number of times the vibration will occur; you can pick from 1, 2, 3, 5, and 10.

   - *Vibrate:* Here you can specify whether the vibration will occur while your BlackBerry is in or out of holster or always vibrate.

5. **Press the Menu key, and then select Save**

Creating your own profile

You need to know which applications on your BlackBerry Bold have alert capabilities because you can then personalize each "Hey, you!" to your liking. You can have your BlackBerry Bold so personalized that you can tell whether you have a phone call or an incoming message just by how your BlackBerry Bold sounds.

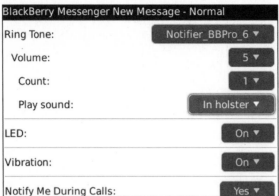

Figure 3-9:
Set ring
tones and
alerts for
Messages
in OS 5.0.

If you're already familiar with the different applications and are clear how you want each one to alert you, go on and create your own profile. As we mention earlier, you can achieve the same result by personalizing the predefined profiles that come with your BlackBerry Bold. But if you like to keep the predefined profiles the way they are, create a new profile by following the steps for your OS version.

If you have OS 4.6, follow these steps to create a new profile:

1. **From the BlackBerry Bold Home screen, select the Profile application.**

   A pop-up screen appears, listing different profiles (Quiet, Vibrate, Normal).

2. **Scroll to the end of the list and select Advanced.**

   A screen appears listing different profiles.

3. **Press the Menu key, and then select New.**

   A new Profile screen appears, as shown in Figure 3-10, prompting you to name your profile.

4. **In the Name field, enter a name for your profile.**

   For this example, just type **My Profile**.

5. **Configure your new profile.**

   Refer to Steps 3–7 of the previous section to customize each one of the seven applications.

6. **Press the Menu key, and then select Save.**

   Your newly created profile appears in the Profile screen.

7. **Select My Profile.**

   You can start to use your newly created profile.

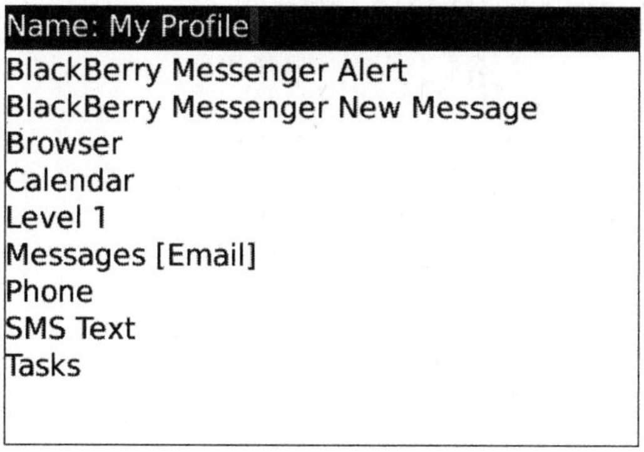

```
Name: My Profile
BlackBerry Messenger Alert
BlackBerry Messenger New Message
Browser
Calendar
Level 1
Messages [Email]
Phone
SMS Text
Tasks
```

Figure 3-10: Create your own profile from this menu in OS 4.6.

If you have OS 5.0, follow these steps to create a new profile:

1. **From the BlackBerry Bold Home screen, select the Sound application.**

   A pop-up screen appears, listing different profiles.

2. **Scroll to the end of the list and select Edit Profiles.**

   A screen appears with a line Add Custom Profile and also listing different profiles.

3. **Select Add Custom Profile.**

   A New Custom Profile screen appears, as shown in Figure 3-11, prompting you to name your profile.

4. **In the Name field, enter a name for your profile.**

   For this example, just type **My Profile**.

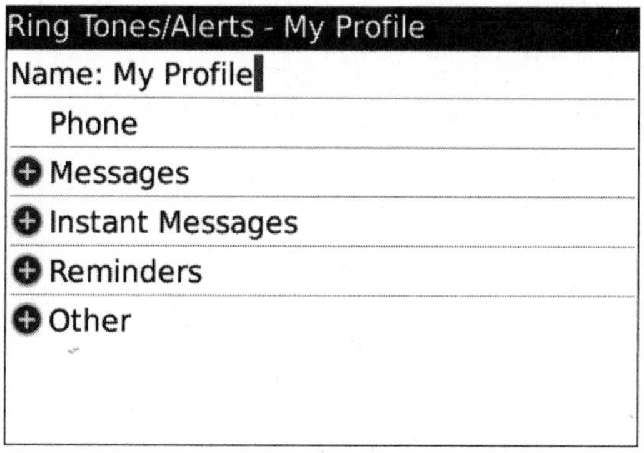

```
Ring Tones/Alerts - My Profile
Name: My Profile
   Phone
⊕ Messages
⊕ Instant Messages
⊕ Reminders
⊕ Other
```

Figure 3-11: Create your own custom profile here in OS 5.0.

5. **Configure your new profile.**

Refer to Steps 3–7 of the previous section to customize each one of the categories of applications.

6. **Press the Menu key, and then select Save.**

Your newly created profile appears in the Profile screen.

7. **Select My Profile, as shown in Figure 3-12.**

You can start to use your newly created profile.

You can switch between your current profile and the Quiet profile by pressing and holding the # key.

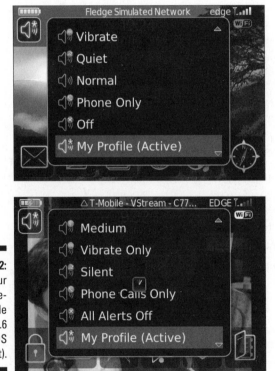

Figure 3-12: See your newly created profile in OS 4.6 (left) or OS 5.0 (right).

Regardless of whether the ring tone is for an incoming call or an incoming e-mail, you can download more ring tones to personalize your BlackBerry Bold. Also, you can use any MP3 files in your Media application as your personalized ring tone. Follow these steps:

1. **From the Home screen, press the Menu key, and then select the Media application.**

2. **In Media, select the Music category.**

   Doing so brings up folders named Preloaded Media and Device Memory. If you have a microSD card inserted, you also see the Media Card folder.

3. **Select one of the folders.**

   This lists all the music in this folder.

4. **Highlight the music file you want to use for your ring tone.**

5. **Press the Menu key, and then select Set as Phone Tune.**

   This sets the music file as your new phone tune.

6. **Press and hold the Escape key (to the right of the trackball) to return to the Home screen.**

Keeping Your BlackBerry Bold Safe

The folks at RIM take security seriously, and so should you. Always set up a password on your BlackBerry Bold. If your BlackBerry Bold hasn't prompted you to set up a password, you should immediately do so. Here's how it's done:

1. **From the BlackBerry Bold Home screen, select the Options (wrench) icon.**

2. **Select the Password option.**

3. **Highlight the Password field, and then select Enabled.**

   All this does for now is enable the Password feature. You won't be prompted to type a password until you save the changes you just made.

4. **Click the Set Password button.**

   At this time, you should be prompted to enter a new password, as shown in Figure 3-13.

   If you have set a password before, the button will be called Change Password.

5. **Type a password, and then type it again for verification.**

   From this point on, whenever you lock your BlackBerry Bold and want to use it again, you have to type the password. How do you lock your BlackBerry Bold? Good question. Keep reading.

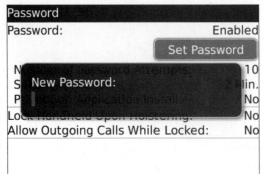

Figure 3-13:
It's time to
enter a new
password.

When you set your password on a BlackBerry Bold, you must make sure that you know what letters your password uses and not just which keys you pressed. You need the same password if you link your BlackBerry Bold with BlackBerry Bold Desktop Manager for synchronization. For more on BlackBerry Bold Desktop Manager, read Chapters 15, 16, 18, and 19.

Setting up your password is a good first step, but just having a password won't help much if you don't take the further step of locking your BlackBerry Bold when you aren't using it. (You don't want people at the office or sitting at the next table at the coffee shop checking out your e-mails or phone history when you take a bathroom break, do you?) So, how do you lock your BlackBerry Bold? Let us count the ways. . . . we came up with two.

You can go the Autolock after Timeout (also known as Security Timeout) route by following these steps:

1. **From the BlackBerry Bold Home screen, select the Options icon.**

2. **Select the Password option.**

   The Password screen appears.

3. **Highlight the Security Timeout field, and then select the desired minutes.**

   The preset times range from 1 minute to 1 hour.

4. **Press the Menu key, and then select Save.**

If you're more the hands-on kind of person, you can go the Manual Lockout route by scrolling to the keyboard Lock icon on your Home screen and pressing the trackball. (Pressing K while at the Home screen does the same thing. Make sure to turn off the Dial from Home Screen option. See Chapter 2 for more info on using Home screen shortcuts.)

As a shortcut, to lock your BlackBerry Bold, just press and hold the asterisk (*) key.

No matter what route you take to lock your BlackBerry Bold, you use your (newly created) password to unlock it when you get back from wherever you've been.

Block That Spam

With your BlackBerry Bold, you can block certain e-mails, SMS numbers, or BlackBerry PINs from getting to your inbox. It's like having your own spam blocker on your BlackBerry Bold!

To set up your personal spam blocker, follow these steps:

1. **From the BlackBerry Bold Home screen, select the Options icon.**

2. **Select the Security option.**

3. **Highlight the Firewall option and press the trackball.**

   This opens the Firewall screen.

4. **Highlight the Status field and select Enable.**

   This enables the spam blocker.

5. **Under Block Incoming Message, make sure what you want to block is selected:**

   • *SMS:* Blocks SMS messages.

   • *PIN:* Blocks BlackBerry PIN messages.

   • *BlackBerry Internet Service:* Blocks e-mail messages (for example, the e-mail account that you set up from Google or Yahoo! Mail).

   • *Enterprise Email:* Blocks enterprise e-mail (if you're in a corporate e-mail network).

6. **In the Except Messages From area, select the desired options:**

   • *Contact:* Blocks everything except the e-mails and phone numbers in your Contacts.

   • *Specific Address:* Blocks everything specified by you (you can set up the list below).

7. **Press the Menu key and select Configure Exception.**

   This opens the Firewall exception screen.

8. Press the Menu key and select the desired options:

- *Add Email:* Specify the e-mail you want to block by selecting this check box.

- *Add PIN:* Specify the BlackBerry Bold PIN you want to block by selecting this check box.

- *Add Phone Number:* Specify the SMS number you want to block by selecting this check box.

Part II
Organizing with Bold

The 5th Wave
By Rich Tennant

In this part . . .

This part covers how to use your BlackBerry Bold to its fullest to get — and keep — you organized. Peruse the chapters here to find out how to use Contacts, keep appointments, keep on track with to-do lists, and keep your passwords safe and easy to retrieve.

Chapter 4

Remembering and Locating Your Acquaintances

A ddress books were around long before the BlackBerry was conceived. And BlackBerry Bold Contacts serves the same function as any address book: a place where you record and organize information about people. However, Contacts also affords you a central place to reach your contacts in myriad ways: by landline phone; cellphone; e-mail; or the speedy messaging of PIN, SMS, MMS, or BlackBerry Messenger.

Most likely, in your busy lifestyle, you can benefit from using your BlackBerry Contacts if any of the following fit:

✔ You travel.

✔ You meet clients frequently.

✔ You spend a lot of time on the phone.

✔ You ask people for their phone number or e-mail address more than once.

✔ You carry around a paper day planner.

✔ Your wallet is full of important business cards, with phone numbers written on the backs, that you can never find.

If you're one of those stubborn folks who insist they don't need an address book — "I'm doing just fine without one, thank you very much!" — think of it this way: You've probably been using a virtual address book all the time: the one buried in your cellphone. That address book probably isn't even a very good one! Read this chapter to see how to transfer all that good contact info from an old phone into your new BlackBerry-based Contacts.

Accessing Contacts

The Contacts icon looks like an old-fashioned address book. (Remember those?) You can see it highlighted in Figure 4-1. Opening Contacts couldn't be simpler: Highlight the Contacts icon and press the trackball.

Figure 4-1:
The
Contacts
icon.

You can also access Contacts from Phone, Messages, BlackBerry Messenger, and Calendar. For example, say you're in Calendar and you want to invite people to one of your meetings. Look no further — Contacts is in the menu, ready to lend a helping hand.

Another way to get to Contacts is by pressing A while on the Home screen. Go to Chapter 2 for more on Home screen shortcuts.

Working with Contacts

Getting a new gizmo is always exciting because you just know that your newest toy is chock-full of features you're dying to try out. Imagine having a new BlackBerry Bold, for example. The first thing you'll want to do is try to call or e-mail someone, right? But wait a sec. You don't have any contact information yet, which means you have to type in someone's e-mail address each time you send an e-mail — what a hassle.

It's time to get with the plan. Most of us humans — social creatures that we are — maintain a list of contacts somewhere, like an e-mail program, on an old cellphone, or on a piece of paper kept tucked away in a wallet. We're pretty sure that you have some kind of list somewhere. The trick is getting that list into your BlackBerry Bold so that you can access your info more efficiently. The good news for you is that getting contact info into your BlackBerry Bold isn't hard.

Often, the simplest way to get contact information into your BlackBerry Bold is to enter it manually. However, if you've invested a lot of time and energy in maintaining some type of Contacts application on your desktop computer, you may want to hot-sync that data into your Bold. For more on synchronizing data, check Chapter 15.

Creating a contact

Imagine that you just ran into Jane Doe, an old high school friend whom you haven't seen in years. Jane is about to give you her number, but you don't have a pen or pencil handy to write down her information. Are you then forced to chant her phone number to yourself until you can scare up a writing implement? Not if you have your handy BlackBerry Bold on you.

With BlackBerry in hand, follow these steps to create a new contact:

1. **On the BlackBerry Home screen, select the Contacts application.**

   As we mention earlier, you can also access Contacts from different applications. For example, see Chapter 7 to find out how to access Contacts from Messages.

2. **In Contacts, highlight Add Contact, and then press the trackball.**

   The New Contact screen appears, as shown in Figure 4-2.

3. **Enter the contact information in the appropriate fields.**

   Use your BlackBerry Bold keyboard to enter this information. Scroll down to see more of the contact fields.

   When entering an e-mail address, press the Space key to insert an at symbol (@) or a period (.). BlackBerry is smart enough to figure out that you need an @ or a period.

   We don't think you can overdo it when entering a person's contact information. Enter as much info as you possibly can. Maybe the benefit won't be obvious now, but when your memory fails you or your boss needs a critical piece of info that you happen to have, you'll thank us for this advice.

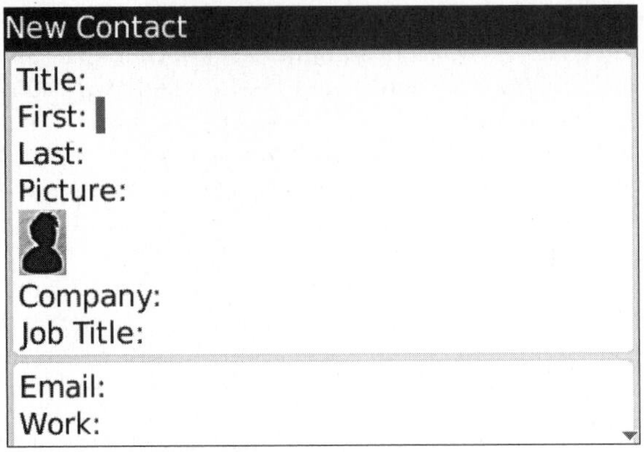

New Contact
Title:
First: |
Last:
Picture:

Figure 4-2:
Create a
new contact
here.

Company:
Job Title:

Email:
Work:

4. **(Optional) For those contacts who have more than one e-mail address —
say, work and home — just create another new, blank E-mail field for the
same contact.**

You can have up to three e-mail addresses per contact.

   a. Press the Menu key.

   b. Select Add Email Address.

5. **Press the trackball, and then select Save.**

You should see your new contact added to the list, as shown in Figure 4-3.

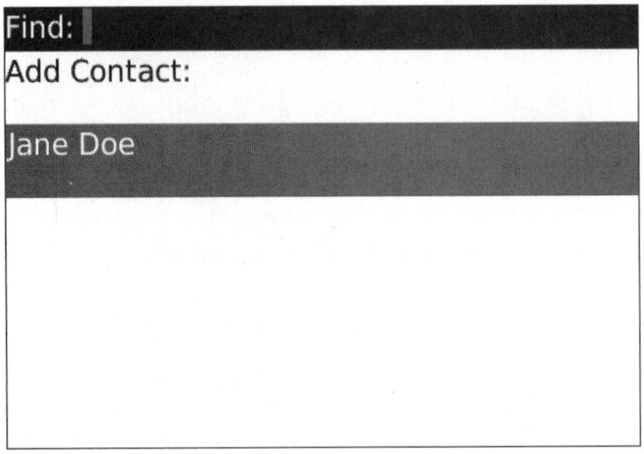

Find: |
Add Contact:

Jane Doe

Figure 4-3:
The
Contacts
screen after
adding a
contact.

Here's something slick to know when you're entering phone information for a
contact: BlackBerry Bold can also dial an extra number after the initial phone
number. That extra number can be someone's extension, or a participant
code on a conference number, or simply your voice mail PIN. When you're
entering the contact's phone number, type the primary phone number, press

the Alt key and press X, and then add the extension number. Say you enter 11112345678X1111; when you tell your Bold to call that number, it will dial 11112345678 first. Then you'll see a prompt asking you to continue or skip dialing the extension.

The menu is always available through the Menu key, but just for convenience, we prefer to use the trackball, which displays a shortened menu list based on where you are.

Adding notes

The Notes field on the New Contact screen (you may need to scroll down a bit to see it) is useful for adding a unique description about your contact. For example, use the field to hold info to jog or refresh your memory with tidbits such as *Knows somebody at ABC Corporation* or *Can provide introduction to a Broadway agent.* Or perhaps your note is something personal, such as *Likes golf; has 2 children: boy, 7, & girl, 3; husband's name is Ray.* It's up to you. Again, the more useful the information, the better it will serve you.

Customizing with your own fields

Perhaps you'd like to add contact information that doesn't fit into any of the available fields. Although you can't really create additional fields from scratch, you can commandeer one of the User fields for your own purposes.

The User fields are located at the bottom of the screen; you have to scroll down to see them. Basically, you can use these fields any way you want (which is great), and you can even change the field's name. (Face it, *User field* isn't that helpful as a descriptive title.) For example, you can rename User fields to capture titles that follow a name (such as MD, PhD, and so on). Or how about profession, birth date, hobbies, school, or nickname? When it comes down to it, you decide what information is important to you.

Changing the field name for this particular contact changes it for all your contacts.

To rename a User field, follow these steps:

1. **Scroll to the bottom of the screen to navigate to one of the User fields.**

2. **Press the Menu key, and then select Change Field Name.**

   The Change Field Name selection on the menu appears only if the cursor is in a User field.

3. **Use the keyboard to enter the new User field name.**

4. **Press the trackball or the Enter key to save.**

   You're all set.

Adding a picture for a contact

Like most phones, your BlackBerry Bold can display a picture of the caller. Here's how to add a photo for a contact:

1. **Have access to a digital picture of the person.**

   See Chapter 12 for more about taking photos with your BlackBerry Bold.

2. **Get the photo to your BlackBerry Bold.**

   You can send it via e-mail, copy it to the microSD card, or copy it to the built-in memory of Bold. If you don't know how to use the microSD, Chapter 13 is your gateway to media satisfaction.

3. **From the Home screen, select the Contacts icon.**

4. **Highlight a contact.**

5. **Press the Menu key, and then select Add Picture (see Figure 4-4).**

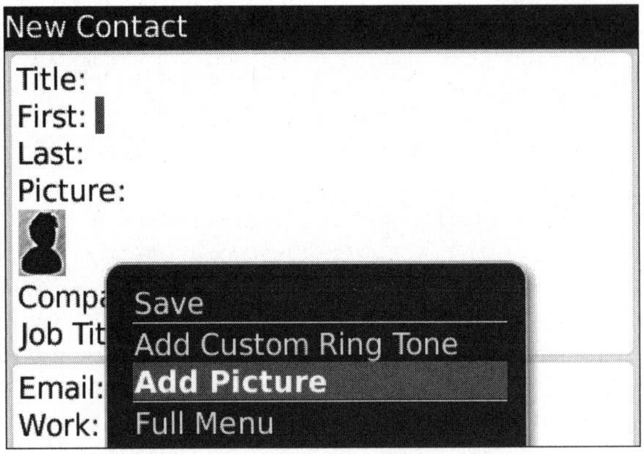

New Contact

Title:
First:
Last:
Picture:

Comp Save
Job Tit Add Custom Ring Tone
  Add Picture
Email: Full Menu
Work:

Figure 4-4:
Add a
picture
here.

6. **Use the trackball to navigate to the drive and folder that contain the picture.**

   You can use multiple locations for storing media files, such as pictures. Chapter 12 gives you the scoop.

7. **Select the picture.**

   The picture you choose is displayed in full onscreen with a rectangle on it.

8. **Scroll the trackball to position the rectangle on the face.**

   Contacts uses a tiny image, just enough to show the face of a person. The rectangle you see here indicates how the application crops the image.

9. **Press the trackball, and then select Crop and Save.**

   You're all set. Just save this contact to keep your changes.

10. **Press the Menu key, and then select Save.**

Assigning a tone

Oh, no, your ringing Bold has woken you. Ring tones help you decide whether to ignore the call or get up. Hopefully, you can easily switch to Sleep mode if you decide to ignore the call.

If you have OS 4.6, follow these steps to assign a ring tone to one of your contacts:

1. **While editing a contact, press the trackball, and then select Add Custom Ring Tone from the menu (refer to Figure 4-4).**

2. **Press the trackball.**

   A screen similar to Figure 4-5 gives you an option to customize the ring tone settings. From this screen, you can select a ring tone; set the volume; and control whether to make the LED blink, the phone vibrate, and the settings work while on a call.

3. **Select the ring tone you want.**

4. **Press the Menu key, and then select Save.**

If you have OS 5.0, follow these steps to assign a ring tone to one of your contacts:

1. **While editing a contact, scroll to the Ring Tones/Alerts section.**

   Under the Ring Tones/Alerts section, you should see Phone and Messages. You can customize the ring tone when you receive a call and when you have a new message such as e-mail or SMS.

2. **Select Phone.**

   Customize the ring tone on the screen that follows. You will see and be able to change the following options:

   • *Ring Tone:* You select from a list of ring tones here.

   • *Volume:* Allows you to control the volume. The default is set to use the Active Profile settings. Other values are from 1 to 10; 10 is the loudest.

   • *Play Sound:* Lets you control in what state to play the tone. Values are Active Profile, In holster, Out of holster, and Always; the default is set to Active Profile, which uses the settings on the Active Profile.

   • *LED:* Allows you to use LED to indicate a call. Displays only if you have work address information filled up. This allows you to map the location using Maps.

- *Vibration:* Allows you to enable vibration as a way of notification. Choices are Active Profile, Off, On, and Custom. The default is Active Profile. Choosing Custom allows you to control how long you want the vibration to last.

- *Vibrate with Ring Tone:* Allows you to choose between vibration and play the tone. Choices are Active Profile, On, and Off. The default value is Active Profile.

3. **Press the Escape key.**

   You're back to the Edit Contact screen.

4. **Select Messages.**

   You'll be presented with the Messages screen, allowing you to customize the ring tone when you receive a message.

   All the customization that you can do is the same as in Step 2 except for this addition:

   - *Notify Me During calls:* Allows you toggle notification while you are actively on a call. Your choices are Yes or No, and it defaults to No.

5. **Press the Escape key.**

6. **Press the Menu key, and then select Save.**

 Spend a little bit of time adding your own contact record(s). We recommend adding at least one record for your business contact info and one for your personal contact info. This saves you time having to type your own contact information every time you want to give it to someone. You can share your contact record by sending it as an attachment to an e-mail. (See the later section, "Sharing a Contact.")

Adding contacts from other BlackBerry applications

When you get an e-mail message or a call, that person's contact information is in Messages or Phone. It's just logical to add the information. You may have noticed that Phone lists only outgoing numbers. That's half of what you need. You can access incoming phone calls in Messages:

1. **On the BlackBerry Home screen, select Messages.**

2. **In Messages, press the Menu key, and then select View Folder.**

3. **Select Phone Call Logs.**

A phone log entry stays only as long as you have free space on your BlackBerry Bold. When BlackBerry runs out of space (which could take years, depending on how you use it), it deletes read e-mails and phone logs, starting from the oldest.

You can view your device memory information by going to Options from the Home screen and selecting Memory. The next screen shows you two types of memory, Application Memory and Media Card. Pay close attention to Application Memory. This is where your applications are installed, including data from out of the box applications like Contacts, Messages, and Calendar. Your Bold has 128MB total Application Memory, and you should see how much is free from this screen.

Creating a contact from an existing e-mail address or phone number in Messages is easy:

1. **On the BlackBerry Home screen, select Messages.**

2. **In Messages, select the e-mail address or the phone number.**

3. **From the menu that appears, select Add to Contacts.**

   A New Contact screen appears, filled with that particular piece of information.

4. **Enter the rest of the information you know.**

5. **Press the Menu key, and then select Save.**

The best solution for capturing contact information from e-mail is an application called gwabbit. The app has the intelligence of detecting any contact information and gives you a quick and easy way to add them to Contacts. You can purchase gwabbit for $9.99 a year, and download the app from their Web site at www.gwabbit.com.

Viewing a contact

Okay, you just entered your friend Jane's name into your BlackBerry, but you have this nagging thought that you typed the wrong phone number. You want to quickly view Jane's information. Here's how you do it:

1. **On the BlackBerry Home screen, select Contacts.**

2. **In Contacts, scroll to and highlight the contact name you want, and then press the trackball.**

   Pressing the trackball or the Enter key while a name is highlighted is the same as opening the menu and choosing View — just quicker.

   View mode displays only information that's been filled in, as shown in Figure 4-5. It doesn't bother showing blank fields.

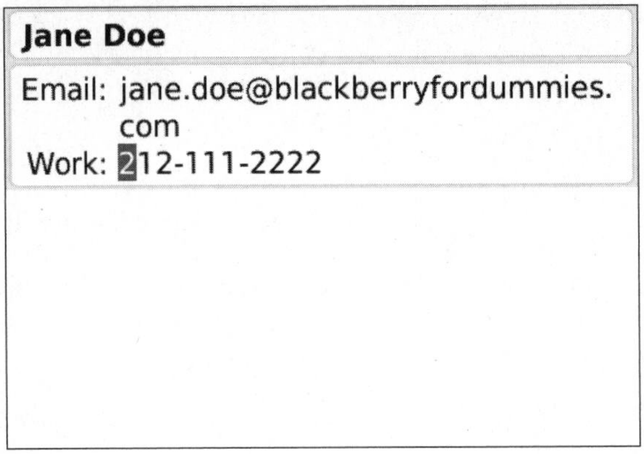

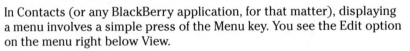

Jane Doe

Email: jane.doe@blackberryfordummies.
com
Work: 212-111-2222

Figure 4-5:
View mode
for a
contact.

Editing a contact

Change is an inevitable part of life. Given that fact, your contact information is sure to change as well. To keep current the information you diligently put in Contacts, you have to do some updating now and then. To update a contact, follow these steps:

1. **On the BlackBerry Home screen, select Contacts.**

2. **In Contacts, scroll to and highlight a contact name, press the Menu key, and then select Edit.**

   The Edit Contact screen for that contact makes an appearance.

   In Contacts (or any BlackBerry application, for that matter), displaying a menu involves a simple press of the Menu key. You see the Edit option on the menu right below View.

3. **Scroll through the various fields of the Edit Contact screen, editing the contact information as you see fit.**

   If you want to edit only a few words or letters in a field (instead of replacing all the text), scroll the trackball while pressing and holding the Alt key (located to the left of the Z key) to position your cursor precisely on the text you want to change. Then make your desired changes.

4. **Press the Menu key, and then select Save.**

   The edit you made for this contact is saved.

When you're editing information and you want to totally replace the entry with a new one, it's much faster to first clear the contents, especially if you have a lot of old data. When you are in an editable field (as opposed to a selectable field), just press the Menu key, and then select Clear Field. This feature is available in all text-entry fields and for most BlackBerry applications.

Deleting a contact

It's time to get rid of somebody's contact information in your Contacts. Maybe it's a case of duplication or a bit of bad blood. Either way, BlackBerry Bold makes it easy to delete a contact.

1. **On the BlackBerry Home screen, select Contacts.**

2. **In Contacts, scroll to and highlight a contact name you want to delete, press the Menu key, and then select Delete.**

   A confirmation screen appears, as shown in Figure 4-6.

3. **Select Delete.**

   The contact you selected is deleted and disappears from your contact list.

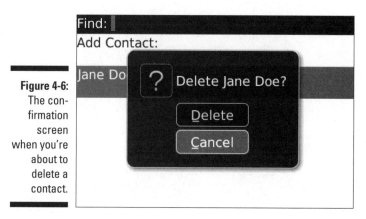

Figure 4-6: The confirmation screen when you're about to delete a contact.

Dealing with the confirmation screen can be a pain if you want to delete several contacts in a row. If you are 100 percent sure that you want to ditch a number of contacts, you can suspend the Confirmation feature by setting the Confirm Delete option to No on the Contacts Options screen. See the "Setting preferences" section, later in this chapter, for more on Contacts Options.

Copying Contacts from Desktop Applications

Most people use desktop applications to maintain their contacts — you know, Microsoft Outlook, IBM Lotus Notes, or Novell GroupWise. And a word to the wise: You don't want to maintain two address books. That's a recipe for disaster. Luckily for you, RIM (Research In Motion) makes it easy to get your various contacts — BlackBerry, desktop, laptop, whatever — in sync.

Your BlackBerry Bold comes with a collection of programs, BlackBerry Desktop Manager (BDM). One of the BDM programs is Synchronize. You can use Synchronize to

✔ Sync between your device and the PC software for managing contacts like Outlook.

✔ Set up and configure the behavior of the program, including how the fields in the desktop version of Contacts map to the Contacts fields in your BlackBerry.

Chapter 15 shows how to use Synchronize.

Looking for Someone?

Somehow — usually through a combination of typing skills and the shuttling of data between various electronic devices — you've created a nice, long list of contacts in Contacts. Nice enough, we suppose, but useless unless you can find the phone number of Rufus T. Firefly at the drop of a hat.

That's where the Find screen comes in. In fact, the first thing you see in Contacts when you open it is the Find screen, as shown in Figure 4-7.

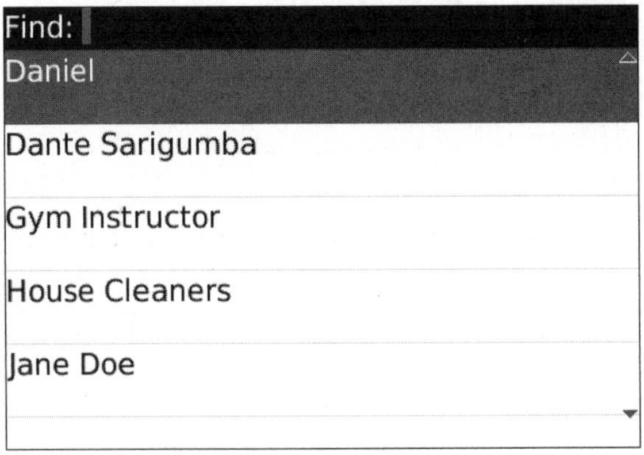

Find:
Daniel

Dante Sarigumba

Gym Instructor

House Cleaners

Figure 4-7:
Your search
starts here.

Jane Doe

You can conveniently search through your contacts by following these steps:

1. **In the Find field, enter the starting letters of the name you want to search for.**

   Your search criterion is the name of the person. You could enter the last name or first name or both, although the list is usually sorted by first name, and then last name. As you type the letters, the list shrinks based on the matches. Figure 4-8 illustrates how this works.

2. **Using the trackball, scroll and highlight the name from the list of matches.**

   If you have a long list in Contacts and you want to scroll down a page at a time, just hold down the Alt key (it's located to the left of the Z key) and scroll. You get where you need to go a lot faster.

3. **Press the Menu key and select from the possible actions listed on the menu that appears.**

   After you find the person you want, you can select from these options, as shown in Figure 4-9:

   - *Activity Log:* Opens a screen listing e-mails, calls, and SMS messages you've made to the contact.

   - *View Work Map:* Displays only if you have work address information filled up. This allows you to map the location using Maps.

   - *Email:* Starts a new e-mail message. See Chapter 8 for more information about e-mail.

   - *PIN:* Starts a new PIN-to-PIN message, which is a messaging feature unique to BlackBerry. With PIN-to-PIN, you can send a quick message to someone with a BlackBerry. See Chapter 9 for more details about PIN-to-PIN messaging.

   - *Call:* Uses Phone to dial the number.

   - *SMS:* Starts a new SMS message. SMS stands for Short Messaging Service, which is used in cellphones. See Chapter 9 for more details about SMS.

   - *Send to Messenger Contact:* Adds this contact to your contacts list in BlackBerry Messenger. (Note that this option appears only if you have BlackBerry Messenger installed.)

   - *MMS:* Starts a new MMS message. MMS is short for Multimedia Messaging Service, an evolution from SMS that supports voice and video clips. See Chapter 9 for more details about MMS.

     The item only appears in the menu if the contact has the Mobile field filled up.

   - *Send as Attachment:* Starts a new e-mail message attaching the contacts. See Chapter 8 for more information.

If you have a finger-fumble and press a letter key in error, press the Escape key (the arrow key to the right of the trackball) once to return to the original list (the one showing all your contacts), or press the trackball once, and then select View All.

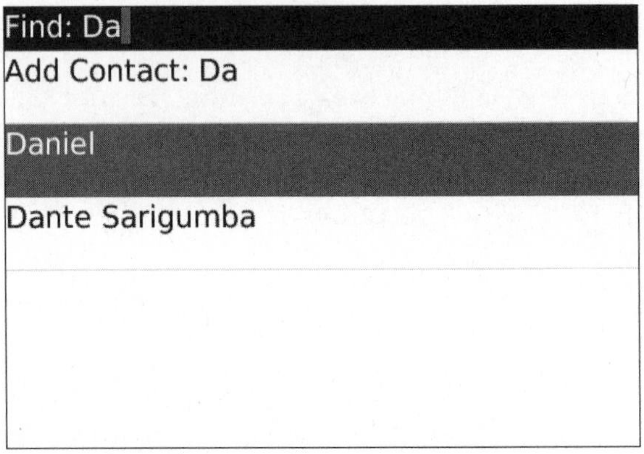
Find: Da
Add Contact: Da
Daniel
Dante Sarigumba

Figure 4-8: Enter more letters to shorten the potential contact list search.

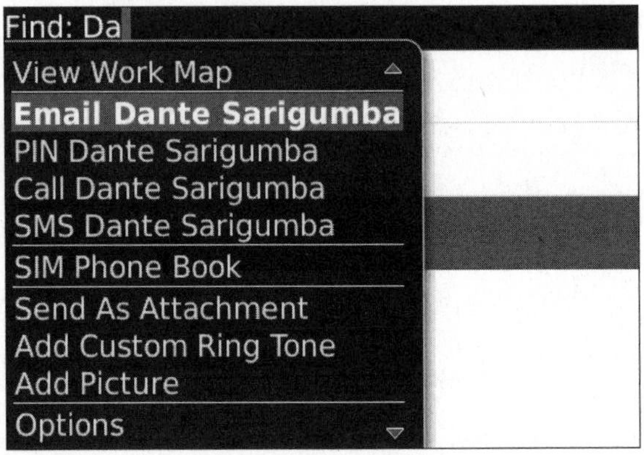
Find: Da
View Work Map
Email Dante Sarigumba
PIN Dante Sarigumba
Call Dante Sarigumba
SMS Dante Sarigumba
SIM Phone Book
Send As Attachment
Add Custom Ring Tone
Add Picture
Options

Figure 4-9: Action options for the selected contact.

TECHNICAL STUFF

You aren't hallucinating: Sometimes `Email` *`<contact name>`* or `Call` *`<contact name>`* appears on the menu and sometimes it doesn't. Contacts knows when to show those menu options. If a contact has a phone number, `Call` *`<contact name>`* and `SMS` *`<contact name>`* show up, and the same is true for e-mail and the personal identification number (PIN). In fact, this list of actions is a convenient way to find out whether you have particular information — a phone number or an e-mail address — for a particular contact.

TECHNICAL STUFF

In a corporate environment, your BlackBerry Enterprise server administrator may disable PIN-to-PIN messaging because it doesn't go to the corporate e-mail servers and, therefore, can't be monitored. If this is the case, the menu option `PIN`*`<contact name>`* won't appear, even though you entered PIN information for your contacts. Note that you'll still be able to receive a PIN-to-PIN message, but you won't be able to send one.

Organizing Your Contacts

You've been diligent by adding your contacts to Contacts, and your list has been growing at a pretty good clip. It now has all the contact information for your business colleagues, clients, and (of course) family and friends. In fact, Contacts has grown so much that it holds hundreds of contacts, and it's taking more time to find somebody.

Imagine that you just saw an old acquaintance and you want to greet the person by name. You know that if you see the name, you'd recognize it. The trouble is that your list has 300-plus names, which would take you forever to scroll through — so long, in fact, that this acquaintance would surely come right up to you in the meantime, forcing you to hide the fact that you can't remember his name. (How embarrassing.) In this scenario, the tried-and-true Find feature wouldn't be much help. What you need is a smaller pool of names to search.

This isn't rocket science. You'll want to do one of the following:

- ✔ **Organize your contacts into groups.** Using groups (as every kindergarten teacher could tell you) is a way to arrange something (in your case, contacts) to make them more manageable. How you arrange your groups is up to you. You should base the principle on whatever makes sense to you and fits the group you set up. For example, you can place all your customer contacts within a Clients group and family members in a Family group.

- ✔ **Set up your contacts so that you can filter them.** Use the Filter feature in combination with BlackBerry's Categories. (*Categories* is labeling your contacts to make it easy to filter them.) Using the Filter feature narrows the Contacts list to such an extent that you have to only scroll down and find your contact — no need to type search keywords, in other words.

Whether you use the Group or Filter feature is up to you. You find out how to use both methods in the next sections of this chapter.

Creating a group

A BlackBerry group in Contacts — as opposed to any other kind of group you can imagine — is just a simple filter or category. In other words, using a group just arranges your contacts into subsets without affecting the contact entries themselves. In Contacts, a group shows up in the contact list just like any other contact. The only wrinkle here is that when you select the group, the contacts associated with that group — and only the contacts associated with that group — appear onscreen.

Need some help visualizing how this works? Go ahead and create a group, following these steps:

1. **On the BlackBerry Home screen, select Contacts.**

2. **In Contacts, press the Menu key, and then select New Group.**

   A screen similar to that shown in Figure 4-10 appears. The top portion of the screen is where you type the group name, and the bottom portion is where you add your list of group members.

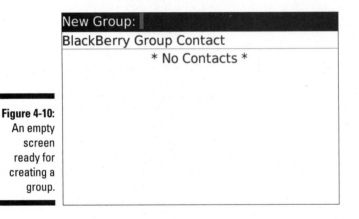

Figure 4-10: An empty screen ready for creating a group.

3. **Type the name of the group in the New Group field.**

   You can name it anything. For this example, let's name it Poker Buddies.

4. **Press the trackball, and then select Add Member.**

   The main Contacts list shows up in all its glory, ready to be pilfered.

5. **Select the contact you want to add to your new group list, press the trackball, and then select Continue from the menu that appears.**

   Everybody knows a Rob Kao, so select him. Doing so places Rob Kao in your Poker Buddies group list, as shown in Figure 4-11.

   You can't add a contact to a group if that contact doesn't have at least an e-mail address or a phone number. (It's very strict on this point.) Skirt this roadblock by editing that contact's information and putting in a fake (and clearly inactive) e-mail address, such as `notareal@email address.no`.

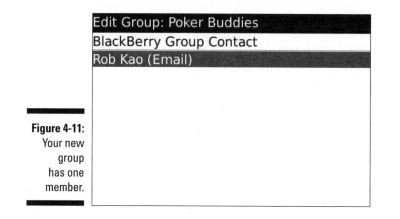

Edit Group: Poker Buddies
BlackBerry Group Contact
Rob Kao (Email)

Figure 4-11:
Your new
group
has one
member.

6. **Repeat Steps 4 and 5 to add more contacts to your list.**

   After you're satisfied, save your group.

7. **Press the trackball, and then select Save Group from the menu that appears.**

   Your Poker Buddies group is duly saved, and you can now see Poker Buddies in your main Contacts list.

Using the Filter feature on your contacts

Are you a left-brainer or a right-brainer? Yankees fan or Red Sox fan? Innie or Outie? Dividing up the world into categories is something everybody does (no divisions there), so it should come as no surprise that BlackBerry divides your contacts into distinct categories as well.

By default, two categories are set for you on the BlackBerry Bold:

✔ Business
✔ Personal

Why stop at two? BlackBerry makes it easy to create more categories. In this section, you first find out how to categorize a contact, and then you see how to filter your Contacts list. Finally, you find out how to create categories.

Categorizing your contacts

Whether you're creating one or editing one, you can categorize a particular contact as long as you're in Edit mode.

If the trick is getting into Edit mode, it's a pretty simple trick. Here's how that's done:

1. **On the BlackBerry Home screen, select Contacts.**

2. **In Contacts, highlight the contact, press the Menu key, and then select Edit.**

   Contacts is now in Edit mode for this particular contact, which is exactly where you want to be.

3. **Press the Menu key, and then select Categories.**

   A Categories list appears, as shown in Figure 4-12. By default, you see only the Business and the Personal categories.

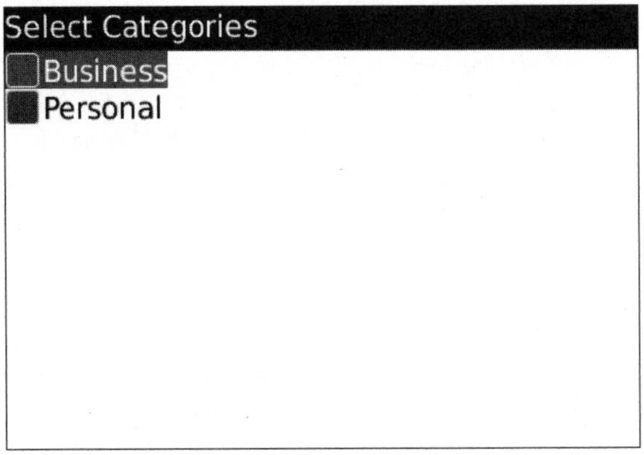

Figure 4-12:
Default
categories.

Select Categories
☐ Business
☐ Personal

4. **Press the Space key or the trackball to select the check box next to Personal.**

5. **Press the Menu key, and then select Save.**

   You are brought back to the Edit screen for this particular contact.

6. **Press the trackball, and then select Save (again) from the menu that appears.**

You now have one — count 'em, one — contact with Personal as its category, which means you can filter your Contacts list by using a category. Here's how:

1. **On the BlackBerry Home screen, select Contacts.**

2. **Press the Menu key, and then select Filter.**

   Your Categories list appears.

If you haven't added any categories in the meantime, you see only the default Business and Personal categories.

3. **Press the Space key or the trackball to select the Personal check box.**

Your Contacts list shrinks to just the contacts assigned to the Personal category, as shown in Figure 4-13.

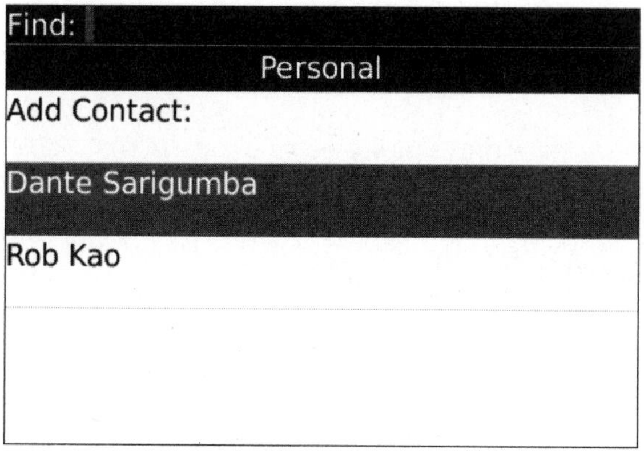

Find:

Personal

Add Contact:

Dante Sarigumba

Rob Kao

Figure 4-13:
The Contacts list after a filter is applied.

As you add contacts to a category, you can use Find. Enter the first few letters of the name to further narrow the contact search. If you need a refresher on how Find works, see the "Looking for Someone?" section, earlier in this chapter.

Adding a category

Whoever thought the default categories (Business and Personal) were enough for the complexities of the real world probably didn't know many people. BlackBerry makes it easy to add categories, so you can divide your world as much as you like:

1. **On the BlackBerry Home screen, select Contacts.**

2. **In Contacts, press the Menu key, and then select Filter.**

You get a view of the default categories. Refer to Figure 4-12.

3. **Press the Menu key (again), and then select New.**

A pop-up screen asks you to name the new category.

4. **Type the name of the category in the Name field, and then press Enter.**

The category is automatically saved. The Filter screen lists all the categories, including the one you just created. Just press the Escape key (the arrow key next to the trackball) to get back to the Contacts main screen.

Setting preferences

Vanilla, anyone? Some days you'll wish that your Contacts list were sorted differently. For example, there's the day when you need to find the guy who works for ABC Company but has a foreign name that you can hardly pronounce, let alone spell. What's a body to do?

You're in luck. Contacts Options navigates some out-of-the-ordinary situations. Figure 4-14 shows the Contacts Options screen. Despite its simplicity, it provides you with three important options that change Contacts behavior:

✔ **Sort By:** Changes how the list is sorted. You can use First Name, Last Name, or Company. Use the Space key to toggle among the choices. Remember that guy from ABC Company? You can use the Sort By option to sort by company. By doing that, all contacts from ABC Company are listed next to each other, and with any luck, the guy's name will jump out at you.

✔ **Separators:** Changes the dividers in the Contacts list. It's purely aesthetics, but check it out — you may like the stripes.

✔ **Allow Duplicate Names:** Self-explanatory. If you turn this on, you can have multiple people who happen to share the same name in your Contacts. If you disable this option, you get a warning when you try to add a name that matches one already on your list. Maybe you're just tired and mistakenly try to add the same person twice to your list. Then again, sometimes people just have the same name. We recommend keeping the default value of Yes, allowing you to have contacts with the same names.

✔ **Confirm Delete:** Displays a confirmation screen for all contact deletions.

Always keep this feature turned on for normal usage. Because there are many ways you could delete somebody from your Contacts, this feature is a good way of minimizing accidents.

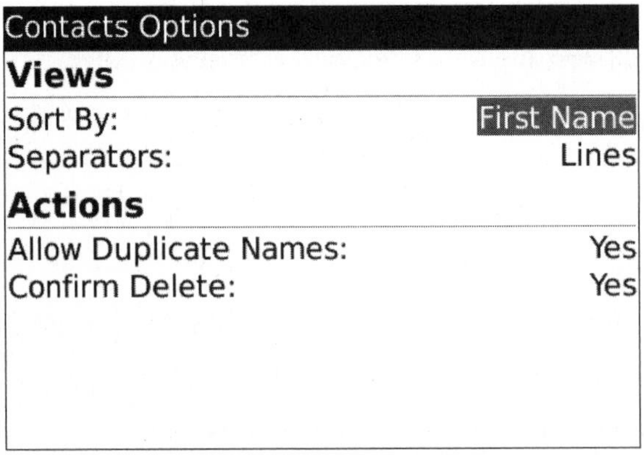

Contacts Options	
Views	
Sort By:	First Name
Separators:	Lines
Actions	
Allow Duplicate Names:	Yes
Confirm Delete:	Yes

Figure 4-14:
Choose your sort type here.

How do you change any of these options? The fields behave like any other on a BlackBerry application. Simply highlight the field, and then press the trackball to bring up a menu from which you can select the possible Options values. For example, Figure 4-15 shows the possible Sort By fields.

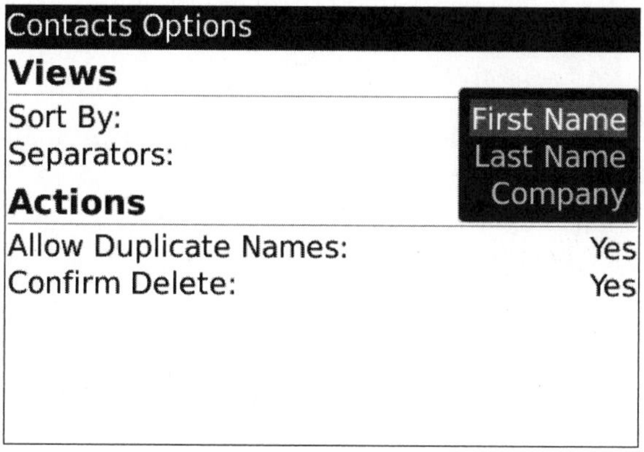

Contacts Options	
Views	
Sort By:	First Name
Separators:	Last Name
Actions	Company
Allow Duplicate Names:	Yes
Confirm Delete:	Yes

Figure 4-15:
The Sort
By field
options.

Sharing a Contact

Suppose you want to share your contact information with a friend who also has a BlackBerry. A *vCard* — virtual (business) card — is your answer and can make your life a lot easier. In BlackBerry Land, a vCard is a contact in Contacts that you send to someone as an attachment to an e-mail.

At the receiving end, the BlackBerry Bold (being the smart device that it is) recognizes the attachment and informs the BlackBerry owner that she has the option of saving it, making it available for her viewing pleasure in Contacts.

Sending a vCard

Because a vCard is nothing more than a Contacts contact attached to an e-mail, sending a vCard is a piece of cake. (Of course, you do need to make sure that your recipient has a BlackBerry device to receive the information.)

Here's how you go about sending a vCard:

1. **On the BlackBerry Home screen, select the Messages application.**

2. **In Messages, press the Menu key, and then select Compose Email.**

   A screen where you can compose a new e-mail appears.

3. **In the To field, start typing the name of the person you want to receive this vCard.**

4. **When you see the name in the drop-down list, highlight it, and then press the trackball.**

   You see an e-mail screen with the name you just selected as the To recipient.

5. **Type the subject and message.**

6. **Press the Menu key, and then select Attach Contact.**

   Contacts opens.

7. **Highlight the name of the person whose contact information you want to have attached, and then press the trackball.**

   The e-mail composition screen reappears, and an icon that looks like a book indicates that the e-mail now contains your attachment. Now all you have to do is send your e-mail.

8. **Press the trackball, and then select Send from the menu that appears.**

   You just shared the specified contact information. (Don't you feel right neighborly now?)

Receiving a vCard

If you get an e-mail with a contact attachment, here's how you save it to your Contacts:

1. **On the BlackBerry Home screen, select Messages.**

2. **Select the e-mail that contains the vCard.**

   The e-mail with the vCard attachment opens.

3. **Scroll down to the attachment. When the cursor is hovering over the attachment, press the trackball, and then select View Attachment from the menu that appears.**

   The vCard makes an appearance onscreen. Now save the contact in Contacts.

4. **Press the Menu key, and then select Add to Contacts.**

   The vCard is saved and is available in Contacts.

Transferring Contacts

Are you switching to BlackBerry Bold from an old AT&T or Cingular cell-phone? You've probably accumulated contacts on that phone by painstakingly typing them. Good news! Maybe you don't have to type them into BlackBerry Bold!

The trick is to use the old phone's *SIM card* (see Figure 4-16) as an external storage device, like a flash drive. The SIM card is an electronic chip that can store information, such as your phone numbers and contacts.

Figure 4-16:
Transfer contacts with a SIM card.

This should work on almost any GSM-compatible phone. The big U.S. GSM carriers are AT&T (including old Cingular phones) and T-Mobile; in Canada, Rogers. To find whether you have a GSM phone, look for the SIM card. Take the battery out of your cellphone; behind the battery, you should see a SIM card. If you don't see a SIM card, you don't have a GSM phone.

Copying contacts from a GSM phone

The process for copying contacts on a BlackBerry Bold is pretty straightforward, but the steps for retrieving them depend on your old phone.

For the purpose of showing you what's what, we use a Nokia 6300 phone as an example. You probably need the manual for your old phone. It's likely that the exact steps aren't the same for your old phone.

To copy contacts from an old GSM cellphone to a BlackBerry Bold, follow these steps:

1. **Take out the SIM card out of your BlackBerry Bold and put it in the old cellphone.**

   Moving a SIM card is no big deal. The SIM card is usually behind the battery, so you have to remove the back cover of the device to get to it:

   • On the Bold, there's a lock at the bottom of the back of the device. Just press this with your thumb to unlock the cover. You can pull the cover out starting from where the lock is located. You should be able to gently pry the BlackBerry Bold battery out with your fingernail.

   • Follow the instructions from the old cellphone's owner's manual to open it and remove the old SIM card, and then insert the BlackBerry Bold SIM card into the old cellphone. Put the battery back in the old cellphone and switch it on.

2. **Use the old cellphone's menu to copy the old contact list to the SIM card.**

The contact list may be called something like *Contacts* or *Names.* You'll probably need the old cellphone owner's manual to work through the process. The sidebar "Copying the contact list" shows how it works on a Nokia 6300.

If your old cellphone phone doesn't recognize your BlackBerry SIM card, perhaps the phone is *locked.* Phone providers can "lock" phones to their network, making it unusable in other networks. If this is the case, call your phone provider and ask for instructions to unlock your phone.

 3. **Put the SIM card back into your BlackBerry.**

Reinserting the SIM card and battery resets your BlackBerry.

Don't forget to put the old SIM card back into the old phone!

 4. **On the BlackBerry Home screen, select Contacts.**

Contacts opens.

 5. **In Contacts, press the Menu key, and then select SIM Phone Book.**

It might take some time to load the contacts from your SIM card; how long depends on how many contacts you've saved to the card. (You'll see a progress bar on the screen.) After the contacts are loaded, they are listed on the screen, and you can start browsing or copying them to your Contacts list.

The SIM Phone Book menu item is located toward the bottom of the menu, as shown in Figure 4-17. You need to scroll down to see it.

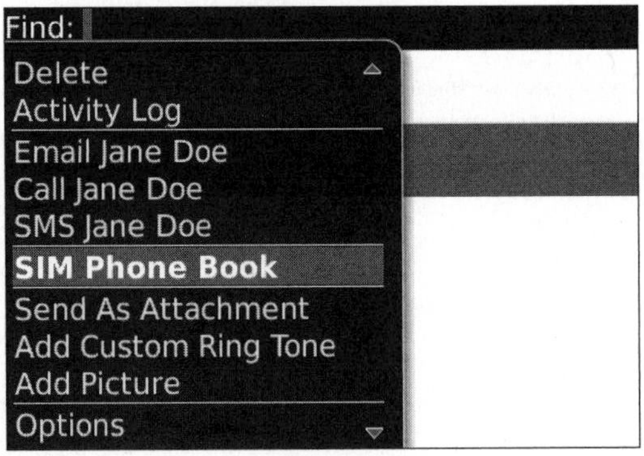

Figure 4-17:
The
Contacts
menu,
showing the
SIM Phone
Book option.

Find:
Delete
Activity Log
Email Jane Doe
Call Jane Doe
SMS Jane Doe
SIM Phone Book
Send As Attachment
Add Custom Ring Tone
Add Picture
Options

 6. **Copy each contact you want on your new BlackBerry Bold:**

   a. Highlight the contact.

   b. Press the Menu key.

   c. Select Add to Contacts.

Repeat this step for each contact you want to copy. (It's still a lot better than actually *typing* each contact on your BlackBerry.)

Copying the contact list

The steps for copying the contact list depend on your old phone. You probably need the owner's manual for your own phone, but here's how it works on a Nokia 6300:

1. **Select Names by pressing the top of the rightmost top button.**

   On this phone, Names is the equivalent of Contacts. The phone displays a list of contacts.

2. **Select Options by pressing the leftmost top button.**

   The Names menu appears, as shown in the figure.

3. **On the Names menu, select Mark All.**

4. **Select Options by pressing the leftmost top button.**

   The Names menu appears.

5. **Select Copy Marked.**

   A menu displays two options: From Phone to SIM Card and From SIM Card to Phone.

6. **Select From Phone to SIM Card.**

7. **Select All, and then select Keep Original from the next menu.**

   A confirmation screen appears.

8. **Select OK to confirm the copy.**

   The Nokia 6300 phone starts copying the contents of the Phone Book to the SIM

card. While it's making the copy, the screen displays a bar that moves back and forth. If you have many contacts on your phone, this process can take some time, so be patient. When the contacts are loaded into the SIM card, the screen displays the number of contacts that were copied.

When the contacts are copied, you can switch the SIM card back to the BlackBerry Bold.

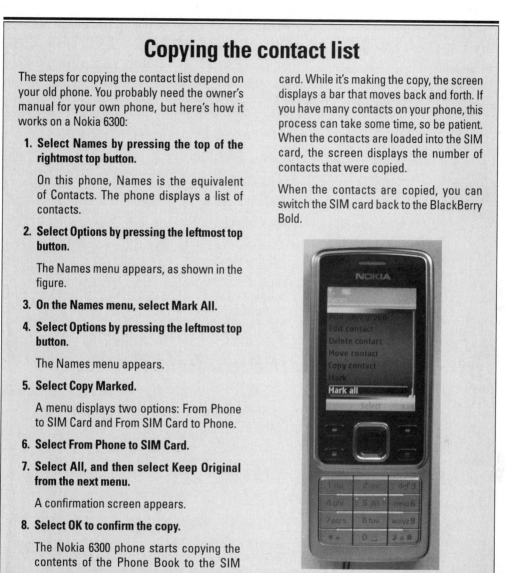

SIM cards have a limited capacity. If one or two old contacts don't fit on your SIM card, just type them into your BlackBerry Bold. But if you need to move many more contacts, you can clear and refill the SIM card as many times as you need to move all of your old contacts:

1. **On your Bold, launch Contacts.**

2. **Press the menu key, and then select SIM Phone Book.**

   On this screen, you should see the already copied contacts in your SIM card. Deleting the contact here only deletes it from the SIM card and not on the Contacts applications. There's no facility to delete all at once, only one at a time.

3. **Press the Del key to delete a contact, and then select Delete on the confirmation screen.**

   This is the best time to disable the confirmation screen and speed up the deletion. If you need a refresher on how it's done, check the section earlier on this chapter titled "Setting Preferences."

4. **Swap the BlackBerry SIM card back into the old cellphone.**

5. **Use the old cellphone's menu to copy individual contacts that didn't fit when you copied "all" contacts.**

   Put the BlackBerry SIM card back in the BlackBerry Bold, and follow Steps 4—6 of the preceding instructions to copy the extra contacts from the SIM card to BlackBerry Contacts.

Copying a BlackBerry Bold contact

Someday, you may want to copy your carefully curated BlackBerry Contacts list to another cellphone. It's possible, with a little help from two BlackBerry experts.

This is one of the most difficult tricks unless someone shows you how.

So here's how to copy each contact you want to move:

1. **View the contact information.**

   Follow the steps in the "Viewing a contact" section, earlier in this chapter.

2. **On the view screen, scroll to a Phone Number field, press the Menu key, and then select Copy to SIM Phone Book.**

   The Copy to SIM Phone Book feature (see Figure 4-18) shows up only when you position the cursor in a Phone Number field.

3. **On the Phone Book Entry screen, press the trackball, and then select Save.**

   The screen immediately returns to the View contact screen. You can repeat these steps to copy more contacts from the BlackBerry Bold.

When all the contacts you want are on the BlackBerry SIM card, insert the SIM card in the other phone and follow its instructions to copy contacts from the SIM card.

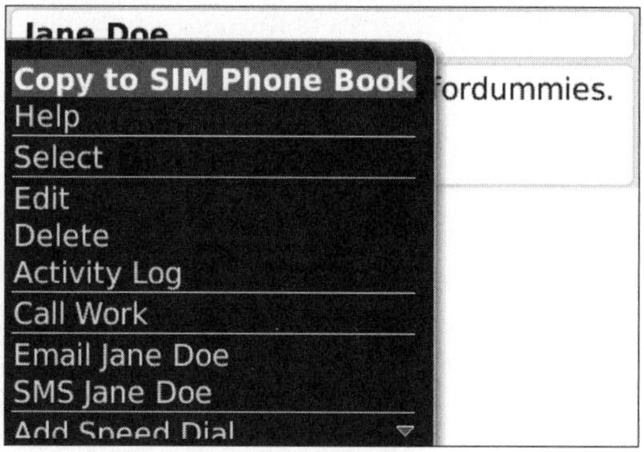

Jane Doe

Copy to SIM Phone Book ordummies.
Help
Select
Edit
Delete
Activity Log
Call Work
Email Jane Doe
SMS Jane Doe
Add Speed Dial

Figure 4-18:
Copy
BlackBerry
info to a
cellphone.

If your other phone doesn't recognize your BlackBerry SIM card, perhaps the phone is locked. Phone providers do this all the time: They lock the phones to their network, making it unusable in other networks. If this is the case, call your phone provider and ask for instructions on how to unlock your phone.

Searching for Somebody Outside Your Contacts

Does your employer provide your BlackBerry Bold? Do you use Outlook or Lotus Notes on your desktop machine at work? If you answer yes to both questions, this is for you.

BlackBerry Contacts allows you to search for people in your organization, basically using any of the following software which contains employee databases:

✔ Microsoft Exchange (for Outlook)

✔ IBM Domino (for Lotus Notes)

✔ Novell GroupWise

Exchange, Domino, and GroupWise serve the same purposes:

✔ Facilitate e-mail delivery in a corporate environment.

✔ Enable access to a database of names:

• Global Address Lists (GALs) in Exchange

• Notes Address Books in Domino

• GroupWise Address Books in GroupWise

To search for somebody in your organization through a database of names, simply follow these steps:

1. **On the BlackBerry Home screen, select Contacts.**

2. **Press the Menu key, and then select Lookup.**

   Some corporations may not enable the Lookup feature. Please check with your IT department for more information.

3. **Type the name you're searching for, and then press the trackball.**

   You could enter the beginning characters of either a person's last or first name. You aren't searching your Contacts but your company's database, so this step may take some time.

   For big organizations, we recommend being more precise when searching. For example, searching for *Dan* yields more hits than searching for *Daniel*. The more precise your search criteria, the fewer hits you'll get, and the faster the search will be.

   While the search is in progress, you see the word Lookup and the criteria you put in. For example, if you enter **Daniel,** the top row reads Lookup: Daniel. After the search is finished, BlackBerry displays the number of hits or matches, for example, 20 matches: Daniel.

4. **Select the matches count to display the list of matches.**

   The matches appear. A header at the top of this screen details the matches displayed in the current screen as well as the total hits. For example, if the header reads something like Lookup Daniel (20 of 130 matches), 130 people in your organization have the name *Daniel,* and BlackBerry is displaying the first 20. You have the option of fetching more by pressing the trackball, and then choosing Get More Results from the menu that appears.

   You can add the listed name(s) to your Contacts by using the Add command (for the currently highlighted name) or the Add All command for all the names in the list. (As always, press the trackball to call up the menu that contains these options.)

5. **Select the person whose information you want to review.**

   The person's contact information is displayed on a read-only screen (you can read but not change it). You may see the person's title; e-mail address; work, mobile, and fax numbers; and the snail-mail address at work. Any of that information gives you confirmation about the person you're looking for. Of course, what shows up depends on the availability of this information in your company's database.

Synchronizing Facebook Contacts

Do you network like a social butterfly? You must be using one of the popular social networking BlackBerry applications, such as MySpace or Facebook. You must have tons of friends from these networking sites and want to copy their contact information down to your Bold. There are ways to achieve this, and individual networking sites will have their own unique way. But if you are in Facebook, you're lucky.

With the latest Facebook application (version 1.6 as of this writing), it's much easier to get Facebook contacts to your Bold. Not only a one-time copying of contact information, but the Facebook app also allows you to synchronize information between your Bold and your friend's information in Facebook.

Upon running the Facebook app for the first time, you're asked to enable synchronization. Here are Facebook and BlackBerry connections you can choose from:

- **BlackBerry Message application:** When enabled, you'll see new Facebook notifications in your Messages application.

- **BlackBerry Calendar application:** When enabled, it automatically creates a calendar item in your Bold whenever you have a new Facebook event.

- **BlackBerry Contacts application:** When enabled, your Bold contacts are periodically updated with the latest information from Facebook, including the profile pictures. In order for this to happen, your Bold contacts also will be sent to Facebook.

If you opted out from these options during the first run, you can still enable them from the Facebook app Options screen. The following steps enable Contacts synchronization:

1. **Select Facebook icon from home screen.**

   Facebook application is filed under Downloads folder.

2. **Press the Menu key, and then select Options.**

   The Options screen appears. A lot of information and text are on this screen, and you have to scroll down to see all the options. Feel free to check other options, but for the purposes of synchronizing contacts, refer to the first two pages of the screen, which should look like Figure 4-19.

3. **Check BlackBerry Contacts application.**

   There's explanation text right below this check box. If you scroll down, you should see another check box, which allows you to include Facebook profile photo synchronization with Contacts photo.

4. **Check Update existing photos in your BlackBerry contacts list with Facebook friend profile photos.**

5. **Press the Escape key, and select Yes on the Save Changes prompt.**

   Your Contacts will now be periodically updated with Facebook friends.

Figure 4-19:
Enable
Facebook
friends
synchroni-
zation with
Facebook
Options.

facebook   ✎ **Options**

You are currently logged in as Dante Sarigumba.

                                        Logout

                              Run Setup Wizard

Connect your Facebook account with:
- ☑ BlackBerry Calendar application   ❷
- ☑ BlackBerry Message application   ❷
- ☑ BlackBerry Contacts application   ❷
(Enabling this feature will periodically send copies

facebook   ✎ **Options**

of your BlackBerry device Contacts to Facebook Inc. to match and connect with your Facebook Friends. Profile pictures and information about you and your Facebook Friends will also be periodically sent from Facebook to your BlackBerry Contact list and Calendar, and you acknowledge that access to this data (e.g. by applications) will no longer be subject to you and your Facebook Friends privacy settings once stored on your BlackBerry device.)

☑ Update existing photos in your BlackBerry contacts list with Facebook friend profile photos

Chapter 5

Never Miss Another Appointment

. . . .

In This Chapter

▶ Seeing your schedule from different time frames

▶ Making your Calendar your own

▶ Scheduling a meeting

▶ Viewing an appointment

▶ Sending and receiving meeting requests

. . . .

*T*o some folks, the key to being organized and productive is mastering time management and using their time wisely (and we aren't just talking about reading this book while you're commuting to work). Many have discovered that there is no better way to organize their time than to use a calendar — a daily planner tool. Some prefer digital to paper, so they use a planner software program on their PC, whether installed on their hard drive or accessed through an Internet portal (such as Yahoo!). The smartest of the bunch, of course, use their BlackBerry handheld because it has the whole planner thing covered in handy form with its Calendar application.

In this chapter, we show you how to keep your life (personal and work) in order by managing your appointments with your BlackBerry Bold Calendar. What's great about managing your time on a BlackBerry instead of on your PC is that your BlackBerry is always with you to remind you. Just remember that you won't have any more excuses for forgetting that important quarterly meeting or Bertha's birthday bash.

Accessing BlackBerry Calendar

BlackBerry Calendar is one of the BlackBerry core applications, like Contacts or Phone (read more about the others in Chapter 2), so it's easy to get to. From the Home screen, press the Menu key, and then select Calendar. *Voilà!* You have Calendar.

Choosing Your Calendar View

The first time you open Calendar, you'll likely see Day view, the default setting, as shown in Figure 5-1. However, you can change the Calendar view to a different one that works better for your needs:

- ✔ **Day:** Gives you a summary of your appointments for the day. By default, it lists all your appointments from 9 a.m. to 5 p.m.

- ✔ **Week:** Shows you a seven-day summary view of your appointments. In this view, you can see how busy you are in a particular week.

- ✔ **Month:** Shows you every day of the month. You can't tell how many appointments are in a day, but you can see on which days you have appointments.

- ✔ **Agenda:** A bit different from the other views. It isn't a time-based view like the others; it basically lists your upcoming appointments. And in the list, you can see details of the appointments, such as where and when.

20 Nov 2008	19:16	◁M T W T F S S▷
10:00	Director's Meeting	🔔
11:00		
12:00	Lunch with Sales Team	🔔
13:00		
14:00		
15:00		
16:00	Jade's Piano Lesson	🔔
17:00		

Figure 5-1:
Day view in
Calendar.

Different views (like Week view shown in Figure 5-2) offer you a different focus on your schedule. Select the view you want based on your scheduling needs and preferences. If your life is a little more complicated, you can even use a combination of views for a full grasp of your schedule.

To switch between different Calendar views, simply follow these steps:

1. **From the Home screen, press the Menu key and then select Calendar.**

   Doing so calls up the Calendar application in its default view — Day view.

2. **Press the Menu key, and then select the view of your choice from the menu that appears (shown in Figure 5-3).**

   As we mention earlier, your view choices are Day, Week, Month, and Agenda.

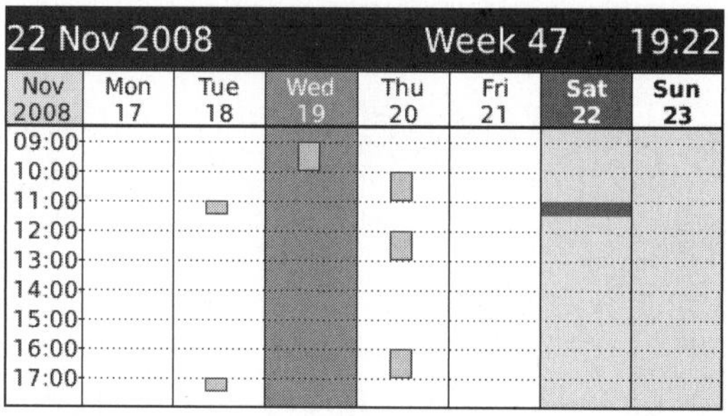

Figure 5-2:
Change your
Calendar
view to fit
your life.

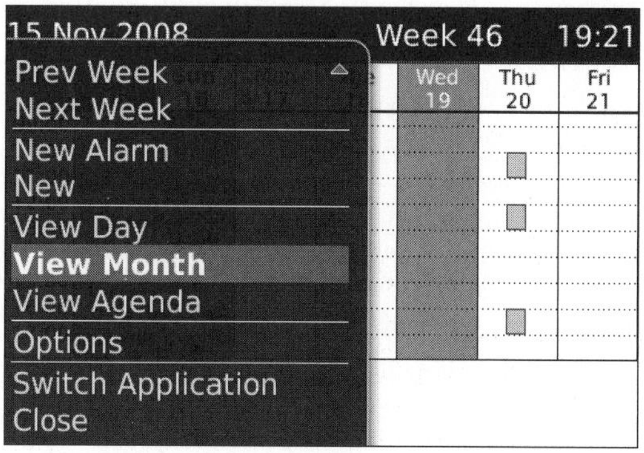

Figure 5-3:
Choose your
Calendar
view here.

Moving between Time Frames

Depending on what view of Calendar you're in, you can easily move to the preceding or next day, week, month, or year. For example, if you're in Month view, you can move forward to the next month (um, relative to the currently displayed month). Likewise, you can also move back to the preceding month. In fact, if you like to look at things in the long term, you can jump ahead (or back) a year at a time. (See Figure 5-4.)

You have similar flexibility when it comes to the other Calendar views. See Table 5-1 for a summary of what's available.

Table 5-1	Moving between Views
Calendar View	*Move Between*
Day	Days and weeks
Week	Weeks
Month	Months and years
Agenda	Days

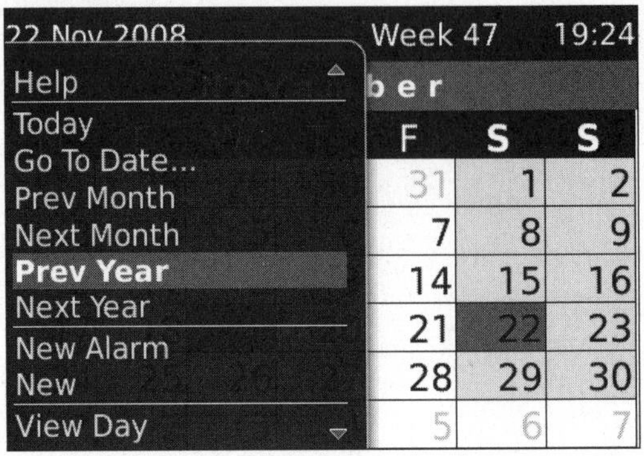

22 Nov 2008	Week 47	19:24
Help	b e r	
Today	F	S	S
Go To Date...	31	1	2
Prev Month	7	8	9
Next Month	14	15	16
Prev Year	21	22	23
Next Year	28	29	30
New Alarm	5	6	7
New			
View Day			

Figure 5-4:
Move
among
months or
years in
Month view.

You can always go to today's date regardless of what Calendar view you're in. Just press the Menu key, and then select Today from the menu that appears.

Furthermore, you can jump to any date you choose by pressing the Menu key, and then selecting Go to Date. Doing so calls up a handy little dialog box that lets you choose the date you want. To change the date, scroll the track-ball to the desired day, month, and year, as shown in Figure 5-5.

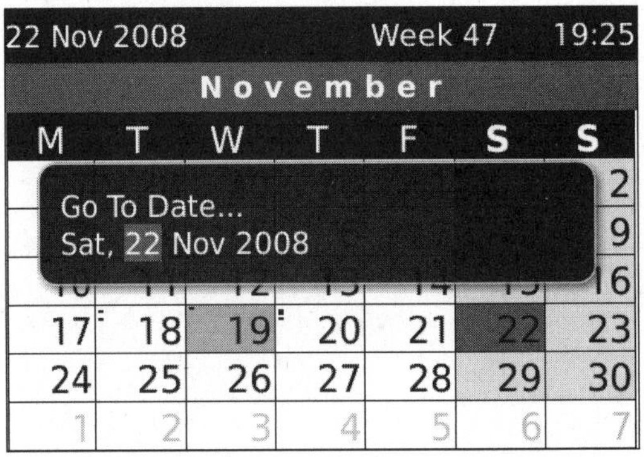

22 Nov 2008	Week 47	19:25
N o v e m b e r		
M T W T F S S		
		2
Go To Date...		9
Sat, 22 Nov 2008		16
17 18 19 20 21 22 23		
24 25 26 27 28 29 30		
1 2 3 4 5 6 7		

Figure 5-5:
Go to any
date you
want.

Customizing Your Calendar

To change the initial (default) view in your Calendar — from Day view to Month view, for example — Calendar Options is the answer. To get to Calendar Options, open Calendar, press the Menu key, and select Options from the menu that appears. You see choices similar to the ones shown in Table 5-2.

Table 5-2	Calendar Options
Option	*Description*
Formatting	
First Day of Week	The day that first appears in your Week view.
Start of Day	The time of day that defines your start of day in Day view. The default is 9 a.m. If you change this to 8 a.m., for example, your Day view starts at 8 a.m. instead of 9 a.m.
End of Day	The time of the day that defines the end of day in Day view. The default is 5 p.m. If you change this to 6 p.m., for example, your Day view ends at 6 p.m. instead of 5 p.m.
Views	
Initial View	Specifies the Calendar view that you first see when opening Calendar.
Show Free Time in Agenda View	If Yes, this field allows an appointment-free day's date to appear in Agenda view. If No, Agenda view doesn't show the date of days on which you don't have an appointment.
Show End Time in Agenda View	If Yes, this field shows the end time of each appointment in Agenda view. If No, Agenda view shows only the start time of each appointment.
Actions	
Snooze	The snooze time when a reminder appears. The default is 5 minutes.
Default Reminder	How far in advance your BlackBerry notifies you before your appointment time. The default is 15 minutes.
Enable Quick Entry	Day view only. Allows you to make a new appointment by typing characters. This way, you don't need to press the trackball and select New. *Note:* If you enable this, Day view shortcuts described on the online Cheat Sheet don't apply.
Keep Appointments (OS 5.0)	This is the number of days your BlackBerry Bold will save your calendar item. We recommend keep it on Never.
Show Tasks (OS 5.0)	A scheduled task will be shown on your calendar just like a Calendar event. (Scheduled task is a task with a due date.)
Show Alarms (OS 5.0)	You can see alarms in your calendar if you set this option to Yes.

Managing multiple calendars

Like your e-mail accounts, you may have multiple calendars. For example, say you have a calendar from your day job and a calendar from your personal life or softball club. Whatever the reason, your BlackBerry Bold has a great way for you to manage multiple calendars.

From Calendar Options, you see a screen similar to the following figure. The colored squares represent different calendars to give you a better view of which event belongs to which calendar. For example, you can assign your day job calendar as red and your softball club calendar as green. When you have two events conflict at the same time slot, you can better prioritize with the color.

To change the color of each calendar, follow these steps:

1. **Open Calendar.**

2. **Press the Menu key and select Options Menu.**

   This opens a screen similar to the following figure.

3. **Select a calendar of your choice.**

   The calendar properties screen opens.

4. **Highlight the colored square, and then select the desired color (six colors to choose from).**

   If you have more than one e-mail address "hooked" into your BlackBerry, you will see them here.

5. **Press the Menu key and tap the Save button.**

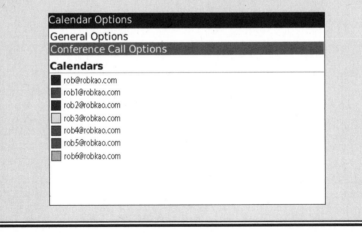

All Things Appointments: Adding, Opening, and Deleting

After you master navigating the different Calendar views (and that should take you all of about two minutes) and you have Calendar customized to your heart's content (another three minutes, tops), it's time (pun intended) to set up, review, and delete appointments. We also show you how to set up a meeting with clients or colleagues.

Creating an appointment

Setting up a new appointment is easy. You need only one piece of information: when your appointment occurs. Of course, you can easily add related information about the appointment, such as the meeting's purpose, its location, and whatever additional notes are helpful.

In addition to a standard one-time, limited-duration meeting, you can also set all-day appointments, recurring meetings, and reminders. Sweet!

Creating a one-time appointment

To add a new one-time appointment, follow these steps:

1. **Open Calendar.**

2. **Press the Menu key, and then select New.**

   The New Appointment screen appears.

3. **Fill in the key appointment information.**

   Type all the information regarding your appointment in the appropriate spaces. You should at least enter the time and the subject of your appointment. See Figure 5-6.

4. **Press the Menu key, and then select Save.**

   This saves your newly created appointment.

```
New Appointment
─────────────────────────────────
Subject: Meeting with BigWig▌
Location:
─────────────────────────────────
■ All Day Event
Start:              Fri, 21 Nov 2008 09:00
End:                Fri, 21 Nov 2008 10:00
Duration:                 1 Hour 0 Mins
Time Zone:             Casablanca (GMT)
Show Time As:                      Busy
Reminder:                       15 Min.
Recurrence:                       None
```

Figure 5-6: Set an appointment here.

Your new appointment is now in Calendar and viewable from any Calendar view.

You can have more than one appointment in the same time slot. Your BlackBerry Calendar allows conflicts in your schedule because it lets you make the hard decision about which appointment to forgo.

Creating an all-day appointment

If your appointment is an all-day event — for example, if you're in corporate training or have an all-day doctor's appointment — select the All Day Event check box on the New Appointment screen, as shown in Figure 5-7. You can do so by scrolling to the check box and pressing the trackball. When this check box is selected, you can't specify the time of your appointment — just the start date and end date (simply because it doesn't make sense to specify a time for an all-day event).

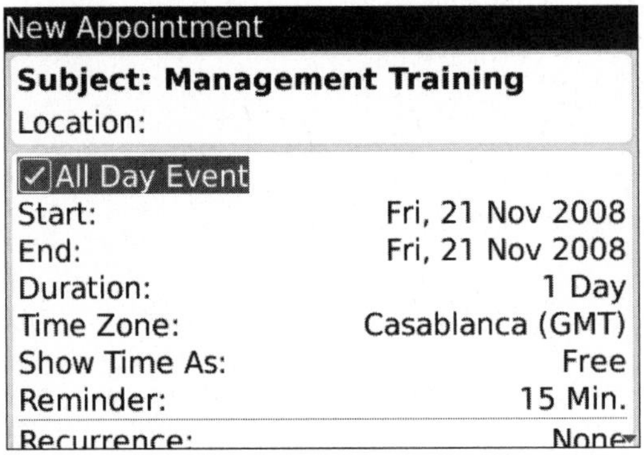

Figure 5-7: Set an all-day event here.

> New Appointment
>
> **Subject: Management Training**
> Location:
>
> ☑ All Day Event
> Start: Fri, 21 Nov 2008
> End: Fri, 21 Nov 2008
> Duration: 1 Day
> Time Zone: Casablanca (GMT)
> Show Time As: Free
> Reminder: 15 Min.
> Recurrence: None

Setting your appointment reminder time

Any appointment you enter in Calendar can be associated with a reminder alert — either a vibration or a beep, depending on how you set things up in your profile. (For more on profiles, see Chapter 3.) You can also choose to have no reminder for an appointment. From the New Appointment screen, simply scroll to the Reminder field and select a reminder time anywhere from None to 1 Week before your appointment time.

Profile is simply another useful BlackBerry feature that allows you to customize how your BlackBerry alerts you when an event occurs. Examples of events are an e-mail, a phone call, or a reminder for an appointment.

By default, whatever reminder alert you set goes off 15 minutes before the event. However, you don't have to stick with the default. You can choose your own default reminder time. Here's how:

1. **Open Calendar.**

2. **Press the Menu key, and then select Options.**

   Doing so calls up the Calendar Options screen.

3. **Select Default Reminder.**

4. **Choose a default reminder time anywhere from None to 1 Week before your appointment.**

So from now on, any new appointment has a default reminder time of what you just set up. Assuming that you have a reminder time other than None, the next time you have an appointment coming up, you see a dialog box like the one shown in Figure 5-8, reminding you of the appointment.

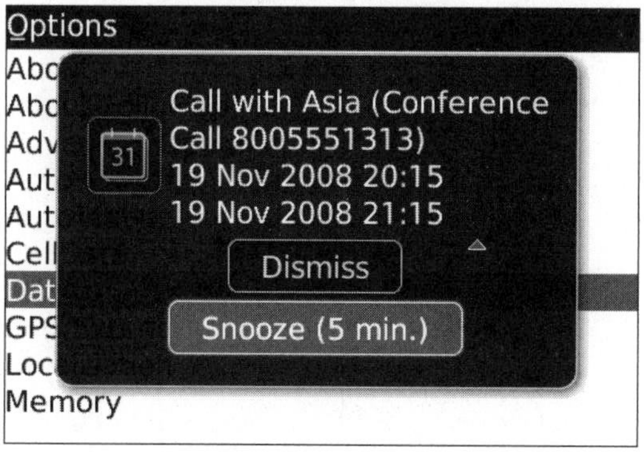

Options	
Abo	

Call with Asia (Conference Call 8005551313)
19 Nov 2008 20:15
19 Nov 2008 21:15

Dismiss

Snooze (5 min.)

Figure 5-8:
You get a
reminder
dialog box if
you want.

Creating a recurring appointment

You can set up recurring appointments based on daily, weekly, monthly, or yearly recurrences. Everyone has some appointment that repeats, such as birthdays or anniversaries (or taking out the trash every Thursday at 7:30 a.m. — ugh).

For all recurrence types, you can define an Every field. For example, say you have an appointment that recurs every nine days. Just set the Recurrence field to Daily and the Every field to 9, as shown in Figure 5-9.

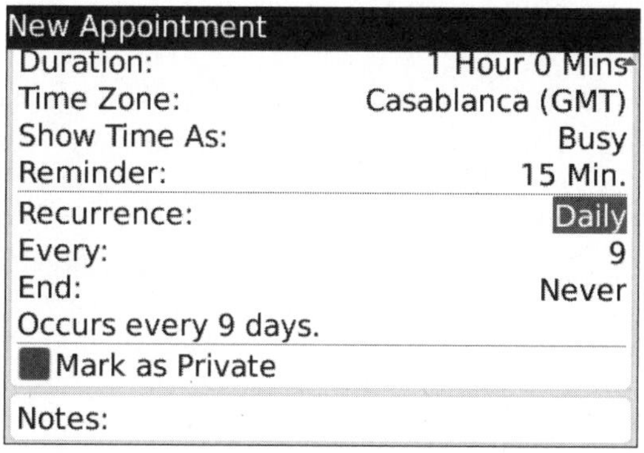

New Appointment

Duration:	1 Hour 0 Mins
Time Zone:	Casablanca (GMT)
Show Time As:	Busy
Reminder:	15 Min.
Recurrence:	Daily
Every:	9
End:	Never
Occurs every 9 days.	
▪ Mark as Private	
Notes:	

Figure 5-9:
An
appointment
recurring
every nine
days.

Depending on what you select in the Recurrence field, you have the option to fill in other fields. If you enter Weekly in the Recurrence field, for example, you have the option of filling in the Day of the Week field. (It basically allows you to select the day of the week on which your appointment recurs.)

If you enter Monthly or Yearly in the Recurrence field, the Relative Date check box is available. With this check box selected, you can ensure that your appointment recurs relative to today's date. For example, if you choose the following, your appointment occurs every two months on the third Sunday until July 31, 2012:

> **Start:** Sunday, June 21, 2009 at 12 p.m.
>
> **End:** Sunday, June 21, 2009 at 1 p.m.
>
> **Recurrence:** Monthly
>
> **Every:** 2
>
> **Relative Date:** Selected
>
> **End:** Saturday, July 31, 2012

On the other hand, if all options in this example remain the same except that Relative Date isn't selected, your appointment occurs every two months, on the 21st of the month, until July 31, 2012.

If all this "relative" talk has you dizzy, don't worry: The majority of your appointments won't be as complicated as this.

Opening an appointment

After you set an appointment, you can view it in a couple of ways:

✔ If you set up reminders for your appointment and the little Reminder dialog box appears onscreen at the designated time before your appointment, you can view your appointment by clicking the box's Open button. In the same dialog box, you can Snooze the reminder (refer to Figure 5-8).

✔ In Calendar, go to the exact time of your appointment and view it there.

While looking at an appointment, you can make changes (a new appointment time and new appointment location), and then save them.

Appointments versus Meetings

Technically, any event in your Calendar counts as an appointment, whether it's a reminder for your best friend's birthday or a reminder of a doctor's appointment for a checkup. However, when you invite people to an appointment or you get invited to one, regardless of whether it's a face-to-face meeting or a phone conference, that appointment becomes a *meeting*.

Sending a meeting request

Sending a meeting request to others is similar to creating a Calendar appointment. Follow these steps:

1. **Open Calendar.**

2. **Press the Menu key, and then select New.**

3. **Fill in the key appointment information (subject, location, and time).**

4. **Press the Menu key, and then select Invite Attendee.**

   You're taken to Contacts to select your meeting attendee.

5. **Select your contact via Contacts:**

   • *If your contact is in Contacts:* Highlight the contact you want, and then press the trackball.

   • *If you don't yet have contacts or if the one you want isn't in Contacts:* Select the Use Once option to enter the appropriate e-mail address, and then press the Enter key to finish and return to Calendar.

6. **After returning from Contacts, you see the attendees in your Calendar meeting notice.**

7. **Press the Menu key and then select Save.**

   An e-mail is sent to your meeting attendees, inviting them to your meeting.

Responding to a meeting request

Whether for work or a casual social event, you've likely received a meeting request by e-mail, asking you to respond to the meeting by choosing one of three options: Accept, Tentative, or Decline. (If it's from your boss for an all-staff meeting and you just can't afford to decline again because it's so close to Christmas bonus time, that's an Accept.)

You can accept any meeting request from your managers or colleagues on your BlackBerry just as you would on your desktop PC. In the PC world, you respond to an e-mail request for a meeting by clicking the appropriate button in your e-mail client (Microsoft Outlook, for the vast majority of you). In the BlackBerry world, a meeting request also comes in the form of an e-mail; after reading the e-mail, just choose Accept, Tentative, or Decline in the Messages application. Your response is sent back in an e-mail. We go into more detail about the Messages application in Chapter 8.

After you respond to the meeting request, the meeting is added to your Calendar automatically. If you have a change of heart later, you can change your response (yes, you can later decline that useless meeting after all) in Calendar, and the declined event disappears from your Calendar.

Setting your meeting dial-in number

You may have colleagues and friends all over the country or even on another continent. Group phone meetings may require

- ✔ A dial-in number
- ✔ Moderator code (if you are the moderator)
- ✔ Participation code

If you have a BlackBerry Bold with OS 5.0, you can store and display these numbers when you create a new appointment in the BlackBerry Calendar.

To set your phone conference dial-in details with OS 5.0, follow these steps:

1. **Open Calendar.**

2. **Press the menu key and select Options menu item.**

3. **Select Conference Call Options.**

   A screen similar to Figure 5-10 appears.

4. **Enter the appropriate numbers.**

5. **Press the menu key and select Save.**

   Your conference call number is saved.

   The next time you create a new appointment, if you tap the Conference Call check box in the Appointment Screen, you see the conference number, as shown in Figure 5-11.

If your BlackBerry Bold has OS 4.6, you'll have to keep writing conference call access numbers on a sticky note. Sorry.

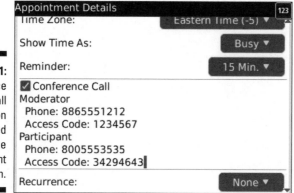

Figure 5-10:
Setting up
Conference
Call dial-in
details.

Figure 5-11:
Conference
Call
information
displayed
in the
Appointment
screen.

Chapter 6

Creating To-Do's and Keeping Your Words

*U*sing your BlackBerry Bold as an organizational tool is one of the key themes in this book. And speaking of organization, what better tool for your impressive organizational skills is there than using task, or to-do, lists? Knowing what you need to do today, tomorrow, the entire week, or perhaps the whole month makes you more efficient in your job and personal life. Not only do you need to know what your tasks are, but you also need to prioritize them — and reprioritize them, if necessary. And with your BlackBerry Bold as your able assistant, you can.

Your BlackBerry Bold has another handy application — Tasks — that saves you from having to lug around a portfolio notebook. This will at least take you a step closer to keeping your desk from drowning in a sea of sticky notes.

To top it off, we'll make sure that you'll get a scoop on keeping your passwords safe by using the Password Keeper application.

If you keep a to-do list on your desktop (Outlook, anyone?), consider switching to all BlackBerry, all the time. You'll love the greater flexibility that comes with greater mobility. Or, if you just can't give up your desktop application, you have the option of using both and just synchronizing them. (More about that in chapter 15.)

Accessing Tasks

Tasks can be found in the Applications folder on the Home screen, as you can see in Figure 6-1. Just look for the icon of a clipboard with a check mark.

Changing the theme might alter the icons used (refer to Chapter 3 on changing themes). Just remember that Tasks is always in Applications. If you can locate the Applications icon, it's just a matter of scrolling the trackball and pressing to locate the Tasks icon.

Figure 6-1:
Going from
Applications
to Tasks.

Recording a Task

The first step when building a to-do list is to start recording one. Don't groan and roll your eyes. This is easy. Relax, and you'll be finished in a snap.

Follow these simple steps:

1. **Select Tasks.**

   The Tasks application opens. Similar to Contacts and MemoPad, the screen that appears is divided into two parts: The top shows the Find field, followed by the list of tasks or *No Tasks*.

2. **Highlight Add Task and press the trackball.**

   Alternatively, you can press the Menu key, and then select New (as shown on the left in Figure 6-2).

   The New Task screen appears, as shown on the right side of Figure 6-2, ready and willing to document your new task. This simple screen features easy-to-understand fields that describe the task you're about to enter.

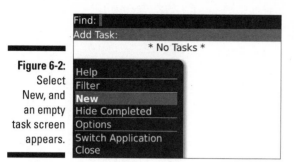

Figure 6-2:
Select
New, and
an empty
task screen
appears.

3. **Use the trackball to move to each field and enter information for your task.**

   Some fields are for text that you enter yourself, and some fields hold items you select from a menu specific for that field. In other words, for text fields, you have to enter the stuff you want; but for nontext fields, you select the field, press the trackball again, and then make your choice from the selection that appears.

   To update a field from a list of choices, select that field, and then press the trackball.

4. **After filling in the relevant fields, press the Menu key, and then select Save.**

   Your task is saved and listed on the main Tasks screen.

Navigating the Tasks Fields

The New Task screen (refer to Figure 6-2) is straightforward and contains a few fields.

Task field

Log the subject or short description of your task here.

Make this field as descriptive as you can: The subject you type here should be specific enough that you can differentiate this task from the rest in your list. For example, if you make several presentations to clients, you don't want to call your task Prepare Presentations. You want to be specific so that you can distinguish it from other tasks. Perhaps name it Product X Benefit Forecast to XYZ CFO.

You can search on this field from the main Tasks screen.

Status field

Indicate the current state of your task using this field. Status is a *selection field* — that is, after highlighting the field, you press the trackball and select a value from the list.

You can choose from these values:

- ✔ **Not Started:** You haven't started this task yet. Because this choice is the most common, Not Started is the default choice when creating a task.

- ✔ **In Progress:** You're in the midst of the task.

- ✔ **Completed:** You're finished with the task.

- ✔ **Waiting:** Your task is ongoing and depends on another task or another event. For example, you're waiting for Joe in Accounting to get you a spreadsheet, which you need to work on this task.

- ✔ **Deferred:** Your task is on hold. Maybe you just don't need to work on this task at the moment, or you need more information before you decide whether this task is worth doing. Either way, you want to keep the task listed so that you can track it or resurrect it later. Perhaps this task isn't a big deal today, but it could become important in a month or two. By tagging a task as Deferred, you keep yourself aware of a task that might or might not ramp up.

Priority field

Specify the timeliness or urgency of the task using this field. Like the Status field, the choices here are selections you make from a menu:

- ✔ **High:** This is the highest possible setting. You should consider the most urgent task to be of high priority.

- ✔ **Normal:** This is the default value, which applies to most tasks. In reality, a Normal task can jump to become a high priority when it isn't finished in time, but you have to decide and assign that yourself.

- ✔ **Low:** Just like you'd surmise, a Low rating tags a task as being less critical: tasks that you can put off until you're finished with the High and Normal tasks. You can rate all your nice-to-have tasks with this priority. *Hint:* When you're finished with your High and Normal tasks, reprioritize your Low tasks.

Due field

Consider this your deadline. Here, you can enter a due date for your task. The default here is None; to change the value to a specified due date, follow these steps:

1. **Select the field.**

   A pop-up menu appears onscreen offering two options: None and By Date.

2. **Select the By Date option.**

   A date field appears on the next line, as shown in Figure 6-3. The value of the date defaults to the current date. If the current date isn't your intended due date, proceed to Step 3 to change the value of this date.

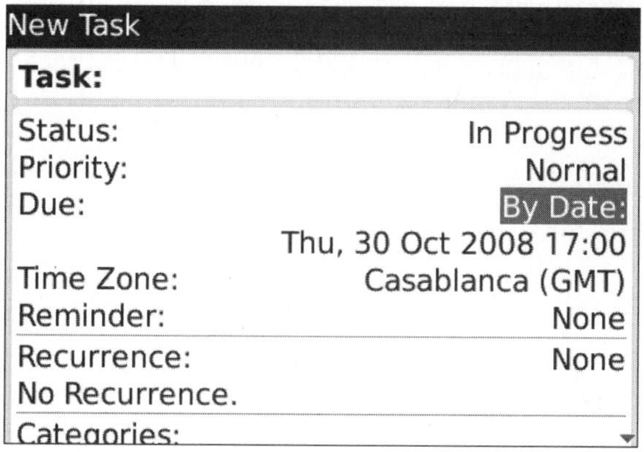

Figure 6-3:
Set a task's
due date
here.

> New Task
>
> **Task:**
>
> | Status: | In Progress |
> |---|---|
> | Priority: | Normal |
> | Due: | By Date: |
> | | Thu, 30 Oct 2008 17:00 |
> | Time Zone: | Casablanca (GMT) |
> | Reminder: | None |
> | Recurrence: | None |
>
> No Recurrence.
>
> Categories:

3. **Select the specific portion of the date that you want to change.**

   Any highlighted portion of the date is editable. You can change the year, month, day, and time. Although this is a date field — like any date field in Tasks, for that matter — setting its value doesn't create an entry in Calendar.

4. **Using the trackball, scroll to the specific date value you want, and then press the trackball to accept the change.**

   At this point, you should have the right value of the date component you want.

Say you modified the day but you want a specific time on that day. Repeat Steps 3 and 4, but this time, highlight (and edit) the time component of the date.

The Recurrence and No Recurrence fields you see in Figure 6-3 show up only when you select By Date in the Due field. Intrigued? Check out the "Creating Recurring Tasks" section, later in this chapter.

Time Zone field

The Time Zone field holds the time zone related to the date fields used for this task: Due (preceding section) and Reminder (following section). If these fields have values of None, this field is irrelevant.

You can specify a time zone different from your locale. For example, if you live in New York but you anticipate completing this task in Mexico City, you can specify the Mexico City time zone. All the times in this task become relative to Mexico City.

Reminder field

You can remind yourself ahead of time about the task using this field. Set this field like you set the Due field. (See the earlier section "Due field.") Setting a reminder is useful, especially for important tasks that you can't afford to forget (such as buying a birthday gift for your significant other).

Just like any date field in Tasks, setting its value doesn't make it show up in Calendar. The type of reminder you get is based on your active profile. (See Chapter 3 for details on how to customize notifications in your profile.)

When the reminder date is met, BlackBerry notifies you and displays a reminder screen. On this screen, you will see the name of the task and possible actions:

- ✔ **Open:** Opens the task
- ✔ **Mark Completed:** Shows up for a task with a status other than Completed
- ✔ **Dismiss:** Closes the screen

Categories field

Assign a specific category to a task using this field. That way, you can filter your Tasks list later. By default, this field is blank. However, you can easily assign a value to it from the Categories screen available through the context menu.

The Categories field is important for organizing your list. It's described fully in the section "Organizing Your Tasks List," later in this chapter.

Notes field

This is your free-for-all text field. You can put anything here you want, such as a detailed description of the task or any other info that relates to this task.

Updating Your Tasks

When it's time to update your Tasks list — say, after finishing a high-priority task or when you want to change the due date for a specific task — the Tasks application won't stand in your way. You can quickly go back to your Tasks list and update those records.

To update a specific task, follow these steps:

1. **Select Tasks.**

   The Tasks application opens to the Find screen, which displays your current Tasks list.

2. **In the Tasks list, select the task you need to edit.**

   The screen that opens is the same one you used to create the high-lighted task, although obviously this display has fields filled with the information you already entered.

3. **Update the fields.**

   Go through each of the fields that you want to edit.

   Tasks and Notes fields are text fields that you can edit from here. To update the other fields, you have to highlight the field, and then press the trackball to make those fields editable.

4. **Press the Menu key, and then select Save.**

   This saves your task, and you can see the updated task in the Tasks list.

Deleting a Task

Just like folks make a ritual of spring cleaning when winter fades, the same is true for your tasks. When a task is completed and keeping it just takes up space, here's how you delete it:

1. **Select Tasks.**

2. **In Tasks, use the trackball to highlight the task you want to delete.**

3. **Press the Menu key, and then select Delete.**

   You see the standard Confirmation screen.

4. **If you're sure that this task is doomed for the dustbin, highlight Delete on the Confirmation screen, and then press the trackball.**

   The task is deleted, and your Tasks list is updated.

Organizing Your Tasks List

As time goes by, your Tasks list is sure to grow — which means that the time it takes to find a task in your list is sure to grow as well. Making a habit to delete finished tasks keeps your list short and organized. (The shorter the list, the better.) We recommend weeding out your Tasks list every time a project or a goal is completed.

If you're someone who just loves to document everything you accomplish (or you work in an environment where you're expected to keep a listing of tasks completed — can you say "quarterly employee review"?), you may not relish the idea of deleting. In that case, regularly archive a copy of your entire Tasks list before you do any weeding.

To archive, synchronize your BlackBerry Bold with your desktop and store the data in whatever time-management software you use on your desktop. Your BlackBerry Bold can synchronize to personal as well as enterprise time-management software. (For details on how to synchronize, see Chapter 15.)

After synchronization, you can print the Tasks list related to this completed project (via your desktop application), which you can file. Having a hard copy of those completed tasks can give you peace of mind as you delete tasks from your BlackBerry Bold. The best of both worlds, right? You clean up your Tasks list (making it easier for you to do a search), and you have an archive (in case you need a historical reference).

Another way to quickly find a task is to sort your list. Chances are you know something identifiable about a task, such as its priority or due date. You can use that information as part of a task sort in your BlackBerry Bold. The list is sorted by name, but you can also sort by priority, due date, or status. Sorting involves customization, which we discuss in the next section.

Customizing tasks

You can make two — count 'em, two — Tasks customizations through the Options screen:

✔ Sorting by criteria

✔ Toggling the deletion confirmation screen

Locating the Options screen from the Tasks application is easy. Just press the trackball and select Options. The Tasks Options screen appears, displaying two sections, Views and Actions, as shown in Figure 6-4. You can set the following here:

- ✔ **Sort By:** Here you can change how the list is sorted. The default task listing is the alphabetical order of the subject from *A* to *Z* (no reverse). To change to a different sort field, follow these steps:

  a. *On the Tasks Options screen, highlight the Sort By field, and then press the trackball.*

  Subject, Priority, Due Date, and Status appear as choices.

  b. *Highlight your choice, and then press the trackball.*

- ✔ **Snooze:** For tasks with reminders, this option allows you to snooze the alarm. The default value is None, but you can set it to 1, 5, 10, 15, or 30 minutes.

- ✔ **Confirm Delete:** This displays a confirmation screen upon deleting a task, a common feature to other BlackBerry applications. You can turn this feature off:

  a. *On the Tasks Options screen, select the Confirm Delete field.*

  Yes and No (see Figure 6-5) display as choices. *No* means you want to toggle off the Confirmation screen.

  b. *Select No.*

  c. *Press the trackball, and then select Save.*

  The Tasks application applies the change you made.

The Number of Entries field you see in Figure 6-5 is just informational, showing you how many tasks you have.

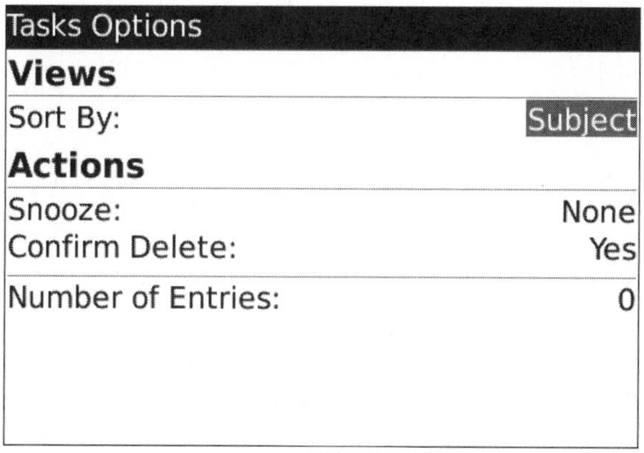

Tasks Options	
Views	
Sort By:	Subject
Actions	
Snooze:	None
Confirm Delete:	Yes
Number of Entries:	0

Figure 6-4: Change your Tasks sort options here.

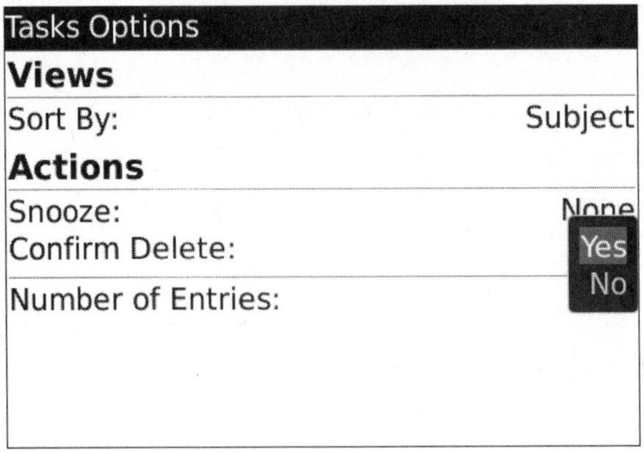

Tasks Options	
Views	
Sort By:	Subject
Actions	
Snooze:	None
Confirm Delete:	Yes / No
Number of Entries:	

Figure 6-5:
Toggle
delete
confirmation
here.

Creating a category

Sometimes sorting doesn't lead you to the right information. For example, if you want to know how many more personal tasks you still have to do as opposed to the more business-oriented stuff you have going, sorting is of no help. What you really need is a way to filter your list based on certain groups that you define. (Hmm. Personal versus Business would be a good start.) Categories is your ticket for filtering.

A *category* is simply a way for you to group your tasks in a manner that you can come back to. When you assign a category on your tasks, you can use the filter feature to view them by category.

To use this feature, start by creating a category:

1. **Select Tasks.**

2. **In Tasks, press the Menu key, and then select Filter.**

   The Select Categories screen appears, listing the default Business and Personal categories. Feel free to use these default categories, but keep in mind that broad categories might not be all that helpful if you have a lot of tasks. (Imagine going to a grocery store with only two sections: perishable and nonperishable.) Our advice to you: Go the extra mile and create some categories to work with.

   Strive to define groups or categories that are meaningful in your line of work: not so broad, but also not too narrow.

3. **Press the Menu key, and then select New.**

   The New Category screen appears. Imagine that.

4. **Type your category name, and then press the trackball.**

   Doing so establishes your category and lists it as an option on the Select Categories screen. See Figure 6-6.

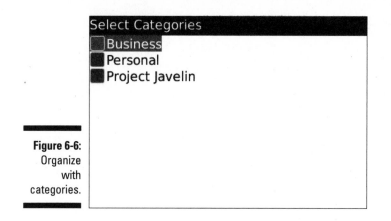

Figure 6-6:
Organize
with
categories.

Define as many categories as necessary upfront so you won't have to go back and create them. After you have the categories, assign them to your tasks.

Categories are shared among applications — specifically, among Contacts, MemoPad, and Tasks. This sibling relationship might sound trivial at first, but don't make the common mistake of assuming that what you change in Tasks doesn't affect other BlackBerry apps. The case of categories shows you how wrong such assumptions are. The importance of this comes into play when you delete a category in an application. For example, if you're working in Tasks and you decide to delete a category, you'll soon discover that you lost that category in Contacts as well — with all its assignments. (The Contacts contact is still intact but will be missing the category assignment.)

Assigning categories to your tasks

Here's how to assign a category to an existing task while you're in the Tasks application:

1. **Launch Tasks and select a task in the list.**

   The Edit Task screen appears, ready for any changes you'd like to make.

2. **Select the Category field.**

3. **In the list that appears, select the category.**

   The category you selected is entered into the field.

4. **Press the Menu key, and then select Save.**

   The task is now associated with the category you selected.

Filtering a Tasks list

Filter is a way for you to view tasks based on a category. Follow these simple steps to use this feature:

1. **Select Tasks.**

   The Tasks application opens.

2. **Press the Menu key, and then select Filter.**

   A screen appears listing all available categories (refer to Figure 6-6).

3. **Select the category you want.**

   A list containing just the tasks associated with the chosen category appears with the category name as the heading, as shown in Figure 6-7.

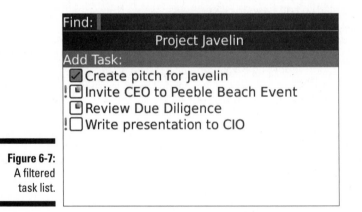

Figure 6-7:
A filtered
task list.

Creating Recurring Tasks

A more-advanced feature in Tasks is to create a *recurring task* — one that repeats periodically. Making a task recurring is the perfect jog for reminding you to pay attention to repeating tasks. Say, buy presents for your significant other (perhaps for a birthday or Valentine's Day), or something a bit more mundane (turning in a weekly status report to your boss).

Making a task recur is simple. If you want a task to repeat every year, follow these steps:

1. **In the Tasks list, select the task you want to recur.**

   The Edit Task screen for the specified task appears.

2. **If the Due field on the Edit Task screen reads None, highlight the field, press the trackball, and then select By Date from the menu.**

   The screen displays a Date field — short for Due Date. The default date is the current date, so if you haven't yet changed the default date to your due date, do that now. (The "Due field" section, earlier in this chapter, has all the details on how to do this.)

   See the Recurrence field farther down the screen, defaulting to None.

   Recurrence appears only after a due date is specified, so you will see it the next time you open this task.

3. **Select the Recurrence field.**

   Daily, Weekly, Monthly, and Yearly selections appear. For this example, you want this task to repeat yearly.

4. **Select Yearly from the list.**

   Your task is set to recur yearly starting on the Due date field (Step 2).

The End field below the Recurrence field is the end of the recurrence and comes in handy when you specify a relative reminder. For example, consider the following:

Due: Mon, Dec 15, 2009 5:00 p.m.

Reminder: Relative

Recurrence: Yearly

Every: 1

End: Mon, Dec 15, 2015

Relative Date: (Checked)

15 Min.

Occurs every year until Dec 15, 2015

Your task will recur every December 15 of each year until 2015. You won't see any difference in the behavior of this task versus a nonrecurring task. You can set up a one-time reminder by choosing either a date or Relative. (Relative means the reminder is active for every recurrence.) For this example, you'll get a reminder at 4:45 p.m. every December 15. By default, your BlackBerry Bold will vibrate. (See Chapter 3 for details on customizing your Tasks notification in Profiles.)

Do you have events that repeat on a particular *day* of the month or year, like the first Tuesday in November? After the End field is a Relative Date check box field. Check this field if the date isn't exact but *relative* on the day: For example, you want the task to recur every fourth Tuesday rather than every 15th of December. This field will appear only for monthly and yearly recurrence.

You can check how your Bold behaves when it reminds you of a task:

✔ In OS 5.0, just press the menu key and select Reminder Alerts.

The same screen you see for the Tasks reminder in the active profile is now available right then and there.

✔ In OS 4.6, you have to go to the active profile.

Chapter 3 shows how to change your profile.

Using Password Keeper

Suppose you're in front of an Internet browser, trying to access an online account. For the life of you, you just can't remember the password of your account. It's your third login attempt, and if you fail this time, your account will be locked. Then you have to call the customer hotline and wait hours before you can speak to a representative. Argghh! We've all done it. Luckily, BlackBerry Bold gives you an application to avoid this headache.

Password Keeper is the simple yet practical BlackBerry Bold application that makes your life that much easier.

Password Keeper is filed in Applications (as shown in Figure 6-8).

Setting a password for Password Keeper

The first time you access Password Keeper, you're prompted to enter a password. *Be sure to remember the password you choose* because this is the password to all your passwords. Forgetting this password is like forgetting the combination your safe. There is no way to retrieve a forgotten Password Keeper password. You are prompted to enter this master password every time you access the application.

Figure 6-8:
Password
Keeper
in the
Applications
folder.

Trust us. One password is much easier to remember than many passwords.

Creating credentials

Okay, so you're ready to fire up your handy-dandy Password Keeper application. Now, what kinds of things does it expect you to do for it to work its magic? Obviously, you'll need to collect the pertinent info for all your various password-protected accounts so that you can store them in the protected environs of Password Keeper. So, when creating a new password entry, be sure you have the following information (see Figure 6-9):

✔ **Title:** This one's straightforward. Just come up with a name to describe the password-protected account — My Favorite Shopping Site, for example.

✔ **Username:** This is where you enter the username for the account.

✔ **Password:** Enter the password for the account here.

✔ **Website:** Put the Web site address (its URL) here.

✔ **Notes:** Not exactly crucial, but the Notes field does give you a bit of room to add a comment or two.

The only required field is Title, but a title alone usually isn't of much use to you. We suggest that you fill in as much other information here as possible, *but at the same time be discreet about those locations where you use your username and password* — so don't put anything in the Website field or use My eBay Account as a title. That way, for the unlikely case of someone gaining access to your password to Password Keeper, the intruder will have a hard time figuring out where exactly to use your credentials.

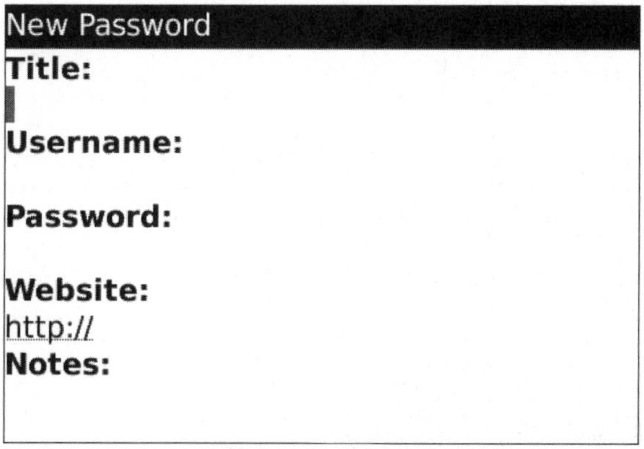

Figure 6-9:
Set your
password
here.

New Password

Title:

Username:

Password:

Website:
http://

Notes:

Random password generation

If you're the kind of person who uses one password for everything but knows deep in your heart that this is just plain wrong, wrong, wrong, random password generation is for you. When creating a new password for yet another online account (or when changing your password for an online account you already have), fire up Password Keeper, press the trackball, and then select Random Password from the menu that appears, as shown in Figure 6-10. *Voilà!* A new password is automatically generated for you.

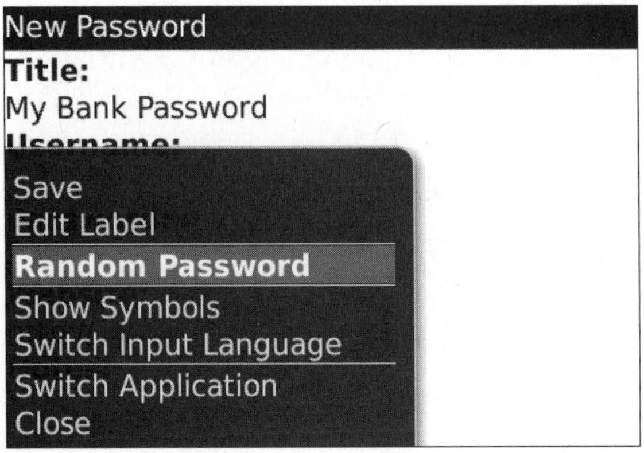

New Password
Title:
My Bank Password
~~Username:~~

Save
Edit Label
Random Password
Show Symbols
Switch Input Language
Switch Application
Close

Figure 6-10:
Generate
a random
password.

Using random password generation makes sense in conjunction with Password Keeper because you don't have to remember the randomly generated password that Password Keeper came up with for any of your online accounts — that's Password Keeper's job.

Using your password

The whole point of Password Keeper is to let your BlackBerry Bold's electronic brain do your password remembering for you. So, imagine this scenario: You can no longer live without owning your personal copy of the *A Chipmunk Christmas* CD, so you surf on over to your favorite online music store and attempt to log in. You draw a blank on your password, but instead of seething, you take out your Bold, open Password Keeper, and do a find.

Type the first letters of your account title in the Find field to search for the title of your password. After you find (and highlight) the title, you press the trackball and the screen for your account appears, conveniently listing the password. All you have to do now is enter the password into the login screen for the online music store and Alvin, Simon, and Theodore will soon be wending their way to your address, ready to sing "Chipmunk Jingle Bells."

Yes, you *can* copy and paste your password from Password Keeper to another application — BlackBerry Browser, for instance. Just highlight the password name, press the trackball, and select Copy to Clipboard from the menu that appears. Then navigate to where you want to enter the password, press the trackball, and select Paste from the menu. Keep in mind, for the copy-and-paste function to work for passwords from Password Keeper, you need to enable the Allow Clipboard Copy option in the Password Keeper options (see the upcoming Table 6-1). You can copy and paste only one password at a time.

After you paste your password in another application, clear the Clipboard by pressing the trackball and choosing Clear Clipboard. The Clipboard keeps your last copied password until you clear it.

Password Keeper options

Password Keeper's Options menu, accessible by pressing the Menu key while in Password Keeper, allows you to control how Password Keeper behaves. For example, you can set what characters can make up a randomly generated password. Table 6-1 describes all these options.

Table 6-1	Password Keeper Options
Option Name	**Description**
Random Password Length	Select between 4 and 16 for the length of your randomly generated password.
Random Includes Alpha	If True, a randomly generated password includes alphabetic characters.
Random Includes Numbers	If True, a randomly generated password includes numbers.
Random Includes Symbols	If True, a randomly generated password includes symbols.
Confirm Delete	If True, all deletions are prompted with a confirmation screen.
Password Attempts	Select between 1 and 20 attempts to successfully enter the password to Password Keeper.
Allow Clipboard Copy	If True, you can copy and paste passwords from Password Keeper.
Show Password	True displays password; otherwise, asterisks take the place of the password characters.

Changing your password to Password Keeper

If you want to change your master password to Password Keeper — the password for opening Password Keeper itself — follow these steps:

1. **Select Password Keeper.**

   The initial login screen for the Password Keeper application appears.

2. **Enter your old password to access Password Keeper.**

3. **In Password Keeper, press the Menu key, and then select Change Password.**

   Doing so calls up the Password Keeper screen that allows you to enter your new password, as shown in Figure 6-11.

4. **Enter a new password, confirm it by entering it again, and then use your trackball to click OK.**

Figure 6-11:
Change your
Password
Keeper
password
here.

Password Keeper

Please choose a new password:
******
Please confirm your new password:
****

OK   Cancel

Chapter 7

Calling Your Favorite Person

. . . .

In This Chapter

▶ Accessing the BlackBerry Phone application

▶ Making and receiving calls

▶ Managing your calls with call forwarding and more

▶ Customizing your BlackBerry Phone setup

▶ Conferencing with more than one person

▶ Talking hands-free on your BlackBerry phone

▶ Multitasking with your BlackBerry phone

. . . .

*T*he BlackBerry phone operates no differently than any other phone you've used. So why bother with this chapter? Although your BlackBerry phone operates like any other phone, it has capabilities that far outreach those of your run-of-the-mill cellphone. For example, when was the last time your phone was connected to your to-do list? Have you ever received an e-mail and placed a call directly from that e-mail? We didn't think so. But with your BlackBerry, you can do all these things and more.

In this chapter, we first cover phone basics, and then show you some of the neat ways BlackBerry Phone intertwines with other BlackBerry applications and functions.

Using the BlackBerry Phone Application

Accessing the Phone application from the BlackBerry is a snap. You can press the green Send button located right below the display screen to get into the Phone application.

You can get to the Phone application also by pressing any of the numeric keys. To do this, however, you have to make sure that the Dial from Home Screen option is enabled in Phone Options. If you're a frequent phone user, we recommend that you enable this option.

To enable dialing from the Home screen, follow these steps:

1. **From your BlackBerry Bold, press the green Send key.**

   Phone opens, showing the dial screen as well as your call history list.

2. **Press the Menu key, and then select the Options (wrench) icon.**

3. **Select General Options.**

4. **Highlight the Dial from Home Screen option, press the trackball, and then select Yes from the drop-down list.**

   This enables you to make a phone call by pressing the numeric keys when at the Home screen.

5. **Press the Menu key, and then select Save.**

Making and Receiving Calls

The folks at RIM have created an intuitive user interface to all the essential Phone features, including making and receiving calls.

Making a call

To make a call, start from the Home screen and type the phone number you want to dial. As soon as you start typing numbers, the Phone application opens. When you finish typing the destination number, press the green Send key.

Calling from Contacts

Because you can't possibly remember all your friends' and colleagues' phone numbers, calling from Contacts is convenient and useful. To call from Contacts, follow these steps:

1. **Open the Phone application.**

2. **Press the Menu key.**

   The Phone menu appears, as shown in Figure 7-1.

3. **Select Call from Contacts.**

   Contacts opens. From here, you can search as usual for the contact you'd like to call.

4. **From Contacts, highlight your call recipient, press the trackball, and then select Call.**

   This makes the call.

1:13 PM	1339	5 f	3G			

Wireless - Misao

Call 2125551212

SMS 2125551212

MMS 2125551212

	(W)	06/20
View History		05/07
Add Speed Dial		05/04
Delete		05/03
View Speed Dial List		04/24
Add to Contacts		04/24
Copy 2125551212		04/23
Set Ring Tones		04/23
Options		04/15
Status		04/15

Figure 7-1: The Phone menu.

Dialing letters

One of the nice features of BlackBerry Phone is that you can dial letters, and BlackBerry will figure out the corresponding number. For example, to dial 1-800-11-LEARN, do the following on your BlackBerry:

1. **From the Home screen or the Phone application, dial 1-8-0-0-1-1.**

   As you type the first number, the Phone application opens (if it isn't open already) and displays the numbers you dialed.

2. **Press and hold the Alt key, and then dial (press) L-E-A-R-N.**

   The letters appear onscreen as you type.

3. **Press the green Send key.**

   The call is initiated.

Receiving a call

Receiving a call on your BlackBerry is even easier than making a call. You can receive calls in a couple of ways. One is by using your BlackBerry's automated answering feature, and the other is by answering manually.

Automated answering is triggered whenever you take your BlackBerry out of your holster; in other words, just taking out the BlackBerry forces it to automatically pick up any call, so you can start talking right away. The disadvantage of this is that you don't have time to see who is calling you (on your Caller ID). *Note:* To disable autoanswering, be sure that your BlackBerry isn't in its holster when an incoming call arrives.

What's the advantage of disabling autoanswering? Well, manual answering prompts you to answer a call or ignore a call when you receive an incoming call (see Figure 7-2). This way, you can see on your Caller ID who is calling you before you decide to pick up or ignore the call.

Figure 7-2:
An incoming call on a
BlackBerry
Bold.

Handling missed calls

So, you missed that call from that important client. What made it worse is that you didn't notice the missed call because you didn't see the little Missed Call icon. This happened because you pay attention only to what is in your e-mail message box. What can you do to make sure that you return that call?

You can make missed calls appear in your e-mail message box so that you are sure to return your missed calls (if you choose to, that is).

To have your missed calls appear in your inbox, follow these steps:

1. **Open the Phone application.**

2. **Press the Menu key.**

   The Phone menu appears (refer to Figure 7-1).

3. **Select Options.**

   The Phone Options screen appears, listing the different categories of options.

4. **Select Call Logging.**

   This opens the Call Logging screen.

5. **Scroll to Missed Calls and press the trackball.**

   You can also select All Calls, which means that incoming and outgoing calls will be displayed in your e-mail inbox.

6. **Press the Menu key and select Save.**

Phone Options while on a Call

When you're on the phone, situations might arise where you'd want to mute your conversation, place a call on hold, or change the call volume. No problem. BlackBerry Bold makes such adjustments easy.

Muting your call

You may want to use the Mute feature while on a conference call (see the upcoming section "Arranging Conference Calls") when you don't need to speak but do need to hear what is being discussed. Maybe you're on the bus or have kids in the background, making your surroundings noisy. By using Mute, these background noises are filtered out from the conference call.

To mute your call, follow these steps:

1. **While in a conversation, press the Menu key.**

   The Phone menu appears in all its glory.

2. **Select Mute.**

   You hear a tone, indicating that your call is being muted.

Follow these steps to unmute your call:

1. **While a call is on mute, press the Menu key.**

   The Phone menu makes another appearance.

2. **Select Turn Mute Off.**

   You hear a tone, indicating that your call is now unmuted.

Placing your call on hold

Unlike muting a call, placing a call on hold prohibits both you and your caller from hearing one another. To put a conversation on hold, follow these steps:

1. **While in a conversation, press the trackball.**

   The Phone menu appears yet again.

2. **Scroll to Hold, and press the trackball.**

   Your call is now on hold.

Follow these steps to unhold your call:

1. **While a call is on hold, press the trackball.**

   A new menu appears.

2. **Scroll to Resume, and then press the trackball.**

   You can continue your conversation.

Adjusting the call volume

Adjusting the call volume, a simple yet important action on your BlackBerry phone, can be performed by simply pressing the volume up or volume down key on the side of your BlackBerry.

Customizing the BlackBerry Phone

For your BlackBerry phone to work the way you like, you have to first set it up the way you want it. In the following sections, we go through some settings that can make you the master of your BlackBerry phone.

Setting up your voice mail number

This section shows you how to set up your voice mail access number. Unfortunately, the instructions for setting up your voice mailbox vary, depending on your service provider. However, most service providers are more than happy to walk you through the steps to get your mailbox set up in a jiffy.

To set up your voice mail access number, follow these steps:

1. **Open the Phone application.**

2. **Press the Menu key, and then select the Options (wrench) icon.**

   A list of phone options appears.

3. **Select Voice Mail.**

   This opens the voice mail configuration screen.

4. **Scroll to access the number field and enter your voice mail access number.**

   If this field is empty and you don't know this number, contact your service provider and ask for your voice mail access number.

5. **Press the Menu key, and then select Save.**

Using call forwarding

On the BlackBerry Bold, you have two types of call forwarding:

- **Forward all calls:** Any calls to your BlackBerry Bold are forwarded to the number you designate. Another name for this feature is *unconditional forwarding.*

- **Forward unanswered calls:** Calls that meet different types of conditions are forwarded to different numbers as follows:

  - *If busy:* You don't have call waiting turned on, and you're on the phone.

  - *If no answer:* You don't hear your phone ring or somehow are unable to pick up your phone (perhaps you're in a meeting).

  - *If unreachable:* You're out of network coverage and cannot receive any signals.

Out of the box, your BlackBerry forwards any unanswered calls, regardless of conditions, to your voice mail number by default. However, you can add new numbers to forward a call to.

You need to be within network coverage before can you change your call forwarding option. After you're within network coverage, you can change your call forwarding settings by doing the following:

1. **Open the Phone application, press the Menu key, and select Options.**

   A list of phone options appears.

2. **Select Call Forwarding.**

   Your BlackBerry now attempts to connect to the server. If successful, you'll see the Call Forwarding screen.

   If you don't see the Call Forwarding screen, wait until you have network coverage and try again.

3. **From the Call Forwarding screen, press the Menu key, and then select Edit Numbers.**

   A list of numbers appears. If this is the first time you're setting call forwarding, most likely only your voice mail number is in this list.

4. **To add a new forwarding number, press the Menu key, and then select New Number.**

   A pop-up menu appears, prompting you to enter the new forwarding number.

5. **In the pop-up window, enter the number you want to forward to, and then press the trackball.**

   The new number you entered now appears on the call forward number list. You can add this new number to any call forwarding types or conditions.

6. **Press the Escape key.**

   (The Escape key is the arrow key to the right of the trackball.) You are returned to the Call Forwarding screen.

7. **Scroll to the If Unreachable field and press the trackball.**

   A drop-down list appears, listing numbers from the call forwarding number list, including the one you just added.

8. **Select the number you want to forward to, and then press the trackball.**

   Doing so places the selected number into the If Unreachable field. You can see this on the Call Forwarding screen.

9. **Confirm your changes by pressing the Menu key, and then selecting Save.**

Configuring speed dial

Speed dial is a convenient feature on any phone. And after you get used to having it on a phone system, it's hard not to use it on other phones, including your BlackBerry phone.

Viewing your speed dial list

To view your speed dial list, follow these steps:

1. **Open the Phone application.**

2. **Press the Menu key, and then select View Speed Dial List.**

    This displays a list of speed dial entries, as shown in Figure 7-3. If you haven't set up any speed dials, this list will be empty.

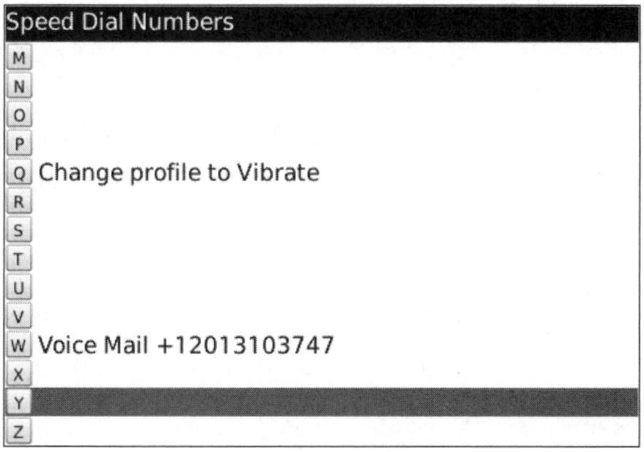

Figure 7-3:
The speed dial list on a BlackBerry Bold.

Adding a number to speed dial

Setting up speed dial numbers is as easy as using them. It takes a few seconds to set them up, but you benefit every time you use this feature.

To assign a number to a speed dial slot, follow these steps:

1. **Open the Phone application.**

2. **Press the Menu key, select Options, and then select View Speed Dial List.**

    This displays your list of speed dial numbers.

3. **Scroll to an empty speed dial slot, press the Menu key, and then select New Speed Dial.**

    BlackBerry Contacts appears so that you can select a contact's phone number.

4. **Select a contact, and then press the trackball.**

    If more than one number is associated with the selected contact, you're prompted to select which number to add to the speed dial list.

    The number appears in the speed dial list.

Using speed dial

After you have a few speed dial entries set up, you can start using them. To do so, while on the Home screen or in the Phone application, press a speed dial key. The call is initiated to the number associated with that particular speed dial key.

Arranging Conference Calls

To have two or more people on the phone with you — the infamous conference call — do the following:

1. **Use the Phone application to place a call to the first participant.**

2. **While the first participant is on the phone with you, press the Menu key, and then select New Call.**

   This automatically places the first call on hold and brings up a New Call screen, as shown in Figure 7-4, prompting you to place another call.

Figure 7-4: A meeting participant is on hold.

3. **Place a call to the second participant by dialing a number, pressing the trackball, and then selecting Call.**

   You can dial the number by using the number pad, or you can select a frequently dialed number from your call log. To place a call from your Contacts, press the trackball from the New Call screen and select Call from Contacts. Your BlackBerry then prompts you to select a contact to dial.

   The call to the second meeting participant is just like any other phone call (except that the first participant is still on the other line).

4. **While the second participant is on the phone with you, press the Menu key, and then select Join Conference, as shown in Figure 7-5.**

   This reconnects the first participant with you, along with the second participant. Now you can discuss away with both participants at the same time.

Figure 7-5:
Join two
other people
in a confer-
ence call.

Another name for having two people on the phone with you is *three-way calling,* which isn't a new concept. If you want to chat with four people or even ten people on the phone at the same time, you certainly can. Simply repeat Steps 2 through 4 until all the participants are on the phone.

Talking privately to a conference participant

During a conference call, you may want to talk to one participant privately. This is called *splitting* your conference call. Here's how you do it:

1. **While on a conference call, press the Menu key and then select Split Call, as shown in Figure 7-6.**

   A pop-up screen appears, listing all the participants of the conference call.

2. **From the pop-up screen, select the participant with whom you want to speak privately.**

   This action places all other participants on hold and connects you to the participant you selected. On the display screen, you can see to whom you are connected — this confirms that you selected the right person to chat with privately.

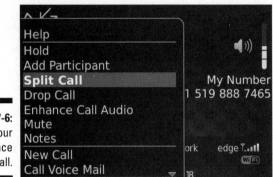

Figure 7-6:
Split your
conference
call.

Help
Hold
Add Participant
Split Call
Drop Call
Enhance Call Audio
Mute
Notes
New Call
Call Voice Mail

My Number
1 519 888 7465

3. **To talk to all participants again, press the Menu key, and then select Join Conference.**

   Doing so brings you back to the conference call with everyone else.

Alternate between phone conversations

Whether you're in a private conversation during a conference call or you're talking to someone while you have someone else on hold, you can switch between the two conversations by swapping them. Follow these steps:

1. **While talking to someone with another person on hold, press the Menu key, and then select Swap.**

   Doing so switches you from the person with whom you're currently talking to the person who was on hold.

2. **Repeat Step 1 to go back to the original conversation.**

Dropping that meeting hugger

If you've been on conference calls, you can identify those chatty "meeting huggers" who have to say something about everything. Don't you wish that you could drop them off the call? Well, with your BlackBerry, you can (as long as you are the meeting moderator or the person who initiates the call). Follow these steps to perform the drop-kick:

1. **While on a conference call, press the Menu key, and then select Drop Call.**

   A pop-up screen appears, listing all conference call participants.

2. **Select the meeting hugger you want to drop.**

   That person is disconnected.

3. **Everyone else now can continue the conversation as usual.**

Communicating Hands-Free

More and more places prohibit the use of mobile phones without a hands-free headset. Here are the hands-free options for your BlackBerry.

Using the speaker phone

The Speaker Phone function is useful under certain situations, such as when you're in a room full of people who want to join your phone conversation. Or you might be all by your lonesome in your office but are stuck rooting through your files — hard to do with a BlackBerry scrunched up against your ear. (We call such moments *multitasking* — a concept so important we devote an entire upcoming section to it.)

To switch to the speaker phone while you're on a phone call on the Pearl Flip, press the OP key. If you are on a non-SureType BlackBerry, press the Menu key, and then select Activate Speaker Phone.

Pairing your BlackBerry with a Bluetooth headset

Because BlackBerry smartphones come with a wired hands-free headset, you can start using yours by simply plugging it into the headset jack on the left side of the BlackBerry. You adjust the volume of the headset by pressing up or down on the volume keys, the same as you would adjust the call volume without the headset.

Using the wired hands-free headset can help you avoid being a police target, but if you're multitasking on your BlackBerry, the wired headset can get in the way and become inconvenient.

This is where the whole Bluetooth wireless thing comes in. You can purchase a BlackBerry Bluetooth headset to go with your Bluetooth-enabled BlackBerry. For a list of BlackBerry-compatible Bluetooth headsets, see Chapter 20.

After you purchase a BlackBerry-compatible Bluetooth headset, you can pair it with your BlackBerry. Think of *pairing* a Bluetooth headset with your BlackBerry as registering the headset with your BlackBerry so that it recognizes the headset.

First things first: You need to prep your headset for pairing. Now, each headset manufacturer has a different take on this, so you'll need to consult your headset documentation for details. With that out of the way, continue with the pairing as follows:

1. **From the Home screen, press the Menu key, and then select Bluetooth.**

2. **Press the Menu key to display the Bluetooth menu.**

   You see the Enable Bluetooth option. If you see the Disable Bluetooth option instead, you can skip to Step 4.

3. **Scroll to Enable Bluetooth, and then press the trackball.**

   This enables Bluetooth on your BlackBerry.

4. **Press the Menu key to display the Bluetooth menu, and then select Add Device.**

   You see the Searching for Devices progress bar, um, progressing, as shown in Figure 7-7. When your BlackBerry discovers the headset, a Select Device dialog box appears with the name of the headset.

Figure 7-7: Searching for a headset.

5. **From the Select Device dialog box, select the Bluetooth headset.**

   A dialog box appears to prompt you for a passkey code to the headset.

6. **Enter the passkey and press the trackball.**

   Normally, the passkey code is 0000, but refer to your headset documentation. After you successfully enter the passkey code, you see your headset listed in the Bluetooth setting.

7. **Press the Menu key to display the Bluetooth menu, and then select Connect.**

   Your BlackBerry now attempts to connect to the Bluetooth headset.

8. **When you see a screen similar to Figure 7-8, you can start using your Bluetooth headset.**

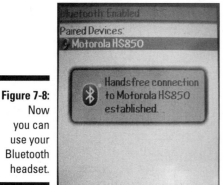

Figure 7-8:
Now
you can
use your
Bluetooth
headset.

Using voice dialing

With your headset and the Voice Dialing application, you can truly be hands-free from your BlackBerry. You may be thinking, how do I activate the Voice Dialing application without touching my BlackBerry? Good question. The majority of hands-free headsets (Bluetooth or not) come with a multipurpose button.

Usually, a multipurpose button on a hands-free headset can mute, end, and initiate a call. Refer to the operating manual of your hands-free headset for more info.

After your headset is active, press its multipurpose button to activate the Voice Dialing application. You will be greeted with a voice stating, "Say a command." At this point, simply say "Call" and state the name of a person or say the number. (For example, say "Call President Obama" or "Call 555-2468.") The Voice Dialing application is good at recognizing the name of the person and the numbers you dictate. However, we strongly suggest that you try out the voice dialing feature before you need it.

Multitasking while on the Phone

One of the great things about the BlackBerry Bold is that you can use it for other tasks while you're on the phone. For example, you can take notes or make a to-do list. Or you can look up a phone number in BlackBerry Contacts that your caller is asking you for. You can even compose an e-mail and receive e-mails while on a call!

It makes sense to multitask while you're using a hands-free headset or a speaker phone. Otherwise, your face would be stuck to your BlackBerry, and you couldn't engage in your conversation and multitask at the same time.

Accessing applications while on the phone

After you have donned your hands-free headset or have turned on a speaker phone, you can start multitasking by doing the following:

1. **While in a conversation, from the Phone application, press the Menu key, and then select Home screen.**

   Alternatively, you can simply press the Escape key (the arrow key to the right of the trackball) while in the Phone application to return to your Home screen. This returns you to the Home screen without terminating your phone conversation.

2. **From the Home screen, you can start multitasking.**

While on the phone and multitasking, however, you can still access the Phone menu from other applications. For example, from your to-do list, you can end a call or put a call on hold.

Taking notes while on the phone

To take notes of your call, follow these steps:

1. **During a phone conversation, press the Menu key, and then select Notes.**

   This displays the Notes screen.

2. **Type notes for the conversation, as shown in Figure 7-9.**

   When the call ends, the notes are automatically saved for you.

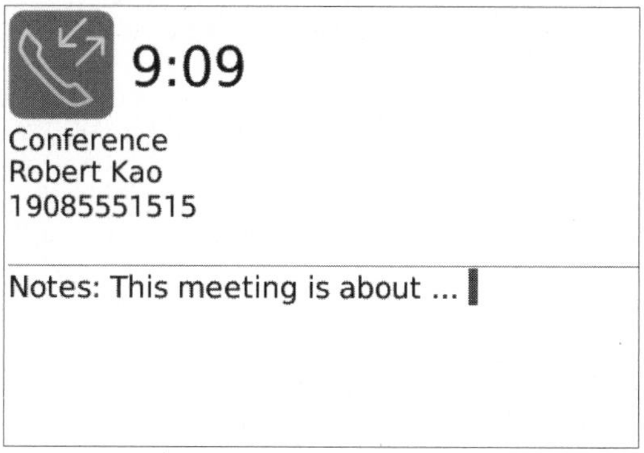

9:09

Conference
Robert Kao
19085551515

Notes: This meeting is about ... |

Figure 7-9:
Take notes
while on a
phone call.

Accessing phone notes

From the call history list (see Figure 7-10), you can access notes that you've
made during a call or a conference call. In addition, you can also edit and add
new notes.

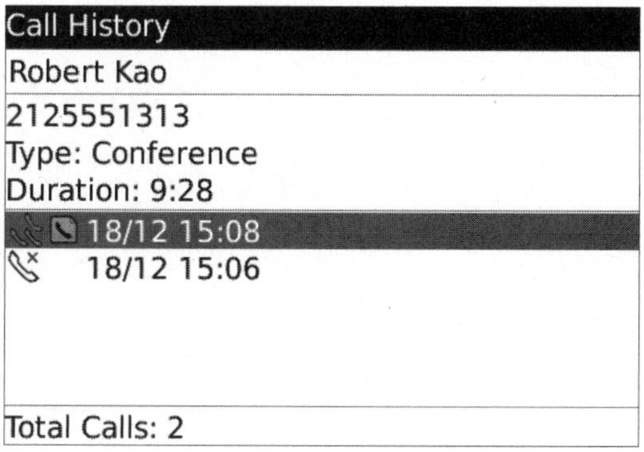

Call History

Robert Kao

2125551313
Type: Conference
Duration: 9:28

  18/12 15:08
  18/12 15:06

Total Calls: 2

Figure 7-10:
Call history,
where you
can see
conversa-
tion notes.

Forwarding phone notes

You can forward your phone notes just like any e-mail. While on the Call
History screen (refer to Figure 7-10), press the Menu key, and then select
Forward.

You can add notes not only while you're on the phone but also afterward.
While you are viewing a call history, press the Menu key. Then select Add
Notes if you have no notes for the call, or select Edit Notes if you already have
notes for the call.

Part III
Getting Online with Your Bold

The 5th Wave   By Rich Tennant

KENNETH BUYS HIS FIRST SMART PHONE

©RICHTENNANT

Exercise more.

In this part . . .

Here's the good stuff — using your BlackBerry for e-mail , text messaging, and going online and Web surfing. You'll also get directions from the BlackBerry GPS.

Chapter 8

You've Got (Lots of) E-Mail

*Y*our BlackBerry Bold brings a fresh new face to the convenience and ease of use that you associate with e-mail. You can direct mail to your Bold from as many as ten e-mail accounts, from your work e-mail to personal e-mail from providers such as Yahoo! and AOL. You can set up an e-mail signature, configure e-mail filters, and search for e-mails.

In this chapter, you find answers on how to use and manage the e-mail capabilities of your Bold to their full potential. From setup to sorts, it's all covered here.

Getting Up and Running with E-Mail

Regardless of your network service provider (such as T-Mobile, or Rogers, or Vodafone), you can set up your Bold to receive mail from at least one of your e-mail accounts. Thus, with whatever address you use to send and receive e-mail from your PC (Yahoo!, Gmail, and so on), you can hook up your Bold to use that same e-mail address. Instead of checking your Gmail from your desktop, for example, you can now get it on your Bold.

Most network service providers allow you to connect as many as ten e-mail accounts to your Bold. This provides you with the convenience of one central point from which you can get all your e-mail, without having to log on to multiple e-mail accounts. Such convenience!

In an enterprise environment — depending on your company policy — you might not be able to access the BlackBerry Internet Service (BIS) site to link your personal e-mail accounts to your Bold. If you work for a Fortune 500 company, most likely you can't access the BIS. However, you can still configure e-mail settings (such as the BlackBerry e-mail filter and BlackBerry e-mail reconciliation) to make your e-mail experience that much better. (See the upcoming section, "Enabling wireless reconciliation." If you're an enterprise user, skip to the parts where you see the Enterprise icon to configure your e-mail settings. If you haven't set up e-mail on your company-owned Bold, see the upcoming section "Setting up e-mail in an enterprise environment."

Using the BlackBerry Internet Service client

You can pull together all your e-mail accounts into one by using the BlackBerry Internet Service (BIS) client (formerly known as the BlackBerry Web client). The BIS client allows you to

- ✔ **Manage multiple e-mail accounts.** As we mention earlier, you can combine as many as ten of your e-mail accounts onto your Bold. See the next section for more details.

- ✔ **Use wireless e-mail reconciliation.** No more trying to match your Bold e-mail against e-mail in your combined account(s). Just turn on wireless e-mail reconciliation, and you're good to go. For more on this, see the upcoming section "Enabling wireless reconciliation."

- ✔ **Create e-mail filters.** You can filter e-mails on your Bold so that you get only those messages that you truly care about. See the "Filtering your e-mail" section, near the end of this chapter.

Think of the BIS client as an online e-mail account manager, but one that doesn't keep your e-mails. Instead, it routes the e-mails from your other accounts to your Bold (because it's directly connected to your Bold).

Combining your e-mail accounts into one

To start aggregating e-mail accounts (such as Gmail) onto your Bold, you must first run a setup program from the BIS client. You can access the Service client from your Bold or from your desktop computer.

To access the Service client from your PC, you need the URL that is specific to your network service. Contact your network service provider (T-Mobile, Verizon, and so on) directly to get that information.

After you've logged on to the Service client, you should see a screen similar to Figure 8-1. If your network provider has activated your account, you should see one e-mail address, the default address of your account.

Figure 8-1:
Set up
an e-mail
account
here.

You see three options on the left navigation bar. The E-mail Accounts option allows you to add, edit, and delete e-mail accounts. In addition, for each e-mail address, you can set up filters and an e-mail signature. We don't cover the other two options here because they're used so infrequently.

As we mention previously, your Bold already has a default e-mail address that you can use to receive and send e-mail. If you don't have any other e-mail account that you want to meld into your BlackBerry e-mail account, simply skip to the upcoming "Customizing Your E-Mail" section.

Adding an e-mail account

To add an e-mail account to your BlackBerry account, follow these steps from your desktop PC:

1. **From the BIS client (refer to Figure 8-1), click the Setup Account button.**

2. **On the e-mail account screen, enter the e-mail address and logon credentials for that e-mail address:**

   • *E-mail address:* The address from which you want to receive e-mail: for example, `myid@yahoo.com`

   • *Account logon:* The one you use to log on to this e-mail account

   • *Password:* The one you use with the logon

3. **Click Next.**

   You're finished. It's that easy!

You can also manage your accounts from your Bold. From the Home screen, press the Menu key and select Set Up Internet E-Mail. The rest is pretty much the same on the Bold as it is on a PC.

With your BlackBerry Bold, you can create and set up the BIS account as you would on your PC. Although you could do this even before OS 5.0, the new interface has made setting up BIS account much easier.

To add an e-mail account to your BlackBerry account from your BlackBerry, follow these steps:

1. **From your BlackBerry Home screen, select Setup Folder**

2. **Select the Person E-mail Setup icon.**

   You will be prompted with a login screen, similar to Figure 8-2. If you haven't created your account, you will see a Create button to create your BIS account.

3. **After you log in, click Add.**

   A screen with different e-mail domains (Yahoo!, Google) appears. See Figure 8-3.

4. **Select an e-mail domain.**

5. **Enter the e-mail address and password, and then select Next.**

   If you entered your e-mail credentials correctly, then you will get a setup confirmation screen.

Figure 8-2:
BlackBerry
Internet
Service
setup on
BlackBerry
OS 5.0.

BlackBerry® Internet Service
Existing Users
If you want to access your email settings or you changed your device, log in.
User name:
mytestbb
Password: Forgot Password?
****
☑ Remember me on this device.
Log In
Close

If you have OS 4.6, follow these steps to add e-mail accounts to your BlackBerry:

1. **From your BlackBerry Home screen, select Setup Folder.**

2. **Select the Person E-mail Setup icon.**

   You will be prompted with a login screen. If you haven't created your account, you will see a Create New Account link to create your BIS account.

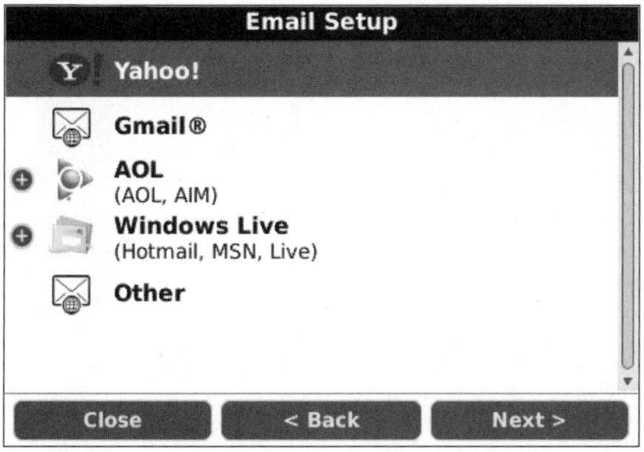

Figure 8-3:
Select
an e-mail
domain.

Email Setup
Ⓨ Yahoo!
✉ **Gmail®**
⊕ 🜁 **AOL** (AOL, AIM)
⊕ 📁 **Windows Live** (Hotmail, MSN, Live)
✉ **Other**

| Close | < Back | Next > |

3. **After you log in, click the Add My Existing E-mail Account link.**

   A screen with different text field appears. Here you can enter an email address and the password associated with that email account.

4. **Enter the e-mail address and password, and click Next.**

   If you enter all the information correctly, you will see a Setup Complete screen.

Setting up e-mail in an enterprise environment

This section is for you if your Bold can't receive and send e-mail yet — like when you first get your Bold or you swap an old model for a new one.

If your e-mail function works properly on your Bold, you can skip this section.

Follow these steps to activate your BlackBerry Bold for enterprise use:

1. **From the Home screen, press the Menu key and select Enterprise Activation.**

The Enterprise Activation screen opens, with two fields for you to fill in:

- *Your corporate e-mail address:* For example, `myaccount@abc Company.com`

- *Your password:* From your IT department

2. **Type your corporate e-mail account along with the appropriate password.**

   If you don't know these pieces of information, contact your corporate system administrator.

3. **Press the Menu key, and select Activate.**

   Your Bold attempts to activate itself with your corporation.

Some corporations don't allow any employee-purchased BlackBerry smartphones to be activated with corporate e-mail. Check with your system administrator for corporate BlackBerry policies.

Getting e-mail in an enterprise environment using Desktop Redirector

If you are a sole proprietor or consultant who works in a corporation that runs Exchange or Lotus, and you would like to get enterprise e-mails on your Bold, this section is for you.

Typically, to get enterprise e-mail, your Bold would have to be configured with the BlackBerry Enterprise Server (BES). Expect this if your employer hands you a Bold. However, if you work for a company as a contractor, you probably won't be getting a BlackBerry from that company. When you want to get enterprise e-mail so that you don't fall behind, you need Desktop Redirector so that you can get company e-mail on your personal BlackBerry.

To start using Desktop Redirector, you first need to install BlackBerry Desktop Manager; see Chapter 15 for details about how to do this. After you install Desktop Manager with Redirector, make sure that Redirector starts every time you boot up your PC.

Depending on the corporate security policy, some corporations allow Desktop Redirector, and some do not. Before you start using Desktop Redirector, contact the IT department in the company you work for.

Here are just a few caveats when using Desktop Redirector:

- ✔ You can get enterprise e-mail as long as your PC is turned on and has an Internet connection.

✔ When someone sends you an attachment, you can't retrieve it from your Bold. Unfortunately, that is the limitation for Desktop Redirector.

✔ When someone sends you a meeting notice, you can't accept or reject it.

Customizing Your E-Mail

In the following sections, we go over the details of the following e-mail configurations:

✔ **Configuring an e-mail signature:** If you're tired of writing *Regards, John Smith* over and over to close an e-mail, set an e-mail signature.

✔ **Enabling wireless e-mail reconciliation:** After enabling e-mail reconciliation, whatever you see on your Bold is what you get in your e-mail account(s). You no longer have to double-delete a message in both your Bold and your e-mail account(s).

✔ **Configuring autoreplies:** Whether you are out of the office or just want a quick response message sent to your senders, this is where you can specify the message they see. This feature is for enterprise users only.

Configuring your e-mail signature

By default, your e-mail signature is something like "Sent via My BlackBerry," which can be cool in the first week, showing off to people that you are *à la mode* with your BlackBerry. But sooner or later, you may not want people to know that you are out and about while answering e-mail. Or, you may want something more personal. Follow these steps to configure your e-mail signature by using the BIS client:

1. **Log on to the client on your PC.**

2. **In the BIS client (refer to Figure 8-1), click the Edit icon for the desired e-mail account.**

   The edit screen appears, as shown in Figure 8-4.

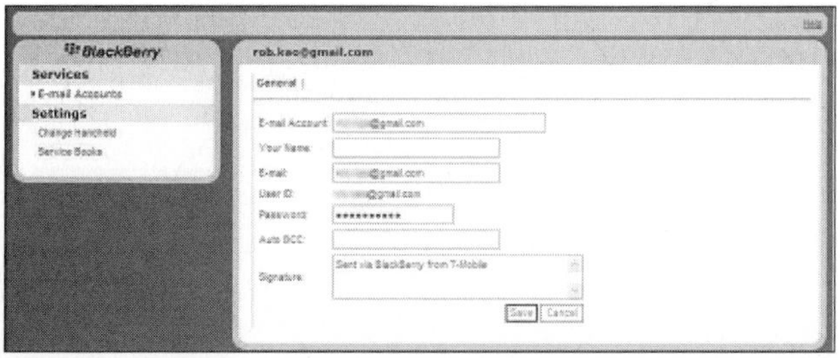

Figure 8-4:
The e-mail account edit screen.

3. **In the Signature field, type the desired text for your e-mail signature.**

4. **Click Save.**

Enabling wireless reconciliation

With wireless reconciliation, you don't need to delete the same e-mail in two places (on your computer and on your Bold). The two e-mail inboxes reconcile with each other: hence, the term *wireless reconciliation.* Convenient, huh?

Enabling wireless e-mail synchronization

You can start wireless e-mail synchronization by configuring your Bold. Follow these steps:

1. **From the Home screen, press the Menu key, and select Messages.**

   This opens the Messages application. You see the message list.

2. **In the message list, press the Menu key, and select Options.**

   The Options screen appears, with two option types: General Options and E-mail Reconciliation.

3. **Select E-mail Reconciliation.**

   This opens the E-mail Reconciliation screen, which has the following options:

   - *Delete On:* Configures how BlackBerry handles your e-mail deletion

   - *Wireless Reconciliation:* Turns on or off the wireless sync function

   - *On Conflict:* Controls how BlackBerry handles any inconsistencies between e-mail on your Bold and the BIS client

     With this option, you can choose who "wins": your Bold or the BIS client.

4. **Select Delete On, and then select one of the following from the drop-down list:**

   - *Handheld:* A delete on your Bold takes effect only on your Bold.

   - *Mailbox & Handheld:* A delete on your Bold takes effect on both your Bold and your inbox on the BIS client.

   - *Prompt:* This option prompts your Bold to ask you at the time of deletion where the deletion takes effect.

5. **Select Wireless Reconciliation, and then select On from the drop-down list.**

6. **Select On Conflict, and make a selection from the drop-down list.**

   If you choose Handheld Wins, the e-mail messages in your e-mail account will match the ones on the handheld.

Unfortunately, some e-mail accounts might not work well with the e-mail reconciliation feature of the BlackBerry, so you still may have to delete an e-mail twice.

Permanently deleting e-mail from your Bold

When deleting e-mail on your Bold, the same message in that e-mail account is placed in the Deleted folder. You can set up your Bold to permanently delete e-mail, but use this option with caution because after that e-mail is gone, it's truly gone.

To permanently delete e-mail on your BIS client from your Bold, follow these steps:

1. **Open the Messages application.**

2. **In the message list, press the Menu key, and select Options.**

3. **On the Options screen, select E-mail Reconciliation.**

4. **On the E-mail Reconciliation screen, press the Menu key, and select Purge Deleted Items.**

   You see all your e-mail accounts.

5. **Choose the e-mail account from which you want to purge deleted items.**

   A screen appears, warning you that you are about to purge deleted e-mails on your Service client.

6. **Select Yes.**

   Deleted e-mails in the selected e-mail account are purged.

Unfortunately, some e-mail accounts may not work with the Purge Deleted Items feature.

Accessing Messages

From Messages, you send and receive your e-mails and also configure wireless e-mail reconciliation with your e-mail account(s).

To access Messages, press the Menu key from the Home screen and select Messages. The first thing you see after opening Messages is the message list. Your message list can contain e-mail, voice mail messages, missed phone call notices, Short Messaging Service (SMS) messages, and even saved Web pages.

Receiving e-mails

Whether you're concerned about security or speed of delivery, with BlackBerry's up-to-date secured network, you're in good hands when receiving e-mail on your Bold.

And whether you've aggregated accounts or just use the plain-vanilla BlackBerry e-mail account, you receive your e-mail the same way. When you receive an e-mail message, your Bold notifies you by displaying a numeral next to a mail icon (an envelope) at the top of the screen. This number represents how many new (unread) e-mails you have. See Figure 8-5. A red asterisk next to the envelope indicates new mail and that you haven't opened the Messages application yet.

Your Bold can also notify you of new e-mail by vibration, a sound alert, or both. You can customize this from the Profile application, detailed in Chapter 3.

Figure 8-5:
You've got (333) e-mails!

Retrieving e-mail

Retrieving your e-mail is simple. Follow these steps:

1. **From the Home screen, press the Menu key, and select Messages.**

2. **In the message list, scroll to any e-mail, and press the trackball.**

   You can tell whether an e-mail is unopened by the small, unopened envelope icon on the left side of the e-mail. A read e-mail bears an opened envelope icon, a sent e-mail has a check mark as its icon, and a document icon represents a draft e-mail.

3. **After you finish reading the message, press the Escape key (the arrow key to the right of the trackball) to return to the message list.**

Sorting the message list

Your Bold mail lists messages in order by the date and time they were received, but you can sort by different criteria. For example, to see only incoming e-mail, press Alt+I.

Sorting and searching are closely related on your Bold. In a sense, searching is really sorting your e-mail based on your search criteria. You can search your e-mail by the name of the sender or by keywords. Or you could run a search as broad as looking through all the e-mail that has been sent to you. See the later section "Searching through Messages like a Pro" for more on searching and sorting. For more predefined hot keys, see the upcoming section "Reusing saved searches."

Saving a message to the saved folder

You can save any important e-mail in a folder so that you can find it without sorting through tons of e-mail. To do so, simply scroll to the e-mail you want to save, press the Menu key, and select Save from the menu. A pop-up message confirms that your e-mail has been saved. Your saved e-mail still remains in the message list.

To retrieve or view a saved e-mail, follow these steps:

1. **Open the Messages application.**

2. **In the message list, press the Menu key, and select View Saved Messages.**

   You see the list of all the messages you saved.

3. **Select the message you want, and press the trackball to open it.**

Viewing attachments

Your Bold is so versatile that you can view most e-mail attachments just like you can on a desktop PC. And we're talking sizeable attachments, too, such as JPEGs (photos), Word docs, PowerPoint slides, and Excel spreadsheets. Table 8-1 shows a list of supported attachments viewable from your BlackBerry.

If you are using BlackBerry Desktop Redirector to get your e-mail on to your Bold, you won't be getting attachments on your Bold.

Table 8-1	BlackBerry-Supported Attachments
Supported Attachment Extension	*Description*
.bmp	BMP image file format
.doc	MS Word document
.dot	MS Word document template
.gif	GIF image file format
.htm	HTML Web page
.html	HTML Web page
.jpg	JPEG image file format
.pdf	Adobe PDF document
.png	PNG image file format
.ppt	MS PowerPoint document
.tif	TIFF image file format
.txt	Text file
.wpd	Corel WordPerfect document
.xls	MS Excel document
.zip	Compressed file format

To tell whether an e-mail has an attachment, look for the standard paper clip icon next to your e-mail in the message list.

You retrieve all the different types of attachments the same way. This makes retrieving attachments an easy task. To open an attachment, follow along:

1. **While reading an e-mail, press the Menu key, and then select Open Attachment.**

You see a screen that contains the name of the file, a Table of Contents option, and a Full Contents option. For MS Word documents, you can see different headings in outline form in the Table of Contents option. For picture files, such as JPEGs, you can go straight to the Full Contents option to see the graphic.

For all supported file types, you see Table of Contents and Full Contents as options. Depending on the file type, use your judgment on when you should use the Table of Contents option.

 2. **Scroll to Full Contents, press the Menu key, and select Retrieve.**

Your Bold attempts to contact the BIS client to retrieve your attachment. This retrieves only part of your attachment. As you peruse a document, your Bold retrieves more as you scroll through the attachment.

Editing attachments

Your Bold comes with Documents To Go, which means that out of the box, you not only can view but also edit Word and PowerPoint documents. You can even save the documents to your Bold and transfer them later to your PC.

As an example, imagine editing a Word document that you received as an attachment to an e-mail:

 1. **Open the e-mail.**

 2. **In the message list, open an e-mail with a Word document attached.**

This opens the e-mail for you to read. Notice the little paper clip, indicating that it has an attachment.

 3. **Press the Menu key, and select Open Attachment.**

You're prompted with a pop-up that asks whether you want to view the Word document or edit with Documents To Go.

 4. **Select Edit with Documents To Go.**

Here you can view and edit a document.

 5. **Press the Menu key, and select Edit Mode.**

In Edit mode, you can edit your document.

 6. **When you are finished editing and viewing, you can either save the document on your Bold or e-mail it:**

   • *To e-mail the edited document:* Press the Menu key, and then select Send via E-mail.

   Here you will see an e-mail message with the Word document. Follow the steps described in the next section to send this e-mail attachment as you would any other e-mail.

   • *To save the document:* Press the Menu key, and then select Save.

If you want to save the attachment to your Bold, you have to navigate its folder structure. For documents, the default save location is usually in the Documents folder.

Sending e-mail

The first thing you probably want to do when you get your BlackBerry is to write an e-mail to let your friends know that you just got a BlackBerry. Follow these steps to send an e-mail message:

1. **Open the Messages application.**

2. **In the message list, press the Menu key, and select Compose E-mail.**

   You are prompted with a blank e-mail that you need to fill out, just like you would do on your PC.

3. **In the To field, type the recipient's name or e-mail address.**

   As you type, you see a list of contacts from your Contacts that match the name or address that you're typing. You can make a selection from this list.

4. **Enter a subject in the Subject field, and type your message in the Body field.**

5. **When you're finished, press the Menu key, and then select Send.**

   Your message has wings.

Forwarding e-mail

When you need to share an important e-mail with a colleague or a friend, you can forward that e-mail. Simply do the following:

1. **Open the e-mail.**

   For information on opening e-mail, see the previous section "Retrieving e-mail."

2. **Press the Menu key, and then select Forward.**

3. **Type the recipient's name or e-mail address in the To field, and then add a message if needed.**

   When you start typing your recipient's name, a drop-down list of your contacts appears and you can choose from it.

4. **Press the Menu key, and then select Send.**

   Your message is on its way to your recipient.

Sending e-mail to more than one person

When you need to send an e-mail to more than one person, just keep adding recipient names as needed. You can also add recipient names to receive a Cc (carbon copy) or Bcc (blind carbon copy). Here's how:

1. **Open the e-mail.**

   For information on opening e-mail, see the previous section "Retrieving e-mail."

2. **Press the Menu key, and select Compose E-mail.**

3. **Specify the To field for the e-mail recipient, and then press the Return key.**

   Another To field is added automatically below the first. The Cc field works the same way.

4. **To add a Bcc recipient, press the Menu key, and select Add Bcc.**

   You see a Bcc field. You can specify a Bcc recipient the same way you do To and Cc recipients.

Whether you're composing a new e-mail, replying, or forwarding an e-mail, you add new Cc and Bcc fields the same way.

Attaching a file to your e-mail

Many people are surprised that you can attach any document on your Bold or on the microSD card. You can attach Word, Excel, and PowerPoint documents as well as pictures, music, and videos. To send an e-mail with a file attached, follow these steps:

1. **Open the Messages application.**

2. **In the message list, press the Menu key, and select Compose E-mail.**

   You are prompted with a blank e-mail that you can fill out as you would on your PC. Enter the recipient's name in the To field, and then enter the subject and body of the message.

3. **Press the Menu key, and select Attach File.**

   You're prompted with a pop-up that shows your folders. Think of this as the folders on your PC.

4. **Navigate to the file of your choice, and press the trackball.**

   After you select a file, you see the file in the e-mail message.

5. **When you're finished, press the Menu key, and select Send.**

   Your message and attached file wing their way to the recipient.

Spell-checking your outgoing messages

Whether you're composing an e-mail message or an SMS text message, you can always check your spelling with the built-in spell checker. Simply press the Menu key, and select Check Spelling. When it finds an error, the BlackBerry spell checker makes a suggestion, as shown in Figure 8-6. To skip the spell check for that word and go on to the next word, press the Escape key. If you want to skip spell-checking for an e-mail, simply press and hold the Escape key.

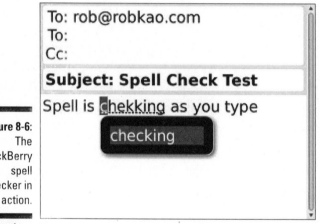

Figure 8-6:
The
BlackBerry
spell
checker in
action.

Your Bold underlines a misspelled word, just like MS Word.

By default, the spell checker doesn't kick in before you send your message, but you can configure it to check spelling before you send an e-mail. Follow these steps:

1. **Open the Messages application.**

2. **Press the Menu key, and select Options.**

3. **Select the Spell Check option.**

4. **Select the Spell Check E-mail before Sending check box.**

5. **Press the Menu key, and select Save.**

The underline feature is a default setting called Check Spelling as You Type. To turn off this feature, disable the Spell Check option in Message Options.

Deleting e-mail

If you want to really clean up your old e-mails and you don't want to scroll through tons of messages, you can do the following:

1. **Open the Messages application.**

2. **From the message list, highlight a horizontal date mark, press the Menu key, and choose Delete Prior.**

   The *date mark* is simply a horizontal bar with dates. Just like you can highlight e-mails in the message list, you can also highlight the date mark.

   A pop-up appears, prompting you for delete confirmation.

   Before you take the plunge, remember that going ahead will *delete all the e-mails before the particular date mark.* You cannot retrieve deleted items from your BlackBerry.

3. **Select Delete to confirm your deletion.**

   All your e-mails prior to the date mark are history.

Filtering your e-mail

Most of us get e-mail that isn't urgent or doesn't really concern us. Instead of receiving these e-mails on your Bold — and wasting both time and effort to check them — you can filter them out. While in the BIS client, set up filters to make your BlackBerry mailbox receive only those e-mails that you care about. (Don't worry; you'll still receive all your e-mails on your main computer.)

To create a simple filter that treats messages as urgent and forwards them to your Bold, follow these steps. In this example, we're setting a filter to mark work-related messages as urgent.

1. **Log on to the BIS client (refer to Figure 8-1).**

2. **Click the Filter icon for the desired e-mail account.**

   The Filter screen that appears shows a list of filters that have been created. See Figure 8-7, which doesn't have any filters yet.

3. **Click the Click Here link.**

   The Add Filter screen appears, as shown in Figure 8-8.

4. **Enter a name in the Filter Name text box.**

   The filter name can be anything you like. We're using WorkUrgent.

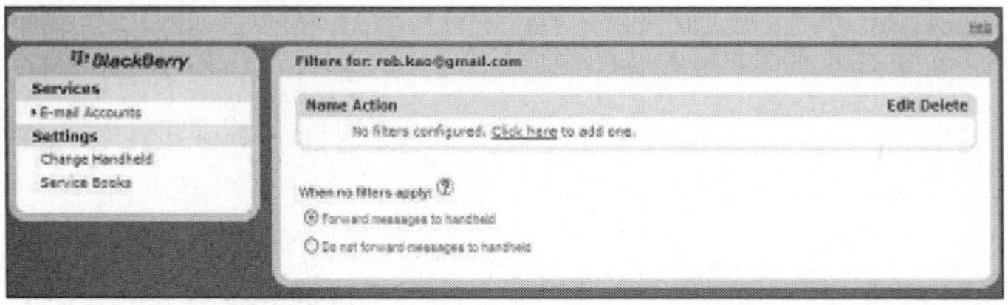

Figure 8-7:
Filter list
screen.

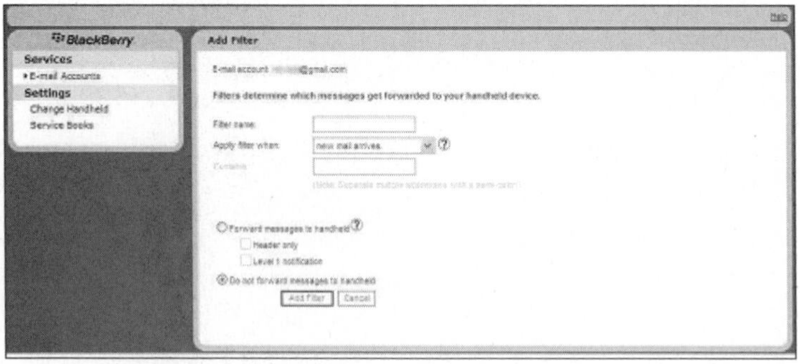

Figure 8-8:
Create a
filter for
your e-mail
here.

5. In the Apply Filter When drop-down list, choose the condition to place on the filter:

- *A High-Priority Mail Arrives:* The filter applies only to urgent e-mail.

- *Subject Field Contains:* The Contains field is enabled (you can type text in it). You can specify what keywords the filter will look for in the subject field. Separate each entry with a semicolon (;).

- *From Field Contains:* The Contains field is enabled (you can type text in it). You can type full addresses or part of an address. For example, you can type **rob@robkao.com** or just **kao**. Separate each entry with a semicolon (;).

- *To Field Contains:* Similar to From Field Contains, enter e-mail address(es).

- *CC Field Contains:* Similar to From Field Contains, enter e-mail address(es).

If you need more conditions, just add filters. Each filter can have one condition.

For this example, we select From Field Contains.

6. Specify the text in the Contains field.

See the details in the preceding step for what to enter in the Contains field. Continuing this example, type in the domain of your work e-mail address. For example, if your work e-mail address is *myName*@XYZCo. com, enter **XYZCo.com**.

7. **Select one of the following options:**

Forward Messages to Handheld: Select this radio button, and you can then select either or both check boxes below it:

- *Header Only:* You want only the header of the e-mails that meets the condition(s) you set in Steps 3, 4, and 5 to be sent to you. (A *header* doesn't contain the body of the e-mail — just who sent it, the subject, and the time it was sent.) Choose this check box if you get automated alerts, where receiving only the subject is sufficient.

- *Level 1 Notification:* Level 1 Notification is another way of saying *urgent e-mail.* When you receive a Level 1 e-mail, it is bold in Messages.

Do Not Forward Messages to Handheld: Any e-mail that meets the conditions you set in Steps 3, 4, and 5 aren't sent to your BlackBerry.

8. **Confirm your filter by clicking the Add Filter button.**

You return to the Filter screen, where you can see your newly created filter in the list.

If you have a hard time setting the criteria for a filter, just take a best guess, and then check it by having a friend send you a test e-mail. If the test e-mail doesn't get filtered correctly, set the conditions until you get them right.

Searching through Messages Like a Pro

Searching is a function you probably won't use every day, but when you run a search, you usually need the information fast. Take a few minutes here to familiarize yourself with general searching.

The BlackBerry Messages application provides three ways to search through your messages. Two of the three ways are specific, and one is a broad search:

- ✔ **Search by sender or recipient:** Specific. This method assumes that you already know the sender or recipient.
- ✔ **Search by subject:** Specific. This approach assumes that you already know the subject.
- ✔ **General search:** Broad. You don't have a specific assumption.

You can search through anything listed in the messages list. This means that you can search through SMS and voice mail as well as e-mail.

Searching by sender or recipient

Search by sender or recipient when you're looking for a specific message from a specific person. For example, suppose your brother constantly sends you e-mail (which means your message list has many entries from him). You're trying to locate a message he sent you approximately two weeks ago regarding a fishing trip location. You scrolled down the message list, but you just can't seem to find that message. Or maybe you want to find a message you sent to Sue but can't lay your hands on it.

To find a message when you know the sender or recipient, follow these steps:

1. **Open the Messages application.**

2. **In the message list, highlight a message that you sent to or received from that particular person.**

   The choice you get in the next step depends on whether you highlighted a sent message or a received message.

3. **Press the Menu key, and then select one of these options:**

   - *To search for a message from someone specific:* Because that certain someone sent you the message, choose Search Sender.

   - *To search for a message to someone specific:* Because you sent that certain someone the message, choose Search Recipient.

   This starts the search. Any results appear onscreen.

Searching by subject

Search by subject when you're looking for an e-mail titled by a specific subject that you already know. As is the case when running a search by sender or recipient, first scroll to an e-mail that bears the same subject you're searching for. Then follow these steps:

1. **Open the Messages application.**

2. **In the message list, highlight an e-mail titled by the specific subject you're searching for.**

3. **Press the Menu key, and then select Search Subject.**

   The search starts, and the results appear onscreen.

Running a general search

A general search is a broad search from which you can perform keyword searches of your messages. To run a general search, follow these steps:

1. **Open the Messages application.**

2. **In the message list, press the Menu key, and then select Search.**

3. **In the Search screen that appears, fill in your search criteria (see Figure 8-9).**

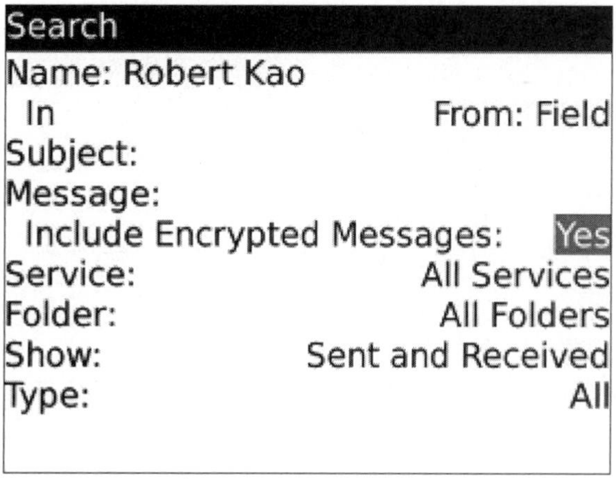

Search

Name: Robert Kao

In   From: Field

Subject:

Message:

Include Encrypted Messages: Yes

Service: All Services

Folder: All Folders

Show: Sent and Received

Type: All

Figure 8-9: The Search screen in Messages.

The search criteria for a general search follow:

- *Name:* This is the name of the sender or recipient to search by.

- *In:* This is related to the Name criterion. Use this drop-down list to indicate where the name may appear, such as in the To or Cc field. From the drop-down list, your choices are From, To, Cc, Bcc, and any address field.

- *Subject:* This is where you type some of or all the keywords that appear in the subject.

- *Message:* Here, you enter keywords that appear in the message.

- *Service:* If you set up your BlackBerry to receive e-mail from more than one e-mail account, you can specify which e-mail account to search.

- *Folder:* This is the folder in which you want to perform the search. Generally, you should select All Folders.

- *Show:* This drop-down list specifies how the search result will appear: namely, whether you want to see only e-mails that you sent or e-mails that you received. From the drop-down list, your choices are Sent and Received, Received Only, Sent Only, Saved Only, Draft Only, and Unopened Only.

- *Type:* This drop-down list specifies the type of message that you're trying to search for: e-mail, SMS, or voice mail. From the drop-down list, your choices are All, E-mail, E-mail with Attachments, PIN, SMS, Phone, and Voice Mail.

From the Search screen shown in Figure 8-9, you can have multiple search criteria or just a single one. It's up to you.

 4. Press the Menu key, and then select Search to launch your search.

   The search results appear onscreen.

You can narrow the search results by performing a second search on the initial results. For example, you can search by sender, and then narrow those hits by performing a second search by subject.

You can also search by sender or recipient when you're looking for a specific message from a specific person. Scroll to an e-mail that bears the specific sender or recipient. Press the Menu key, and select Search Sender or Search Recipient. If the e-mail that you highlighted is an incoming e-mail, you'll see Search Sender. If the e-mail is outgoing, you'll see Search Recipient.

Saving search results

If you find yourself re-searching with the same criteria over and over, you may want to save the search, and then reuse it. Here's how:

 1. Follow Steps 1–3 in the preceding section for an outgoing e-mail search.

 2. Press the Menu key, and then select Save.

   The Save Search screen appears, from which you can name your search and assign it a shortcut key. See Figure 8-10.

 3. In the Title field, enter a name.

   The title is the name of your search, which appears on the Search Results screen.

 4. Scroll to the Shortcut Key field, press the trackball, and select a letter from the drop-down list.

   You have ten letters to choose from.

 5. Confirm your saved search by pressing the Menu key, and selecting Save.

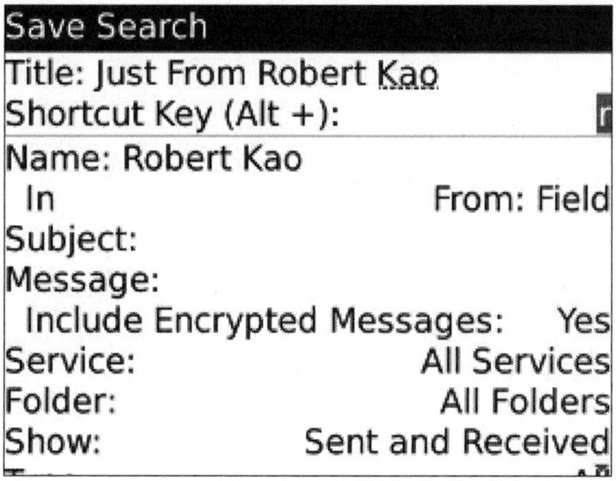

Save Search
Title: Just From Robert Kao
Shortcut Key (Alt +):   r
Name: Robert Kao
   In   From: Field
Subject:
Message:
   Include Encrypted Messages: Yes
Service: All Services
Folder: All Folders
Show: Sent and Received

Figure 8-10:
Name your
search and
assign it a
shortcut
key.

Reusing saved searches

Right out of the box, your BlackBerry comes with five saved search results. Any new saved result will make your search that much more robust.

Follow these steps to see all saved search results:

1. **Open the Messages application.**

2. **In the message list, press the Menu key, and select Search.**

3. **Press the Menu key, and then select Recall.**

   The recall screen opens, and you can see the five preloaded search shortcuts, as well as any searches you saved, as shown in Figure 8-11.

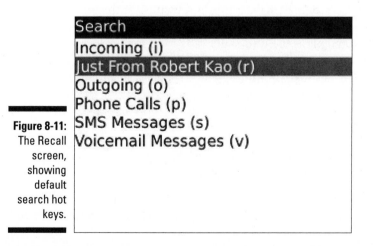

Search
Incoming (i)
Just From Robert Kao (r)
Outgoing (o)
Phone Calls (p)
SMS Messages (s)
Voicemail Messages (v)

Figure 8-11:
The Recall
screen,
showing
default
search hot
keys.

To reuse one of the saved search results, simply select a desired search from the list, press the Menu key, and select Search.

If you have multiple e-mail accounts set up, you can set up a search shortcut so that you view only one specific account. For example, say you have your personal e-mail and your small business e-mail accounts both set up on your BlackBerry. In the Message application, you see e-mails from both, which can be overwhelming at times. From the general Search screen (refer to Figure 8-9), set the Service drop-down list to the one you want, and follow the preceding steps to save the search and assign a shortcut key. The next time you want to see only a certain account, you can get to it in an instant!

Long Live E-Mail

No closet has unlimited space, and your BlackBerry e-mail storage has limits, too. You've likely pondered how long your e-mails are kept in your BlackBerry. (The default is 30 days. Pshew.) You can choose several options: from 15 days to forever (well, for as long as your BlackBerry has enough space for them).

Because any message you save is kept for as long as you want, a good way to make sure that you don't lose an important message is to save it.

To change how long your e-mails live on your BlackBerry, follow these steps:

1. **Open the Messages application.**
2. **Press the Menu key, and select Options.**
3. **Select General Options.**
4. **Scroll to the Keep Messages option, and then press the trackball.**
5. **From the drop-down list that appears, choose the time frame that you want, and then press the trackball:**

    • *Forever:* If you choose Forever, you'll seldom need to worry about your e-mails being automatically deleted. On the downside, though, your BlackBerry will eventually run out of memory. At that point, you must manually delete some e-mails to free space to accept new e-mails.

    A good way to archive your e-mail is to back up your e-mails by using BlackBerry Desktop Manager. See Chapter 18 for more on backing up your BlackBerry on your PC.

- *Time option:* If you choose a time option, any message older than that time frame is automatically deleted from your BlackBerry the next time you reboot your BlackBerry. However, the message will be deleted only on your BlackBerry — even if you turn on e-mail reconciliation — because these deletions are only on the device.

6. **Confirm your changes by pressing the Menu key. and then selecting Save.**

Chapter 9

Too Cool for E-Mail

*Y*our BlackBerry is primarily a communication tool, with e-mail messages and phone conversations as the major drivers. It's a wonderful technology, but sometimes, another means of communication is more appropriate. For instance, e-mail isn't the tool of choice for instant messaging — most people would find that method slow and cumbersome. Nor is e-mail the best tool to use when you want to alert someone to something.

Your BlackBerry offers some less-obvious ways to communicate — ways that may serve as the perfect fit for a special situation. In this chapter, you get the scoop on PIN-to-PIN messaging, messaging using the BlackBerry Messenger and text messaging (also known as *Short Messaging Service,* or *SMS*). We also give you tips on how to turn your BlackBerry into a lean (and not-so-mean) instant messaging (IM) machine.

Sending and Receiving PIN-to-PIN Messages

PIN-to-PIN messaging is based on the technology that underpins two-way pager systems. Unlike sending a standard e-mail, when you send a BlackBerry PIN-to-PIN message, the message doesn't venture outside the RIM infrastructure in search of an e-mail server and (eventually) an e-mail inbox. Instead, it stays solidly in the RIM world, where it is shunted through the recipient's network provider until it ends up on the recipient's BlackBerry.

So, when you use PIN-to-PIN messaging, that's another way of saying *one BlackBerry to another BlackBerry.*

PIN stands for personal identification number (familiar to anyone who's ever used an ATM) and refers to a system for uniquely identifying your device.

Here's the neat part. According to RIM (Research In Motion), the message isn't saved anywhere in this universe *except* on the one device that sends the PIN message and the other device that receives it. Compare that with an e-mail, which is saved in at least four separate locations (the mail client and e-mail servers of both sender and recipient), not to mention all the system's redundancies and backups employed by the server. Think of it this way: If you whisper a little secret in someone's ear, only you and that special someone know what was said. In a way, PIN-to-PIN messaging is the same thing, with one BlackBerry whispering to another BlackBerry. Now, that's discreet.

If you tend to read the financial newspapers — especially the ones that cover corporate lawsuits extensively — you'll know that there's no such thing as privacy in e-mail. PIN-to-PIN messaging, in theory at least, is as good as the old Code of Silence. Now, is such privacy really an advantage? You can argue both sides of the issue, depending on what you want to use PIN-to-PIN messaging for.

Basically, if you like the idea that your communications can be kept discreet, PIN-to-PIN messaging has great curb appeal. If you don't care about privacy issues, though, you still may be impressed by PIN-to-PIN messaging's zippy nature. (It really is the Ferrari of wireless communication — way faster than e-mail.)

The Cone of Silence in an enterprise environment has always been a thorny issue to companies that have strict regulatory requirements. As expected, RIM addressed this issue with a new feature to later operating systems allowing BlackBerry Enterprise Server (BES) administrators to flip a flag, forcing the device to forward all PIN-to-PIN messages to the BES server. Third-party applications are also available now that a company can install on the device to report PIN-to-PIN messages.

Getting a BlackBerry PIN

When you try to call somebody on the telephone, you can't get far without a telephone number. As you may expect, the same principle applies to PIN-to-PIN messaging: no PIN, no PIN-to-PIN messaging.

In practical terms, you need the PIN of any BlackBerry you want to send a PIN message to. (You also need to find out your own PIN so that you can hand it out to folks who want to PIN-message you.)

Earth you'd give your PIN to somebody. Here's the difference: Unlike a PIN for an ATM account, this PIN isn't your password. In fact, this PIN doesn't give anybody access to your BlackBerry or do anything to compromise security. It's simply an ID; think of it like a phone number.

TECHNICAL STUFF

A little bit of RIM history

Sometime during the last millennium, Research In Motion (RIM) wasn't even in the phone business. Before BlackBerry became all the rage with smartphone features, RIM was doing a tidy little business with its wireless e-mail.

Back then, RIM's primitive wireless e-mail service was served by network service providers on a radio bandwidth: DataTAC and Mobitex networks. These were separate from a typical cellphone infrastructure's bandwidth.

RIM devices at that time already had PIN-to-PIN messaging. This type of messaging is akin to a pager, where a message doesn't live in a mailbox but is sent directly to the BlackBerry with no delay. (No one wants a paging system that moves at turtle speed when you can get one that moves like a jack rabbit, right?)

Several interesting facts followed from RIM's initial decision. Of note, most cellphone users in New York City were left without service during the 9/11 disaster. the entire cellphone infrastructure in New York and surrounding areas was overwhelmed when faced with too many people trying to use the bandwidth available.

However, one communication device continued to work during that stressful time: RIM's PIN-to-PIN messaging kept the information flow going.

The cautious side of you may wonder why on Here are three quick paths to PIN enlightenment:

- **From the Help screen:** You can find the PIN for any device right there on its Help screen. Open the Help screen by pressing Alt+Num+H.

- **From the Message screen:** Send your PIN from the Message screen with the help of a keyword. When you type a preset word, your BlackBerry replaces what you type with a bit of information specific to your device.

Sound wacky? It's actually easier than it sounds.

a. *Compose a new message.*

Chapter 8 gives you the basics on the whole e-mail message and messaging thing, if you need a refresher.

b. *In the subject or body of your message, type **mypin** and add a space.*

See the left side of Figure 9-1.

As soon as you type the space, `mypin` is miraculously transformed into your PIN in the format `pin:your-pin-number`, as shown in the right side of Figure 9-1. Isn't that neat? ***Note:*** Case doesn't matter here.

TIP

`mypin` isn't the only keyword that RIM predefines for you. `mynumber` and `myver` give you the phone number and OS version, respectively, of your BlackBerry Bold.

✓ **From the Status screen:** You can also find your PIN on the Status screen. Display the Status screen by choosing the following links in succession, starting from the Home screen: Settings, Options, and Status. Use the trackball to highlight and click the link. Figure 9-2 shows a typical Status screen. (The PIN is fifth on the list of items shown.)

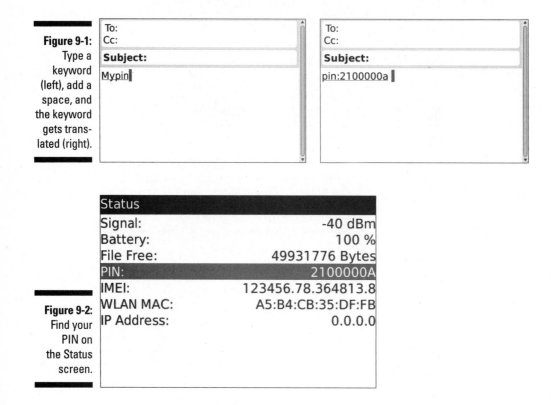

Figure 9-1: Type a keyword (left), add a space, and the keyword gets translated (right).

Figure 9-2: Find your PIN on the Status screen.

Assigning PINs to names

So, you convince your BlackBerry-wielding buddies to go to the trouble of finding out their PINs and passing said PINs to you. Now the trick is finding a convenient place to store your PINs so that you can use them. Luckily for you, you have an obvious choice: BlackBerry Contacts. And RIM, in its infinite wisdom, makes storing such info a snap. To add a PIN to someone's contact info in Contacts, do the following:

1. From the BlackBerry Home screen, select Contacts.

Contacts opens.

2. **Highlight a contact name, press the Menu key, and then select Edit.**

   The Edit Contact screen for the contact name you selected makes an appearance.

3. **On the Edit Contact screen, scroll down to the PIN field (as shown in Figure 9-3).**

4. **Type the PIN.**

5. **Press the Menu key, and then select Save.**

   The edit you made for this contact is saved.

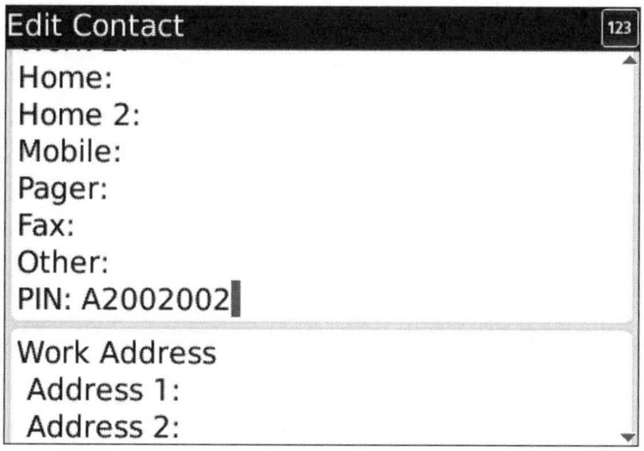

Figure 9-3:
Add a
contact's
PIN info
here.

Edit Contact	123
Home:	
Home 2:	
Mobile:	
Pager:	
Fax:	
Other:	
PIN: A2002002	
Work Address	
Address 1:	
Address 2:	

It's that simple. Of course, it's even easier if you think ahead and enter the PIN information you have when you set up your initial contact info (by using the New Contact screen), but we understand that a PIN isn't the kind of information people carry around.

If all this talk about New Contact screens and Edit Contact screens doesn't sound familiar, check out Chapter 4, which covers the Contacts application in more detail.

Sending a PIN-to-PIN message

PIN-to-PIN just means *from one BlackBerry to another.*

Sending a PIN-to-PIN message is no different than sending an e-mail. Here's how:

1. **From the BlackBerry Home screen, select Contacts.**

2. **In Contacts, highlight a contact name, and then press the Menu key.**

   If a contact has a PIN, you see a menu item titled PIN *<contact name>*. Say, for example, you have a contact named Dante Sarigumba. When you highlight Dante Sarigumba in the list, and then press the Menu key, the menu item PIN Dante Sarigumba appears as an option, as shown in Figure 9-4.

3. **Select PIN *<contact name>* from the menu.**

   The ever-familiar New Message screen, with the PIN of your buddy already entered as an address, makes an appearance.

4. **Enter the rest of text fields — subject, message, and signing off — just as you would with an e-mail.**

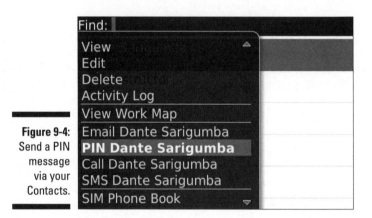

Figure 9-4:
Send a PIN
message
via your
Contacts.

Alternatively, if you know the PIN, you can also type it directly. Here's how:

1. **From the BlackBerry Home screen, select Messages.**

   The Messages application opens.

2. **Press the Menu key, and then select Compose PIN.**

   The ever-familiar New Message screen makes an appearance.

3. **In the To field, enter the PIN, and then press the trackball.**

   You just added a recipient in the To field.

4. **Add a subject line and the message, and then sign off just like you would in an e-mail.**

Unlike e-mails, when you send a PIN-to-PIN message, you can tell almost instantly whether the recipient got your message. Viewing the Message list, you see a letter D — which means *delivered* — on top of the check mark next to the PIN-to-PIN message you sent.

Because of the nature of PIN-to-PIN messaging (the conspicuous lack of a paper trail, as it were), companies can disable PIN-to-PIN messaging on your BlackBerry device. (No paper trail can mean legal problems down the road — can you say *Sarbanes-Oxley?*)

Receiving a PIN-to-PIN message

Receiving a PIN-to-PIN message is no different than receiving a standard e-mail. You get the same entry into your Messages list for the PIN-to-PIN message, and the same screen appears when you open the message.

By default, your BlackBerry vibrates to alert you, but you can change this in Profiles. (Check out Chapter 3 for more details on changing your profile.) When you reply to the message, the reply is a PIN-to-PIN message as well.

Keeping in Touch, the SMS/MMS Way

Short Messaging Service (also known as *SMS,* or *text messaging*) is so popular that you probably have seen TV shows asking for your feedback via SMS. Multimedia Messaging Service (MMS) is a much later evolution of SMS. Rather than a simple text message, you can also send someone an audio or a video clip.

How short is *short?* The maximum size per message is about 160 characters. If you send more than that, it gets broken down into multiple messages.

SMS is an established technology (not a new and unproven thing, in other words) that's been popular for years in Europe and Asia.

Text messaging does pose a challenge for beginners. It isn't tough; it's just cumbersome to type the letters on a small keyboard and keep up with the conversation. Also, you need to know the trends and options for text messaging. In-the-know folks use abbreviations that may be difficult for you to understand in the beginning, so don't dive in without your oxygen tank.

A quick preparation goes a long way toward avoiding being labeled "uncool" when it comes to your SMS syntax. The upcoming sections help smooth your path a bit by filling you in on the basics of SMS-speak.

Using shorthand for speedy replies

On a regular cellphone, three letters share a single key. Typing even a single paragraph can be a real pain.

Human ingenuity prevails. Abbreviations cut down on the amount of text you need to enter. *Texting* (short for "text messaging") language is quite hip, especially among the 14–18-year-old set. Veteran text messagers (the hip ones, at least) can easily spot someone who's new to SMS technology by how that person doesn't use the right lingo — or use such lingo incorrectly.

Awhfy?

In text messaging, the challenge lies in using abbreviations to craft a sentence with as few letters as possible. Because text messaging has been around for a number of years, plenty of folks have risen to this challenge by coming up with a considerable pool of useful abbreviations. Don't feel that you have to rush out and memorize the whole shorthand dictionary at once, though.

Like with mastering a new language, start out with the most commonly used words or sentences. When you become familiar with those, slowly gather in more and more terms. In time, the language will be second nature.

Table 9-1 gives you our take on the most common abbreviations, which are enough to get you started. With these under your belt, you can at least follow the most important parts of an SMS conversation. Feel free to check out the Web site associated with this book (www.blackberryfordummies.com) for a more comprehensive list of shorthand abbreviations.

Showing some emotion

Written words can get folks into trouble every now and then; the very same words can mean different things to different people. A simple example is the phrase, "You're clueless." When you speak such a phrase (with the appropriate facial and hand gestures), your friend knows (you hope) that you're teasing and that it's all a bit of fun. Write that same phrase in a text message, and, well, you may get a nasty reply in return — which you then have to respond to, which prompts another response, and soon enough, you've just ended a seven-year friendship.

Table 9-1	SMS Shorthand and Its Meanings		
Shorthand	**Meaning**	**Shorthand**	**Meaning**
2D4	To die for	CUL8R	See you later
2G4U	Too good for you	CUS	See you soon
2L8	Too late	F2F	Face to face
4E	Forever	FC	Fingers crossed
4YEO	For your eyes only	FCFS	First come, first served
A3	Anytime, anywhere, anyplace	FOAF	Friend of a friend
AFAIK	As far as I know	FWIW	For what it's worth
ASAP	As soon as possible	GAL	Get a life
ASL	Age, sex, location	GG	Good game
ATM	At the moment	GR8	Great
ATW	At the weekend	GSOH	Good sense of humor
AWHFY	Are we having fun yet?	H2CUS	Hope to see you soon
B4	Before	IC	I see
BBFN	Bye-bye for now	IDK	I don't know
BBL	Be back later	IMHO	In my honest opinion
BBS	Be back soon	IMO	In my opinion
BCNU	Be seeing you	IOU	I owe you
BG	Big grin	IOW	In other words
BION	Believe it or not	KISS	Keep it simple, stupid
BOL	Best of luck	LOL	Laughing out loud
BOT	Back on topic	OIC	Oh, I see
BRB	Be right back	RUOK	Are you okay?
BRT	Be right there	W4U	Waiting for you
BTW	By the way	W8	Wait
CMON	Come on	WTG	Way to go
CU	See you	TOM	Tomorrow

SMS is akin to chatting, so *emoticons* show what you mean when you write "You're clueless." (I'm joking! I'm happy! I'm mad!) These cutesy codes help you telegraph your meaning in sledgehammer-to-the-forehead fashion.

We're talking smileys here — those combinations of keyboard characters that, when artfully combined, resemble a human face. The most popular example — one that you've probably encountered in e-mails from especially chirpy individuals — is the happy face, which (usually at the end of a statement) conveys good intentions or happy context, like this :). (Tilt your head to the left to see the face.)

Table 9-2 shows you the range of smiley choices. Just remember that smileys are supposed to be fun. They could be the one thing you need to make sure that your "gently teasing remark" isn't seen as a hateful comment. Smileys help, but if you aren't sure if what you're about to send can be misconstrued even with the help of the smileys, just don't send it.

Table 9-2	Smileys and Their Meanings		
Smiley	*Meaning*	*Smiley*	*Meaning*
:)	Happy, smiling	:(	Sad, frown
:-)	Happy, smiling, with nose	:-(	Sad, frown, with nose
:D	Laughing	:-<	Super sad
:-D	Laughing, with nose	:'-(	Crying
:'-)	Tears due to laughter	:-0	Yell, gasped
:-)8	Smiling with bow tie	:-@	Scream, what?
;)	Winking	:-(o)	Shouting
;-)	Winking, with nose	|-0	Yawn
0:-)	I'm an angel (male)	:----(	Liar, long nose
0*-)	I'm an angel (female)	%-(	Confused
8-)	Cool, with sunglasses	:-|	Determined
:-!	Foot in mouth	:-()	Talking
>-)	Evil grin	:-ozz	Bored
:-x	Kiss on the lips	@@	Eyes
(((H)))	Hugs	%-)	Cross-eyed
@>--;--	Rose	|@@|	Face
:b	Tongue out	#:-)	Hair is a mess
;b	Tongue out with a wink	&:-)	Hair is curly
:-&	Tongue tied	$-)	Yuppie
-!-	Sleepy	:-($)	Put your money where your mouth is
<3	Heart, or love	<(^(oo)^)>	Pig

Shorthand and smileys may not be appreciated in business. Use them appropriately.

Sending a text message

After you have the shorthand stuff and smileys under control, get your fingers pumped up and ready for action: It's message-sending time! Whether it's SMS or MMS, here's how it's done:

1. **From the BlackBerry Home screen, select Contacts.**

2. **In Contacts, highlight a contact who has a cellphone number, press the Menu key, and select SMS (or MMS) *<contact name>* from the menu that appears.**

SMS works only on mobile phones.

The menu item for SMS or MMS is intelligent enough to display the name of the contact. For example, if you choose John Doe, the menu item reads SMS John Doe or MMS John Doe, as shown in Figure 9-5. (Note the space for entering your text message, right underneath the screen heading.)

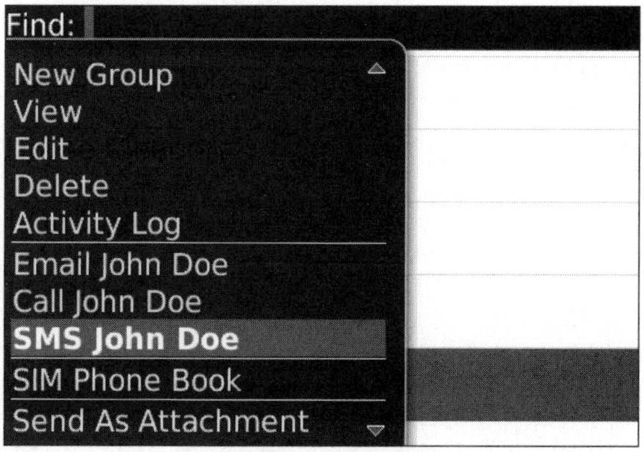

Find:

New Group
View
Edit
Delete
Activity Log
Email John Doe
Call John Doe
SMS John Doe
SIM Phone Book
Send As Attachment

Figure 9-5: Start your text message here.

3. **If you choose MMS, browse from your multimedia folders, and select the audio or video file you want to send.**

When choosing MMS, this extra step allows you to choose the multimedia file, which is the only difference from composing SMS.

4. **Type your message.**

   Remember that shorthand business? You should start taking advantage of it the first chance you get. (Practice makes perfect.)

5. **Press the trackball, and then select Send from the menu that appears.**

   Your message is sent on its merry way.

Viewing a message you receive

If you have an incoming SMS or MMS message, you get a notification just like you do when you receive an e-mail. Also, like e-mail, the e-mail icon at the top of the Home screen indicates a new message. Viewing SMS and MMS is the same as reading an e-mail. The basic run-through is as follows:

1. **Open Messages.**

2. **Scroll and highlight the unread message.**

3. **Press the trackball.**

   Bob's your uncle: The message appears onscreen.

Customize how your BlackBerry notifies you when you receive an SMS. Look for customizing your profile section in Chapter 3 for more details.

Always Online Using Instant Messaging

Real-time (as they happen) conversations with your friends over the Internet are easier with IM. IM allows two or more people to send and receive messages over the Internet. It all started with pure text messages and evolved into a rich medium involving voice and even video conversation in real time.

IM may not be available on your BlackBerry Bold. Service providers choose whether to include it. (Most providers, however, do support it for the BlackBerry Bold.) You can add IM to your BlackBerry even if it didn't come with it.

1. **Open your browser.**

2. **Go to** `http://mobile.blackberry.com.`

3. **Navigate to IM & Social Networking.**

   Here, you'll find download links for all the free applications for the popular IM networks and also a download link for BlackBerry Messenger. (This chapter also covers BlackBerry Messenger.)

Messaging etiquette and a few words of caution

Here are some commonsense messaging rules as well as a few words of caution. Even if you're new to messaging, being a neophyte doesn't give you license to act like a jerk. Play nice and take the following pointers to heart:

✔ **Use smileys to avoid misunderstandings.** Read more about emoticons and smileys earlier in this chapter.

✔ **Don't ever forward chain letters. We** mean it. Never.

✔ **If you need to forward a message, check the entire message content first.** Make sure nothing offends the recipient.

✔ **Some things in this world need to be said face to face, so don't even think of using messaging for it.** Ever try dumping your girl-friend or boyfriend over the phone? Guess what? Using messaging is far worse.

✔ **Keep your tone gender neutral.** Some mes-sages that are forwarded through e-mails are inappropriate to the opposite sex.

✔ **Capital letters are as rude as shouting, so** *DON'T USE THEM.*

✔ **Know your recipient.** A newbie might not easily grasp smileys and shorthand at first, so act accordingly. (Read more about short-hand earlier in this chapter.)

✔ **Don't reply to any message when you're angry.** You can't unsend a sent message. It's better to be prudent than sorry.

✔ **Don't gossip or be rude.** Beware! Your mes-sages can end up in the wrong hands and haunt you in the future.

✔ **Easy does it.** No documented evidence reveals the deleterious effects (physi-cal or psychological) of too much tex-ting. However, don't text as if you want to enter the books as the first recorded case of Instantmessagingitis. As your great-grandma would tell you, too much of any-thing is bad for you. It's easy to lose track of time when IMing.

✔ **Drive safely.** Tuck away your BlackBerry whenever you're in the driver's seat.

Chatting using IM rules

When you're IMing — that's right; it's a verb — you can tell lots of things:

✔ When someone's typing a message to you

✔ Whether your buddies are online

✔ When your buddies are away from their computers

✔ When your buddies are simply too busy to be interrupted at the moment

IM adds a totally different slant on long-distance communication, opening a wide array of possibilities — possibilities that can be used for good (team collaboration) or ill (mindless gossip), depending on the situation.

As you may expect, IM is great for both personal and business applications. Whether you're maintaining friendships or working to create new ones, IM is definitely one powerful tool to consider adding to your social-skills toolbox.

Instant messaging on your BlackBerry

Most network providers dish out the three most popular IM services to their BlackBerry customers:

✔ Google Talk

✔ Yahoo! Messenger

✔ Windows Live Messenger

Those three IM programs aren't the only popular ones. Here are a few more:

✔ AOL Instant Messenger

✔ ICQ Instant Messenger

✔ iChat AV (on the Macintosh)

✔ Jabber (open source)

If you're using an IM network that isn't preloaded, you can always check the RIM Web site to download the applications: `mobile.blackberry.com`. On this page, go to IM and Social Networking. The list of IM applications should be listed on the next page with a link for download.

IM basics: What you need

Assuming that you have the IM application available on your BlackBerry, you just need two things to start using the standard four IM programs:

✔ User ID

✔ Password

Getting a user ID/password combo is a breeze. Just go to the appropriate registration Web page (from the following list) for the IM application(s) you want to use. Using your desktop or laptop machine for signing up is easier and faster.

✔ **Google Talk**

`www.google.com/accounts/NewAccount?service=talk`

✔ **AOL Instant Messenger (AIM)**

`https://reg.my.screenname.aol.com/_cqr/registration/initRegistration.psp`

✔ **ICQ**

```
www.icq.com/register
```

✔ **MSN Live Messenger**

```
http://messenger.msn.com/download/getstarted.aspx
```

✔ **Y! Messenger**

```
http://edit.yahoo.com/config/eval_register?.src=pg&.done=http://
        messenger.yahoo.com
```

Given the many IM network choices available, your friends are probably signed up on a bunch of different networks. You might end up having to sign up for multiple networks if you want to reach them all via IM.

Going online with IM

After you obtain the user ID/password combo for one (or more) of the IM services, you can use your BlackBerry to start chatting with your buddies by following these steps:

1. **From the BlackBerry Home screen, select the IM application of your choice.**

   To illustrate how to do this, we use Google Talk. An application-specific logon screen shows up for you to sign on, similar to the one shown in Figure 9-6. It's straightforward, with the standard screen name or ID line and password line.

2. **Enter your screen name/ID and password.**

Google Talk

talk

Username:

Password:

Sign In

☑ Remember password
☑ Automatically sign me in

Need an account?
Go to google.com/accounts on your computer.
Forgot your password?

Figure 9-6:
Logon
screen for
Google Talk.

3. **(Optional) If you want, select the Remember Password check box. Also if you want, select the Automatically Sign Me In check box.**

We recommend that you select this check box to save time but also set your handheld password to Enabled so that security isn't compromised. Refer to Chapter 3 if you need a refresher on how to enable passwords on your BlackBerry.

When the Remember Password check box is enabled, the ID/password information is pre-entered the next time you come back to this screen. (Um, that is, you don't have to type this stuff every time you want to IM.)

The Automatically Sign Me In check box turns on and off sign-in when your BlackBerry Bold is powered up. This is helpful if you have a habit of turning off your BlackBerry periodically.

4. **Press the trackball, and then select Sign In.**

At this point, IM tries to log you on. This can take a few seconds, during which time the screen reads `Sending request to AOL` or `Sending request to Yahoo!` or `Sending request to ICQ` while it's in this phase. After you're logged on, a simple listing of your contacts, or buddies, appears onscreen.

5. **Select the person you'd like to chat with.**

A menu appears, listing various things you can do. Features could differ a little bit for each IM application, but for Google Talk, here's a sample of what you can do:

- Start Chat
- Send File
- Add a Friend
- Rename
- Remove
- Block

6. **Select the action you'd like.**

Adding a contact/buddy

Before you can start chatting with your buddies, you need to know their user IDs:

Luckily for you, you don't need to search around for IDs every time you want to IM someone. You can store IDs as part of a contact list. Follow these steps:

1. Starting within the IM service of your choice, press the Menu key.

2. Select Add a Friend, as shown in Figure 9-7.

The Add a Friend screen appears.

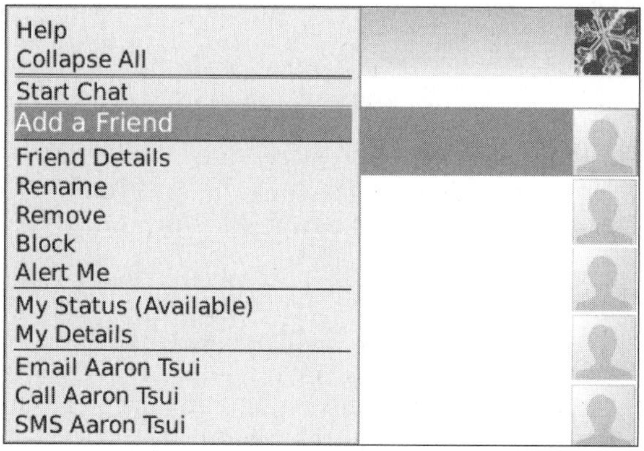

Figure 9-7:
Adding a
friend.

| Help |
| Collapse All |
| Start Chat |
| Add a Friend |
| Friend Details |
| Rename |
| Remove |
| Block |
| Alert Me |
| My Status (Available) |
| My Details |
| Email Aaron Tsui |
| Call Aaron Tsui |
| SMS Aaron Tsui |

3. Enter the user ID of your contact on the Add a Friend screen.

4. Press the trackball.

IM is smart enough to figure out whether this contact has a valid user ID. If the ID is valid, the application adds the ID to your list of contacts. The buddy goes either to the Online or Offline section of your list, depending on whether your buddy is logged on. You'll be warned if the ID you entered isn't valid.

Provider	*Where You Get Someone's User ID*
AIM	Your friend or by searching AOL's directory
Google Talk	The text before the @ sign in his or her Google e-mail address
Yahoo!	The text before the @ sign in his or her Yahoo! e-mail address
ICQ	Your friend's e-mail or the ICQ Global Directory
MSN	MSN passport ID or Hotmail ID

Doing the chat thing

Suppose you want to start a conversation with one of your contacts (a safe assumption, we think). When you send a message within the IM application, you're initiating a conversation. Here's how:

1. **Log on to the IM application of your choice.**

2. **Select the person you want to contact.**

   A typical online chat screen shows up. The top portion lists old messages sent to and received from this contact. You type your message at the bottom part of the screen.

3. **Type your message.**

4. **Press the Enter key.**

   Your user ID and the message you just sent show up in the topmost (history) section of the chat screen. When you get a message, it's added to the history section so that both sides of your conversation stay in view.

Sending your smile

You can quickly add emoticons to your message (without having to remember all the character equivalents in Table 8-1). Follow these steps:

1. **While you're typing your message, press the Menu key.**

2. **From the menu that appears, select Show Symbols.**

   All the icons appear, as shown in Figure 9-8.

3. **Select the emoticon you want.**

   The emoticon is added to your message.

Figure 9-8: You can choose from many smileys.

Using BlackBerry Messenger

RIM has entered the IM horse race in the form of a spirited filly named (you guessed it) BlackBerry Messenger. This application is based on the PIN-to-PIN messaging technology described earlier in this chapter, which means that it is mucho fast and quite reliable.

However, with BlackBerry Messenger, you can chat with only those buddies who have a BlackBerry and also have PIN-to-PIN messaging enabled. The application supports IM features common to many of the other applications, such as group chatting and the capability to monitor the availability of other IM buddies.

Running BlackBerry Messenger

You can access BlackBerry Messenger in the Applications folder from the Home screen, as shown in Figure 9-9. The first time you run BlackBerry Messenger, a welcome screen asks you to enter your display name. This display name is the one you want other people see on their BlackBerry Messenger.

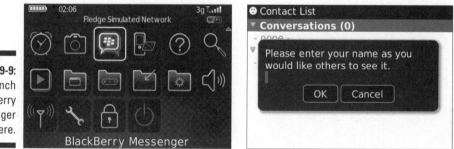

Figure 9-9: Launch BlackBerry Messenger here.

You see a contact list the next time you open the application, as shown on the left in Figure 9-10. (Okay, the picture here shows some contacts already and in yours it should be empty, but we'll show you how to populate it in a minute.)

Pressing the Menu key lets you do these things, as shown on the right side of Figure 9-10:

Figure 9-10:
The
BlackBerry
Messenger
Contact list
(left) and
menu (right).

Figure 9-10: The BlackBerry Messenger Contact list (left) and menu (right).

✔ **Broadcast Message:** Allows you to send a message to multiple contacts in your BlackBerry Messenger. The messages appear as conversations in the recipients' BlackBerry Messenger.

✔ **Start Group Chat:** Initiate a group conversation. See the later section "Starting a group conversation" for details.

✔ **Add Contact:** Add a new contact to BlackBerry Messenger. See the next section.

✔ **Add Group:** Allows you to create custom groupings for your contacts.

This is helpful if you have a lot of contacts in your BlackBerry Messenger. Simply select this menu item and an Add Group screen shows up for you enter a new group name.

✔ **Edit My Info:** Customize your personal information and control how you want others to see you from their BlackBerry Messenger Contacts list. You can set the following (refer to Figure 9-11):

- Change your picture.

- Change your display name.

- Allow others to see the title of the song you're currently listening to.

- Allow others to see that you're currently using the phone.

- Enter a personal message that others could see.

- Set your time zone.

- Allow others to see your country and time zone information.

✔ **Back Up Contacts List:** Allows you to save your list of BlackBerry Messenger contacts into the file system. The location defaults to the media card, but the screen that follows after you select this option allows you to select a different folder and enter a different name of the backup file.

✔ **Restore Contacts List:** Allows you to restore your list of BlackBerry Messenger contacts from the file you created from the Back Up Contacts List.

✔ **Delete Backup Files:** Select this option if you want to delete a backup file. If you have multiple backups, this option allows you to choose which file to delete.

✔ **Options:** Allows you to customize the behavior of your BlackBerry Messenger.

Figure 9-11:
Set your
personal
information,
(left) top and
(right) rest
of Edit My
Info screen.

Adding a contact

With nobody in your contact list, BlackBerry Messenger is a pretty useless item. Your first order of business is to add a contact to your list — someone you know who

✔ Has a BlackBerry

✔ Is entered in your Contacts

✔ Has PIN-to-PIN messaging enabled

✔ Has a copy of BlackBerry Messenger installed on his or her device

If you know someone who fits these criteria, you can add that person to your list by doing the following:

1. **In BlackBerry Messenger, press the Menu key.**

2. **Select Add a Contact.**

   The Add Contact screen appears, listing actions related to adding a contact, as shown in the right of Figure 9-12.

   The two top options in the list are the options you have to add a contact in your BlackBerry Messenger.

   You can *scan* your friend's BlackBerry barcode:

   a. *On the same screen (left of Figure 9-12) but using your friend's BlackBerry, select the third option that says Show your invitation barcode to another BlackBerry. A barcode image similar to the right of Figure 9-13 appears on your friend's BlackBerry.*

b. *On your BlackBerry Bold, select the second option, Scan invitation barcode from another BlackBerry.*

A Camera application appears for you to capture the barcode.

Once captured, it will immediately add the contact information to your contact list.

The following steps show how to enter your contact directly from this screen.

3. **Start typing the name of the contact and select the name you want to add to your BlackBerry Messenger contact list.**

As you start entering letters of the name of the contact, a list of possible contacts shows up, allowing you to quickly select it.

BlackBerry sends the request to the potential contact with the message you see in Figure 9-13. You can edit this message.

Figure 9-12: Many ways to add a contact here (left) and an invitation barcode (right).

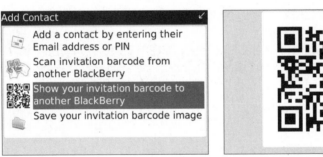

4. **Type your message.**

5. **Select OK, and then select OK again in the screen that follows.**

The application sends your request. As long as the person hasn't responded to your request, his or her name appears as part of the Pending Contacts group, as shown in Figure 9-14. When your contact responds positively to your request, that name goes to the official contact list.

Starting a conversation

You can easily start a conversation with any of your contacts. Follow these steps:

1. **On the BlackBerry Messenger main menu, select the name in your contact list.**

A traditional chat interface opens, with a list of old messages at the top and a text box for typing messages at the bottom.

2. **Type your message.**

3. Press the Enter key.

Any messages you send (as well as any responses you get) are appended to the history list at the top.

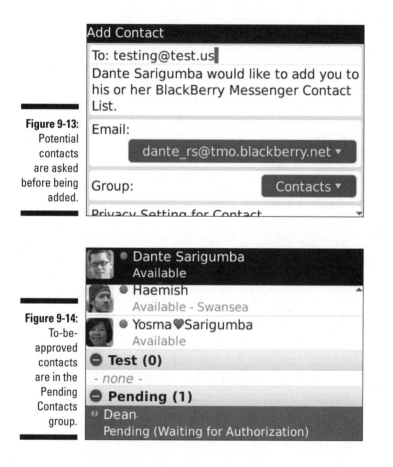

Figure 9-13:
Potential contacts are asked before being added.

Figure 9-14:
To-be-approved contacts are in the Pending Contacts group.

Starting a group conversation

You can easily invite others to your BlackBerry Messenger conversation. Follow these steps:

1. During a conversation, press the Menu key.

The BlackBerry Messenger main menu appears. This time, an Invite option has been added.

2. Select Invite to Group Chat.

The Select Contacts screen opens, listing your BlackBerry Messenger contacts who are currently available. On each contact, you can select the check box to indicate that you want to invite that person to the chat.

3. **Select people by selecting the corresponding check boxes.**

You can choose any number of people.

4. **Select OK.**

You're back to the preceding conversation screen, but this time, the history list shows the contacts you added to the conversation. The newly selected contact(s) can now join the conversation.

You can set a subject on your message. This is especially useful for group conversations:

1. **Press the Menu key while you're in the conversation screen, and then select Set Subject.**

2. **On the screen that follows, enter the subject, and then select OK.**

The conversation screen is updated with the subject, as shown in Figure 9-15.

Figure 9-15:
The conversation screen.

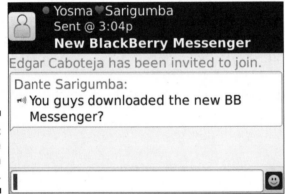

You can make your name appear snazzy by adding symbols, such as Dante☺ and Yosma♨ (see Figure 9-16):

1. **On the BlackBerry Messenger screen, press the Menu key.**

2. **Select Edit My Info.**

3. **Press the menu key and select Add Smiley to choose the symbol you want.**

Taking control of your IM app

If you use IM frequently — and you tend to chat with many contacts at the same time — your BlackBerry's physical limitations may cramp your IM style. No matter whether you use AIM, Y! Messenger, ICQ, MSN Messenger, or BlackBerry Messenger, it's still slower to type words on the tiny keypad than it is to type on your PC.

Do you just give up on the dream of IMing on the go? Not necessarily. The following sections show how you can power up your BlackBerry IM technique.

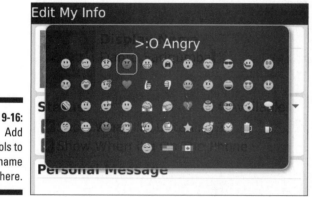

Less is more

If you can't keep up with all your buddies, your best bet is to limit your exposure. Take a whack at your contact list so that only your true buddies remain as contacts whom you want to IM from your BlackBerry. Trimming your list is easy. To delete a contact from your IM application, use the Delete option from your BlackBerry Messenger main menu.

Deleting a contact or buddy from an IM application on your BlackBerry also deletes it from the desktop or laptop computer version of the app. That's because the list of contacts is maintained at a central location — an IM server, to be precise — and not on your BlackBerry.

Set up two accounts of your favorite IM application: one for your BlackBerry and one for your desktop PC. By using these accounts separately, you can limit the number of contacts you have on your BlackBerry and still maintain a full-blown list of contacts on your desktop.

Less typing — use shorthand

Cut down your typing time. Don't forget the shorthand described in Chapter 8. It's widely used in IM as well as texting, so refer to Table 8-1 whenever you can so that you can quickly respond. Before you know it, you'll have the abbreviations memorized and be using them with ease. Emoticons also makes your conversation interesting. Always take them out of your toolbox. Refer to Table 8-2 in Chapter 8 for the list of the most common ones.

SMS versus connecting via the Web

SMS messages are short messages designed for cellphones. IM is a step up, evolving from the Internet where bandwidth is no longer a concern. It provides a better real-time conversation experience across distances. These two technologies evolved in parallel. As more people use IM, it becomes apparent that this technology has a place in handheld devices, where mobility is an advantage. Some of the IM programs developed and used in the BlackBerry in the past use SMS behind the scenes. And because your BlackBerry can connect to the Internet, other programs use the Internet directly. These differences can affect your monthly bill as well as your messaging experience. Read on.

If you don't have unlimited SMS but have an unlimited data plan, be careful with any third-party IM software. Make sure that it uses the Internet instead of SMS. If it uses an SMS, you'll incur charges for every message sent and received, and most network providers charge 20 cents for every SMS message, which can add up quickly and lead to a nasty surprise on your monthly bill.

Jive on

If you want to make sure that you won't have text-messaging fees for using an IM client, check out these IM programs:

✔ **BeejiveIM (`www.beejive.com/download/blackberry.htm`):** This one-time-fee program connects directly to the Web instead of using SMS. It works with multiple IM networks and multiple accounts per network: AIM, Microsoft Live Messenger, Yahoo! Messenger, Google Talk, ICQ, Jabber, and MySpace IM. This is one of the best options.

On their website, they have versions to support old BlackBerry devices, BlackBerry Storm, and high-resolution screens. Download the version for high-resolution screens.

✔ **Nimbuzz (`www.nimbuzz.com`):** Nimbuzz supports many of the popular IM networks. It even supports calls using the Skype network. And the best thing is that it's free and doesn't use SMS.

✔ **IM+ (`www.shapeservices.com/eng/im/blackberry`):** If you don't want to pay annually, consider this service. IM+ asks only for a one-time fee and also supports Yahoo!, MSN, AOL, ICQ, Google Talk, and Jabber networks. The best thing about IM+ is that it sends messages by using the Internet rather than SMS, which is best suited for people who have the unlimited data plan. You have to choose a version: The Regular version connects to BES. (See Chapter 1 for details on BES.) BES is used by companies as a way of connecting the BlackBerry platform to a corporate network and e-mail server. The WAP version allows a personal BlackBerry to use the network provider's WAP gateway to connect to the Internet. The Shape Services Web site has a comprehensive FAQ list for details about the software.

Check out the Web site associated with this book (`www.blackberryfordummies.com`) for updates regarding these (and other) recommendations.

Chapter 10

Surfing the Internet Wave

*I*t's hard to believe that about 15 years ago, more folks didn't have access to the Internet than did. Today, you can surf the Web anytime and anywhere from a desktop computer, a netbook, or even a tiny mobile device such as a PDA or a smartphone. Having said that, it should be no surprise that your BlackBerry Bold has a Web browser of its own.

In this chapter, we show you how to use the BlackBerry Bold Browser. We give you shortcuts and timesaving tips, including the coolest ways to make pages load faster as well as a complete neat-freak's guide to managing your bookmarks.

And because your network service provider may also have its own custom browser for you to use, we compare these proprietary browsers with the default Bold Browser so you can decide which best suits your needs.

Kicking Up the Bold Browser

The BlackBerry Bold Browser comes loaded on your smartphone and accesses the Web by a cellphone connection. Browser can be named differently, depending on how the service provider customizes it. Sometimes it's named *BlackBerry Browser, Internet Browser,* or most likely, just *Browser.* We just use *Browser* to make things easier.

Browser has multiple personalities:

- ✔ **One that's connected to your company's BlackBerry Enterprise Server (BES)**

  BES is a software application from RIM (Research In Motion) that companies can use to control and manage BlackBerry devices. The software also allows your device to see your company's network and connects to your company's databases.

  If you're a corporate BlackBerry user, your company administrator may turn off or not install the other browsers except for the one that connects through the company's BES.

- ✔ **One that goes directly to your service provider's network**

  This might be called by the network service provider's brand name.

- ✔ **A browser that uses a Wi-Fi connection**

- ✔ **A WAP browser**

  Wireless application protocol, or WAP, was popular in the 1990s when mobile device displays were very limited and could display only five or six rows of text. WAP lost its appeal with the advent of high-resolution screens.

The following sections get you started using Browser. After you get your feet wet, we promise that you'll be chomping at the bit to find out more!

Getting to Browser

Browser is one of the main applications of your device, with its Globe icon visible right on the Home screen, as shown in Figure 10-1. In most cases, you open Browser by scrolling to this icon and then pressing the trackball.

If Browser is your default browser, you can access it from any application that distinguishes a Web address. For example, from Contacts, you can open Browser by opening the link on the Web Page field. If you get an e-mail that contains a Web address, just scroll to that link. The link is highlighted, and you can open the page by pressing the trackball.

When you access Browser from another application, you don't have to close that application to jump to Browser. Just press the Alt key (to the left of the Z key) and the Escape key (to the right of the trackball) at the same time to open a pop-up screen with application icons. Use your trackball to highlight the Browser icon; then press the trackball to launch Browser.

By default, accessing Browser by clicking a Web address or a Web link within another application opens the Web page associated with that address. (In

Figure 10-2, we're opening Browser from the Messages application.) Opening Browser by clicking its icon on the Home screen gives you a list of bookmarks.

Figure 10-1: You can open Browser from the Home screen.

Figure 10-2: Open Browser from Messages.

If you haven't yet added bookmarks, the opening Browser screen looks like Figure 10-3. You find out more about adding bookmarks later in this chapter.

Hitting the (air) waves

After you locate Browser, you're ready to surf the Web. Here's how:

1. **Open Browser.**

   Unless the configuration is changed, BlackBerry Bold displays your bookmarks when you open Browser. If you don't yet have any bookmarks or if you want to go to a page that isn't in your bookmarks, skip to Step 3.

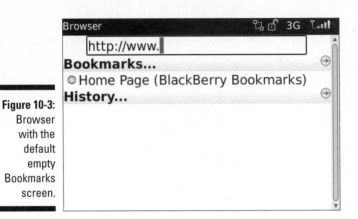

Figure 10-3:
Browser
with the
default
empty
Bookmarks
screen.

2. **Press the Menu key and then select Go To.**

3. **Type a Web address, as shown in Figure 10-4.**

4. **Select OK.**

> The Web page appears. While the page is loading, progress is indicated at the bottom of the screen.

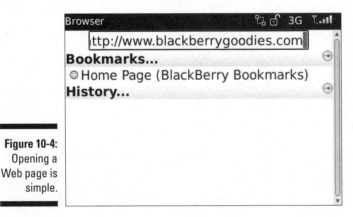

Figure 10-4:
Opening a
Web page is
simple.

Unless you change its configuration (see Start Page in the section "Configuring Browser"), BlackBerry displays your bookmarks when you open Browser. And if you already have bookmarks, just press the Menu key and then select Go To. For the lowdown on adding bookmarks, see upcoming section, "Bookmarking Your Favorite Sites."

When you see a phone number or an e-mail address on a Web page, you can scroll to that information to highlight it. Then, pressing the trackball initiates a phone call or opens a new e-mail message (depending on which type of link you highlighted).

Navigating Web pages

Using Browser to navigate to a Web page is easy. Note that hyperlinks are highlighted onscreen. To jump to a particular hyperlink, scroll to the highlighted link and press the trackball.

Here are a few shortcuts you can use while navigating a Web page:

- ✔ **Move up and down one full display page at a time.** Press 9 (down arrow) or 3 (up arrow).

- ✔ **Switch between full-screen mode and normal mode.** Press the exclamation point (!) key.

  In full-screen mode, the BlackBerry doesn't show anything extra (for example, signals level) on the top portion of the display screen. Normal mode is the default.

- ✔ **Stop loading a page.** Press the Escape key (the arrow key to the right of the trackball).

- ✔ **Go back to the previous page (if there is one).** Press the Escape key (the arrow key to the right of the trackball).

And don't forget the Browser menu (press the Menu key). It has some useful shortcuts, as shown in Figure 10-5.

Figure 10-5:
The
Browser
menu has
lots of good
stuff.

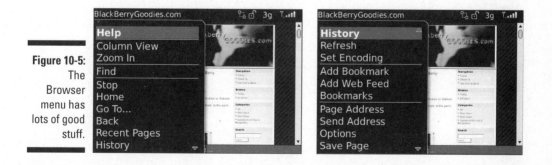

Here are the Browser menu options:

- ✔ **Help:** Like the rest of BlackBerry applications, Help is always available in the menu screen to display a quick guide.

- ✔ **Page View:** Appears only if you are in Column view. (See the upcoming bullet.) This view allows you to see the page like you typically would on a PC's Internet browser. The compressed version of the Web page takes up the entire screen first.

- ✔ **Column View:** The default view; it normally doesn't appear as a menu option. It shows up only if you are in Page view. With this view, the Web page is displayed vertically, meaning that a wide Web page wraps down, and you can use the trackball to scroll up and down the page.

- ✔ **Zoom In/Out:** Zooms in and out.

- ✔ **Find:** Locates and highlights text within the current page. Like any other basic Find tool, choosing this option displays a prompt to enter the text you want to find. After the initial search, a Find Next menu appears for finding the next matching text.

- ✔ **Select:** Appears only if the trackball pointer is placed on text. Use this feature to highlight text onscreen for copying.

- ✔ **Stop:** Appears only if you're in the middle of requesting a page. Use Stop to cancel such request. This is the same as pressing the Escape key.

- ✔ **Copy:** Appears if you have highlighted text. Selecting Copy copies the highlighted text into memory so that you can use it later for pasting somewhere else, such as in MemoPad.

- ✔ **Full Image:** Appears only if you highlight an image and only a portion of the image is displayed onscreen.

- ✔ **Save Image:** Appears only if you highlight an image, allowing you to save the image in the built-in memory or to an SD card.

- ✔ **Home:** The shortcut to your home page. The default home page can vary from carrier to carrier, but to change it, follow these steps:

    a. *Open the Browser menu.*

    b. *Choose Options➪Browser Configuration.*

    c. *Change the Home Page Address field.*

- ✔ **Get Link:** Appears if you have a highlighted link. Choosing this menu item opens that page of the link.

    The faster way to open a link is to press Enter.

- ✔ **Go To:** Opens a Web page when you enter a Web address and press the trackball. As you enter more addresses, they are listed in the History portion of the screen so you don't have to retype them. To find out how to clear that list, see the "Cache operations" section, later in this chapter.

✔ **Back:** Goes back to the preceding page you viewed. This menu item displays only if you have navigated to more than one Web page.

You can achieve the same function by pressing the Escape key (the arrow key to the right of the trackball).

✔ **Forward:** Progresses one page at a time if you've gone back at least one Web page in your browsing travels; otherwise, it isn't a visible option.

✔ **Recent Pages:** Jumps to any of those Web pages when you highlight the history page and press the Enter key twice. Browser can track up to 20 pages of Web addresses you've visited, which you can view on the History screen.

✔ **History:** Displays a list of the Web pages you've visited and allows you to jump back quickly to those pages. It's grouped by date.

✔ **Refresh:** Updates the current page. This is helpful when you're viewing a page with data that changes frequently (such as stock quotes).

✔ **Set Encoding:** Specifies the encoding used in viewing a Web page. This is useful when viewing foreign languages that use different characters. Most BlackBerry users don't have to deal with this and probably don't know what type of encoding a particular language could display.

When you try to open a Web page, indicators that show the progress of your request appear at the bottom of the screen. The left screen in Figure 10-6 shows that Browser is requesting a page. The right screen of Figure 10-6 shows that you've reached the page and that the page is still loading.

Figure 10-6:
Requesting a page (left), and then loading (right) it.

The icons in the upper-right corner of both screens in Figure 10-6 are, from right to left

✔ The **rightmost arrow icon** appears when Browser is processing or receiving data.

✔ The **bars** to the left of the rightmost arrows show the strength of the network signals (the same signal indicators for phone and e-mail).

✔ Your **connection type** also appears. In Figure 10-6, 3g means that the connection is a third-generation network. (Chapter 1 gives you the scoop on connection types.)

✔ The **lock icon** indicates whether you're at a secure Web page. Figure 10-6 shows a nonsecure page. Whether a page is secure depends on the Web site you're visiting. If you're accessing your bank, you most likely see the secured icon (a closed lock). On the other hand, most pages don't need to be secure, so you see the unsecured icon (an open lock).

✔ The **connection information icon** to the left of the lock is a way for you to know the data transferred between your BlackBerry Bold and the network provider. In Browser, you should see a trackball pointer in the screen, which is similar to a PC mouse pointer. Scroll the trackball until the pointer hovers in the connection information icon, then press the trackball. The next screen displays the connection information.

If you lose patience waiting for a page to load and want to browse somewhere else, press the Escape key to stop the page from loading.

Saving a Web page address

Entering a Web address to view a page can get tedious. Fortunately, you can return to a page without typing the same address. While you're viewing a Web page, simply use the Browser menu (shown in Figure 10-7) to save that page's address.

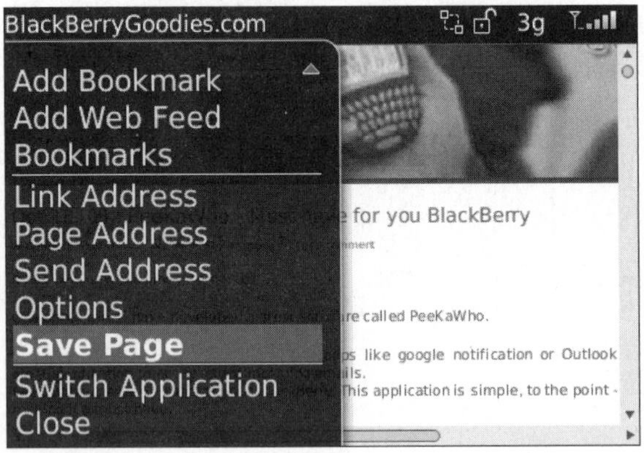

Figure 10-7: Use the Browser menu to save a Web page address.

BlackBerryGoodies.com   3g

Add Bookmark
Add Web Feed
Bookmarks
Link Address
Page Address
Send Address
Options
Save Page
Switch Application
Close

e for you BlackBerry

re called PeeKaWho.

os like google notification or Outlook
ils.
his application is simple, to the point -

You can save a Web page address in a couple of ways:

✔ **Page Address:** This option allows you to view the Web address of the current page through a pop-up screen, which presents you with two options to act upon:

- *Copy Address* saves the page's address on your BlackBerry Clipboard and allows you to paste it somewhere else.

- *Send Address* is the same Send Address you see in the Browser menu (as described in the next item).

✔ **Send Address:** Presents another screen so that you can choose whether to send the address by

- E-mail (Chapter 8)

- MMS (Chapter 9)

- PIN (Chapter 9)

- SMS (Chapter 9)

✔ **Save Page:** Use this option to save the Web address of the current page to Messages. A message appears with the Browser globe icon to indicate that it's a Web link, as shown in Figure 10-8. Scrolling to that entry and pressing the trackball launches Browser and opens the page for your viewing pleasure.

Saving a page to your message list has a different purpose than bookmarking a page. The page initially shows as unread in Messages, to remind you to check back later.

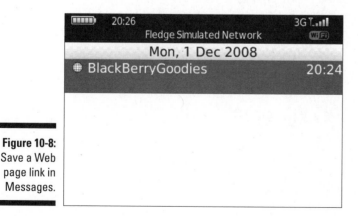

Figure 10-8: Save a Web page link in Messages.

No place like Home

Changing your Home screen background is a neat trick. You can use an image you have saved in your Pictures list as the background on your Home screen. Here's how:

1. **From the Home screen, select the Media icon, and then select Pictures.**

   The Pictures application opens.

2. **Scroll to and select the image you want to set as your background.**

3. **Press the Menu key, and then select Set as Home Screen Image.**

Note: When you don't have network coverage and you try to access a Web page, you're prompted to save your request. When you do, your request is automatically saved in the message list. When you do have coverage later, you can open the same Web page from the message list, with the content loaded already!

Pressing a letter key while a menu appears selects the first menu item that starts with that letter. Pressing the same letter again selects the next menu item that starts with that letter.

Sending an address by e-mail

You can send a Web address to any recipient via an e-mail by using the Page Address option from the Browser menu. For a more direct way, simply select Send Address from the Browser menu while the Web page is displayed. If you know right away that you'll need to send an address to someone, save a couple of clicks and use the more direct method.

Saving Web images

You can save images in JPEG, PNG, GIF, and BMP formats from a Web page. Any saved image is kept in the Pictures application, which enables you to view it later. To save an image, just click the image, and then select Save Image from the menu that appears.

Bookmarking Your Favorite Sites

You don't have to memorize all the addresses of your favorite sites. Instead, use BlackBerry Browser to keep a list of sites you want to revisit. In other words, make a *bookmark* so that you can come back to a site quickly.

Adding and visiting a bookmark

Add a new bookmark this way:

1. **Open Browser and go to the Web page you want to bookmark.**

2. **Select Add Bookmark from the Browser menu.**

   The menu is always accessible by pressing the Menu key.

3. **(Optional) In the Add Bookmark dialog box, change the bookmark name.**

   The name of the bookmark defaults to the Web site title and, in most cases, is appropriate to use as the name. You always have the option to change this name; refer to Modifying a bookmark in the following section.

4. **In the Add Bookmark dialog box, navigate to the folder where you want to save the bookmark.**

   The dialog box is shown in Figure 10-9. The default bookmark save folder is BlackBerry Bookmarks, but you can save the bookmark in any folder you create. To see how to create a bookmark folder, skip to the section, "Adding a bookmark subfolder."

5. **Select Add.**

Figure 10-9:
Name the
bookmark
and specify
where to
store it.

> BlackBerryGoodies.com   3g   📶
>
> **Add Bookmark**
> Name: BlackBerryGoodies.com
> Folder: BlackBerry Bookmarks
> ☐ Available Offline
> Auto Synchronize: Never
> Browser: Browser
> [Add]   [Cancel]

Available offline

In the Add Bookmark dialog box is the Available Offline check box. When that check box is selected, you not only save a page as a bookmark, but you also *cache* it so you can see it even when you're out of range (like when you're stuck deep in a mountain cave). The next time you click the bookmark, that page comes up very fast.

We recommend making bookmarks available offline to pages that don't change from day to day, such as search engines (for example, Google).

Here's how to go to a bookmarked page:

1. **In Browser, select Bookmarks from the Browser menu.**

   You're taken to the Bookmarks screen. From here, you can find all the pages you bookmarked.

2. **Select the bookmark for the page you want to visit.**

Modifying a bookmark

You have the option of changing the attributes of existing bookmarks. Why change? Say you bookmarked a couple of pages from the same Web site but the author of the Web pages didn't bother to have a unique title for each page. While happily bookmarking pages, you didn't bother to change the name of the bookmark that defaults to the Web page title. Now you end up with several bookmarks with the same name. But changing a bookmark is a snap. Follow these steps:

1. **From the Bookmarks screen (select Bookmarks from the Browser menu), highlight the name of the bookmark you want to modify, press the Menu key, and then select Edit Bookmark.**

2. **On the screen that follows, edit the existing name, the address the bookmark is pointing to, or both.**

3. **Select Accept to save your changes.**

Organizing your bookmarks

Over time, the number of your bookmarks will grow. And trying to find a certain site on a tiny screen can be tough. A handy work-around is to organize your bookmarks with folders. For example, you can group related sites in a folder, and each folder can have one or more other folders inside it (subfolders). Having a folder hierarchy narrows your search and allows you to easily find a site.

For example, your sites might fall into these categories:

- ✔ Reference

  NY Times

  Yahoo!

- ✔ Fun

  Flickr

  The Onion

- ✔ Shopping

  Etsy

  Gaiam

Adding a bookmark subfolder

You can add subfolders only to folders that are already listed on the Bookmarks page. That is, you can't create your own root folder. Your choices for adding your first subfolder are under WAP Bookmarks or BlackBerry Bookmarks.

Suppose you want to add a Reference subfolder within your BlackBerry Bookmarks folder. Here are the quick and easy steps:

1. **On the Bookmarks screen, highlight BlackBerry Bookmarks.**

   This is the *parent* of the new subfolder. In this case, the BlackBerry Bookmarks folder will contain the Reference subfolder.

2. **Press the Menu key, and then select Add Subfolder, as shown in Figure 10-10.**

   You see a dialog box where you can enter the name of the folder. (We're using Reference.)

3. **Type the folder name and select OK.**

   The Reference folder now appears on the Bookmarks screen (as shown in Figure 10-11), bearing a folder icon.

Renaming a bookmark folder

Although you can't rename the root bookmark folders like BlackBerry Bookmarks and WAP Bookmarks, the folders you create under them are fair game. Renaming a bookmark folder that you created is as easy as editing a bookmark. Follow these steps:

1. **On the Bookmarks screen, highlight the name of the folder you want to change.**

2. **Press the Menu key and select Rename Folder.**

3. **Type the name of the folder.**

4. **Select OK to save your changes.**

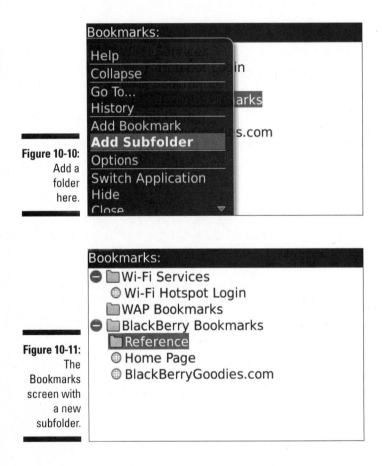

Figure 10-10: Add a folder here.

Figure 10-11: The Bookmarks screen with a new subfolder.

Moving a bookmark

If you keep going astray looking for a bookmark that you think exists in a particular folder but is instead in another, move that bookmark where it belongs. Follow these steps:

1. **Highlight the bookmark, press the Menu key, and select Move Bookmark.**

2. **Use the trackball to move the bookmark to the location in the list where you want it to appear.**

3. **After you find the right location, press the trackball.**

   Your bookmark is in its new home.

Cleaning up your bookmarks

Maybe you really like a site but eventually stop visiting it. Or maybe a site disappears, and every time you click the bookmark, you get a 404 Not Found error. Time for a little spring cleaning. From the Bookmarks screen, highlight the name of the bookmark you want to delete. Press the Menu key and select Delete Bookmark. It's just that easy.

You can — repeat, *can* — clean up bookmarks wholesale by deleting a folder. A word to the wise, though: All the contents of that folder will be deleted, so purge with caution.

Exercising Options and Optimization Techniques

Sure, Browser works out of the box, but folks have their own taste, right? Look to Browser Options for attributes and features you can customize.

Press the Menu key and select Options. The Browser Options screen that opens offers three main categories to choose from, as shown in Figure 10-12:

- ✔ **Browser Configuration:** A place to toggle Browser features
- ✔ **General Properties:** Settings for the general look and feel of Browser
- ✔ **Cache Operations:** Allows you to clear file caches used by Browser

If you feel speed-greedy after adjusting the options, see the sidebar "Speeding up browsing," later in this chapter.

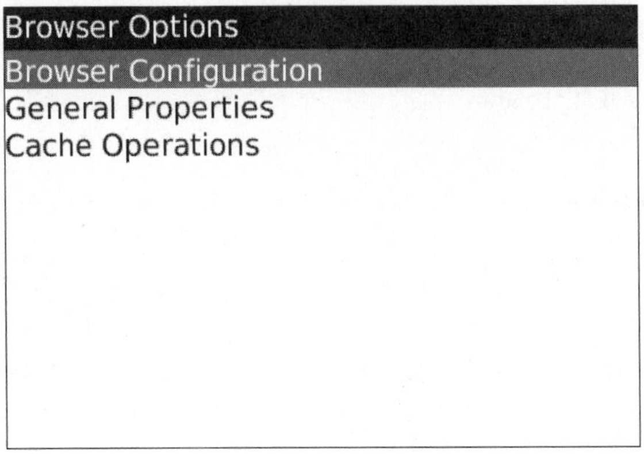

Browser Options
Browser Configuration
General Properties
Cache Operations

Figure 10-12:
The
Browser
Options
screen.

Configuring Browser

You can define browser-specific settings from the Browser Configuration screen, which you access from the Browser Options screen. The customization items you can amend (shown in Figure 10-13) are as follows:

- ✔ **Support JavaScript:** JavaScript is a scripting language used heavily to make dynamic Web pages. A Web page might not behave normally when this option is turned off. This option is off by default.

- ✔ **Allow JavaScript Popups:** Most ad pages are launched as JavaScript pop-ups. So, having this check box selected minimizes these ads. Be aware, though, that some important pages are also displayed as JavaScript pop-ups.

  Note: This option shows up if you select the Support JavaScript check box.

- ✔ **Prompt to enable JavaScript Popups:** This option only shows up and comes into play if you don't have Support JavaScript checked. The default value for this option is checked (if you browse a page that has JavaScript, Browser will prompt you to either enable JavaScript or not).

- ✔ **Terminate Slow Running Scripts:** Sometimes you find Web pages with scripts that aren't written well. Keep this selected to keep Browser from hanging.

  This option shows up only if you select the Support JavaScript check box.

- ✔ **Use Background Images:** A Web page background image can make the page look pleasing, but if the image is big, it could take time to download it.

- ✔ **Support Embedded Media:** Select this option to support media such as SVG (scalable vector graphics). Think of it as Flash for mobile devices such as the BlackBerry Bold. SVG can be a still image or an animated one.

✔ **Show Images:** Controls the display of images depending on the content mode of WML, HTML, or both. Think of WML pages as Web pages made just for mobile devices, such as the BlackBerry. We recommend leaving this selected for both.

Turn on and off the display of image placeholders if you opt to not display images.

✔ **Browser Identification:** This specifies which browser type your browser emulates. The default is BlackBerry, but Browser can also emulate these instead:

- Microsoft Internet Explorer
- Firefox

Keep the default BlackBerry mode. We don't see much difference in any of them.

✔ **Start Page:** Use this to specify a starting page to load when you open Browser.

✔ **Home Page Address:** Use this to set your home page. Note that the home page is always available from the Browser menu.

Figure 10-13:
The
Browser
Configu-
ration
screen.

Browser Configuration	
Browser:	Browser
☐ Support JavaScript	
☑ Prompt to enable JavaScript	
☑ Use Background Images	
☑ Support Embedded Media	
Show Images:	On WML & HTML Pages
Browser Identification:	BlackBerry
Start Page:	Start Page
Home Page Address: http:// mobile.blackberry.com/	

General Browser properties

The General Properties screen is similar to the Browser Configuration screen (see the preceding section) in that you can customize some Browser behaviors. General Properties, however, is geared more toward the features of the Browser content. As shown in Figure 10-14, you can configure features and also turn features off or on.

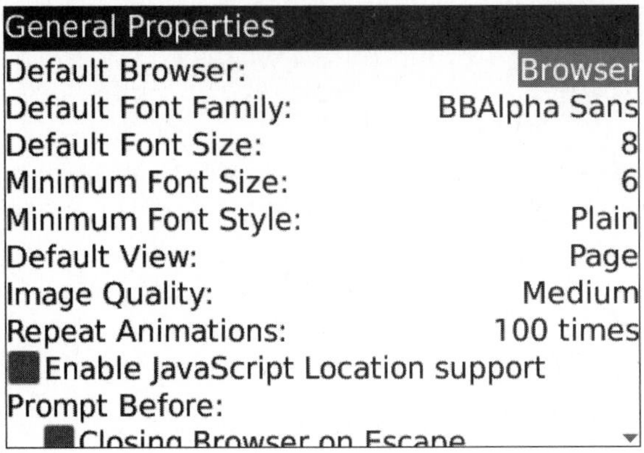

General Properties
Default Browser: Browser
Default Font Family: BBAlpha Sans
Default Font Size: 8
Minimum Font Size: 6
Minimum Font Style: Plain
Default View: Page
Image Quality: Medium
Repeat Animations: 100 times
■ Enable JavaScript Location support
Prompt Before:
   ■ Closing Browser on Escape

Figure 10-14:
The
General
Properties
screen.

From this screen, use the Space key to change the value of a field. You can configure the following features:

- **Default Browser:** If you have multiple browsers available, use this to specify which one you want to use when opening a Web link.

- **Default Font Family:** When a Web page doesn't specify the text font, Browser will use the one you selected here.

- **Default Font Size:** When a Web page doesn't specify the text font size, Browser uses the one you selected here. The smaller the size, the more text that can fit onscreen.

- **Minimum Font Size:** A Web page might specify a font size too small to be legible. Specifying a legible font size will override the Web page.

- **Minimum Font Style:** When Browser is using the minimum font size, you can choose what font to use. Some fonts are more legible, even in small size, than others. If you aren't sure which one to use, leave the default.

- **Default View:** You can toggle the default view:

   - *Column* wraps all Web page elements vertically, so you just scroll up and down by panning the page.

   - *Page* displays the page like you normally see in your PC's Internet browser. Pan the page to scroll left, right, up, and down.

- **Image Quality:** The higher the quality, the slower the page loads. The default quality is medium. You have three options: low, medium, and high.

- **Repeat Animations:** Sets the number of times an animation repeats. This pertains to animated images that most banner ads use. The default is 100, but you can change this setting to

   - Never

   - Once

- 10 Times

- 100 Times

- As Many as the Image Specifies

✔ **Enable JavaScript Location Support:** Web pages that have scripts that take advantage of your BlackBerry's location through GPS will work if you have this selected.

✔ **Prompt Before:** You can have BlackBerry Browser give you a second chance before you do the following things:

- *Closing Browser on Escape:* You're notified right before you exit BlackBerry Browser.

- *Closing Modified Pages:* You're notified right before you exit a modified Web page (for example, some type of online form you fill out).

- *Running WML Scripts:* WML is a script that tells a wireless device how to display a page. It was popular years ago when resolutions of device screens were low, but very few Web sites are using it now. We recommend leaving this field deselected because this type of scripting is old and benign.

Cache operations

At any given time, your BlackBerry uses a few cache mechanisms. A *cache* (pronounced *cash*) temporarily stores information used by Browser so that the next time the info is needed, Browser doesn't have to go back to the source Web site. The cache can speed up displays when you want to view the Web page again and is also useful when you're suddenly out of network coverage. When you visit a site that uses *cookies,* Browser caches that cookie. (Think of a cookie as a piece of text that a Web site created and placed in your BlackBerry's memory to remember something about you, such as your username.)

Browser also caches pages and content so that you can view them offline, which is handy when you're out of network range.

Some Web sites *push* (send information) Web pages to BlackBerry devices. An icon will appear on the Home screen, allowing you to quickly view the page. After the Web page is delivered to your BlackBerry, it becomes available even if you go out of the coverage area. If you subscribe to this service, your device will store Web pages in the cache. Also, the addresses of the pages that you visited (or your latest 20 in your history list) comprise a cache.

The Cache Operations screen, shown in Figure 10-15, allows you to manually clear your cache. To view the Cache Operations screen, follow these steps:

1. From the Browser screen, press the Menu key.

2. Select Options.

3. Select Cache Operations.

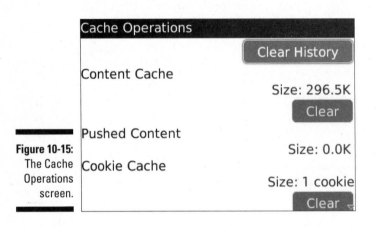

Cache Operations

Clear History

Content Cache

Size: 296.5K

Clear

Pushed Content

Size: 0.0K

Cookie Cache

Size: 1 cookie

Clear

Figure 10-15:
The Cache
Operations
screen.

The size for each type of cache is displayed on this screen. If the cache has content, you also see the Clear button, which you can use to clear the specified cache type. This is true for all types of cache except for history, which has its own Clear History button. You find four types of cache:

✔ **Content Cache:** Any offline content. You may want to clear this whenever you're running out of space on your BlackBerry and need to free some memory. Or maybe you're tired of viewing old content or tired of pressing the Refresh option.

✔ **Pushed Content:** Any content that was pushed to your BlackBerry from Push Services subscriptions. You may want to clear this to free memory on your BlackBerry.

✔ **Cookie Cache:** Any cookies stored on your BlackBerry. You may want to clear this for security's sake. Sometimes you don't want a Web site to remember you.

✔ **History:** The list of sites you've visited by using the Go To function. You may want to clear this for the sake of security if you don't want other people knowing which Web sites you're visiting on your BlackBerry.

You can easily check how much memory your device has in the Help Me! screen. To go to Help Me! screen, and then press and hold these keys: Alt+Shift+H. Shift is the bottom-left key, below the Alt key.

Speeding up browsing

On a wireless network, many factors can affect the speed with which Web pages display. If you find that browsing the Web is extremely slow, you can make your pages load faster but in exchange for not using a few features. Here are some of the speed-enhancing work-arounds you can use:

✔ **Don't display images.** You can achieve a big performance improvement by turning off image display. From the Browser menu, select Browser Options⇨Browser Configuration, scroll to Show Images, and change the value to No.

✔ **Check your BlackBerry memory.** When your BlackBerry's memory is depleted, its performance degrades. The BlackBerry low-memory manager calls each application every now and then, telling each one to free resources.

Hint #1: Don't leave many e-mail messages unread. When the low-memory manager kicks in, Messages tries to delete old messages, but it can't delete unread messages.

Hint #2: Purge the BlackBerry event log to free needed space. Enter the letters **LGLG** while holding the Shift key. This opens an event log. The event log entries may not make sense to you since they're mostly cryptic and in codes. These are usually helpful for technical folks to figure out what's going on on your BlackBerry, but something you don't really need. You can clear the event log to free memory.

✔ **Turn off other features.** If you're mostly interested in viewing content, consider turning off features that pertain to how the content is processed, such as Support HTML Tables, Use Background Images, Support JavaScript, Allow JavaScript Popups, and Support Style Sheets. To turn off other Browser features, navigate to Browser Options⇨General Properties.

Warning: We don't advise turning off features while performing an important task such as online banking. If you do, you may not be able to perform some of the actions on the page. For example, the Submit button might not work. Not good.

Installing and Uninstalling Applications from the Web

You can download and install applications on your BlackBerry via Browser — that is, if the application has a link that lets you download and install the files (see Chapter 19 for other installation options). The downloading and installing parts are easy. Follow these steps:

1. **Click the link from Browser.**

   It displays a simple prompt that looks like the screen shown in the left of Figure 10-16.

2. **Click the Download button.**

   The download starts, as shown in the right of Figure 10-16.

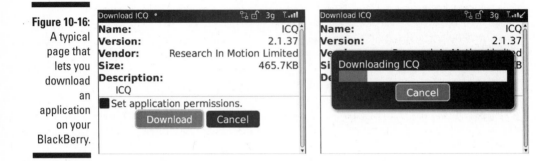

Figure 10-16:
A typical
page that
lets you
download
an
application
on your
BlackBerry.

As long as you stay within network coverage while the download is progressing, your BlackBerry can finish the download *and* install the application for you. If it finishes without any problems, you see a screen similar to Figure 10-17.

Figure 10-17:
The
download
and
installation
were
completed.

Like with a desktop computer, the download might or might not work for a variety of reasons. Sometimes the application

✔ Requires you to install libraries

✔ Works only on a certain version of the BlackBerry OS

These issues can be prevented, depending on the sophistication of the site where the link is published. With most reputable sources, these issues are considered, and successful downloading and installation are a snap.

Installing applications from nonreputable sources can cause your BlackBerry to become unstable. Before you download an application from the Web, be sure to read reviews about that particular application. Most of the time, other people who tried the software provide reviews or feedback. Don't be the first to write the bad review!

Your BES administrator can disable the feature in your BlackBerry to download and install an application. This is mostly the case for a company-issued device. If you have problems downloading and installing an application, check your company policy or contact the BlackBerry support person in your company.

If you download an application that turns out to be a dud, you need to uninstall it. See Chapter 19 for more on uninstalling an application from your BlackBerry.

Browser's Behavior in Business

Getting a device from your employer has both a good and an ugly side:

- ✔ **Good:** Your company foots the bill.
- ✔ **Ugly:** Your company foots the bill.

Because your company pays, the company dictates what you can and cannot do with your BlackBerry Bold. This is especially true with respect to browsing the Web.

Two scenarios come into play when it comes to your browser:

- ✔ Your browser might be running under your company's *BlackBerry Enterprise Server (BES)*. With this setup, your BlackBerry Browser is connecting to the Internet by using your company's Internet connection. It's like using your desktop machine at work.
- ✔ Your browser is connected through a network service provider. Most of the time, this kind of browser is called by the company's name.

In most cases, your device fits in only one scenario, which is the case where your browser is connected through your company's BES server. Some lucky folks may have both. Whatever scenario you're in, the following sections describe the major differences between the two and indicate what you can expect.

Using Browser on your company's BES

In an enterprise setup, your BlackBerry Browser is connected through your company's BES server. With this setup, the browser is actually named *BlackBerry Browser.* BES is located inside your company's intranet. This setup allows the company to better manage the privileges and the functions you can use on your device.

For the BlackBerry Browser application, this setup allows the company to use the existing Internet infrastructure, including the company's firewall. Because you are within the company's network, the boundaries that your network administrator set up on your account apply to your BlackBerry as well. For example, when browsing the Web, your BlackBerry won't display any Web sites that are blocked by your company's server.

The good thing, though, is that you can browse the company's intranet: That is, all the Web pages you have access to inside your company through your company's PC are also available in your BlackBerry.

 Know (and respect) your company's Web-browsing policy. Most companies keep logs of sites you view on your browser and might even have software to monitor usage. Also, your company might not allow downloading from the Web.

Using your network provider's browser

Any new device coming from a network service provider can come with its own branded Web browser. It's the same BlackBerry Browser, but the behavior might differ in the following ways:

- ✔ **The name is different.**
- ✔ **The default home page usually points to the provider's Web site.** This isn't necessarily a bad thing. Most of the time, the network provider's Web site is full of links that you may not find on BlackBerry Browser.
- ✔ **You can browse more sites.** You aren't limited by your company's policy.

 Most of the time, if your browser is through BES, surfing the Web is much faster. This isn't true in all cases, however, because the network bandwidth of your BES affects the speed.

Setting the default browser

If you have two Web browsers on your Bold, you have the option to set the *default* browser. This comes into play when you view a Web address by using a link outside Browser application. For example, when you view an e-mail with a Web link, selecting that link launches the default browser.

To set up the default browser, follow these steps:

1. **Go to the Home screen.**

2. **Select Settings⇨Options⇨Advanced Options⇨Browser.**

3. **Use the Space key to change the value of the default browser configuration, as shown in Figure 10-18.**

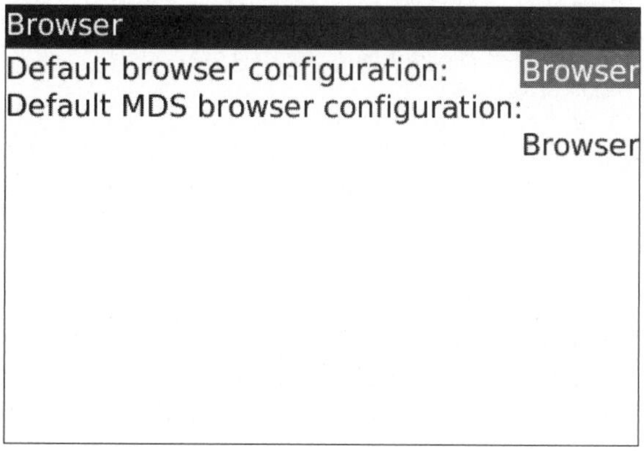

Figure 10-18:
Use the
Space key
to change
the value of
the default
browser.

```
Browser
Default browser configuration:        Browser
Default MDS browser configuration:
                                      Browser
```

Chapter 11

Getting Around with GPS

· ·

In This Chapter

▶ Using GPS safely

▶ Preparing to use GPS on your BlackBerry

▶ Choosing a GPS application

· ·

A few years back when some of the North American network carriers introduced GPS on their versions of the BlackBerry, we was quite impressed . . . until we tried it. The response time was slow, and it wasn't accurate. On top of that, the network carriers charged users an arm and a leg for this inferior service. As it turns out, those GPS functions were implemented by using the network; that is, there wasn't actual GPS embedded in the BlackBerry. How low-tech!

Today, your BlackBerry Bold comes with built-in GPS, which makes finding yourself easy. In this chapter, we show you how to use your BlackBerry's built-in and show you the best GPS applications you can use on your BlackBerry (two of which are free!).

Putting Safety First

Some GPS features are useful while you're driving a car. However, even when tempted to use your BlackBerry GPS while driving, we *strongly* suggest that you *do not* adjust it while you're driving.

Before you start using BlackBerry GPS in your car, you need a BlackBerry car holder — preferably a car kit with a car charger. You can buy a car kit on the Internet; just search for *BlackBerry car kit*. Or go to one of the following Web sites:

▶ www.shopblackberry.com

▶ http://shop.crackberry.com

Now that you have all you need to keep you safe, keep on reading.

What You Need

For GPS to work on your BlackBerry, it needs navigation maps, which are usually downloaded in little pieces as required. And because these maps are downloaded, you must be subscribed to a data plan and have a radio signal to obtain them.

If you didn't subscribe to an unlimited data plan from your network carrier, be aware that the more you use your GPS as you move about, the more data (map pieces) you'll download, which means the more charges you'll incur.

In summary, for your BlackBerry GPS to work, you need

> ✔ **A data plan from your network carrier**
>
> We recommend an unlimited data plan.
>
> ✔ **To be in an area where you have a radio signal**
>
> That way, you can download the maps.

Your GPS Application Choices

The four GPS applications that you can use on your BlackBerry are

> ✔ **BlackBerry Map** (comes with your BlackBerry): Free
>
> ✔ **Google Maps** (m.google.com/maps): Free
>
> ✔ **Garmin Mobile** (garmin.com/mobile/mobilext): $100 per year.
>
> ✔ **TeleNav GPS Navigator** (telenav.com/products/tn/): $10 per month

The icons for all are pictured in Figure 11-1.

BlackBerry Map

As we mention earlier, your BlackBerry comes with the BlackBerry Map application loaded (refer to Figure 11-1).

If you have a BlackBerry with AT&T as your network carrier, you might not have BlackBerry Map installed out of the box. No worries; you can download it via mobile.blackberry.com. (Keep reading, too, for alternatives to BlackBerry Map that still take advantage of your BlackBerry GPS.)

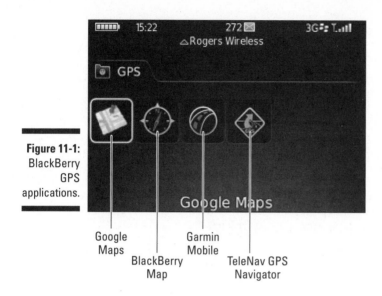

Figure 11-1: BlackBerry GPS applications.

Google Maps

BlackBerry Map

Garmin Mobile

TeleNav GPS Navigator

With or without GPS (built-in or external), you can use BlackBerry Map to do the following (see Figure 11-2):

✔ Find a location by typing an address or by using Contacts.

✔ Get point-to-point directions.

✔ E-mail or SMS a location to colleagues and friends.

✔ Turn GPS on or off.

✔ Zoom in and out of the map.

Of course, with GPS turned on, you can track where you are and follow point-to-point directions.

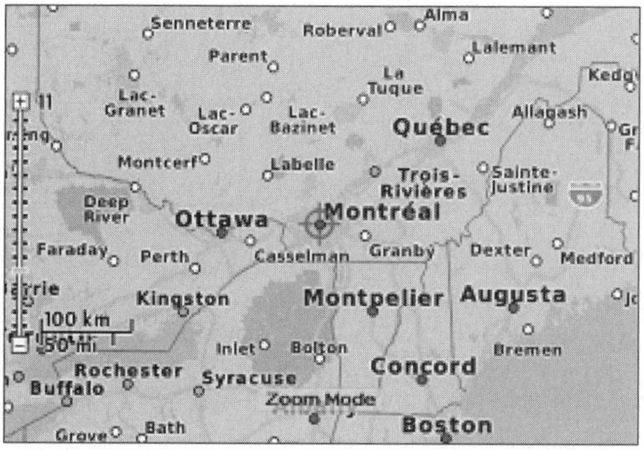

Figure 11-2: BlackBerry Map on the BlackBerry Bold.

Google Maps

Google Maps is the mobile version of `http://maps.google.com`. It has most of the features of the online version, including satellite imaging and traffic information. Best of all, it's free.

Like BlackBerry Map, you can use Google Maps even without a GPS, but it gets better. You can search for businesses and landmarks, just as you do on `http://m.google.com/maps`. It's like having the ultimate 411 (with a map) at the tip of your fingers.

Because Google Maps doesn't come with your BlackBerry, you need to download it. To do so, go to `www.google.com/gmm`. After the program downloads, its icon appears on your Home screen (refer to Figure 11-1).

After Google Maps is loaded, press the Menu key to display the menu shown in Figure 11-3.

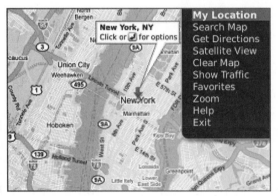

Figure 11-3:
Google
Maps menu.

From the menu, you can do the following:

- ✔ Find businesses and landmarks, including phone numbers, address information, and Web addresses.

- ✔ Find and map exact addresses.

- ✔ Get step-by-step directions from point A to point B.

- ✔ View satellite images of the current map (see Figure 11-4).

- ✔ Get traffic information for major highways.

Figure 11-4:
Google
Maps
showing
a satellite
photo.

With GPS or Google's MyLocation on, you can see your current location as a blue blinking dot.

Here are some keyboard shortcuts for Google Maps:

- ✔ **Zoom in:** I key
- ✔ **Zoom out:** O key
- ✔ **Go to the current location:** 0 (zero) key

You need to have a radio signal to download maps to your BlackBerry. In addition, we recommend that you have an unlimited data plan if you are a frequent user of the GPS feature on your BlackBerry.

TeleNav GPS Navigator

TeleNav GPS Navigator is a full-featured GPS solution. It's meant as a GPS device replacement, which means the folks at TeleNav want you to use your BlackBerry in the car. TeleNav's feature list is extensive. From 3D maps to a real-time compass to finding Wi-Fi hotspots, the list goes on and on. It even lets you input the address by speaking aloud instead of typing and responds by speaking the directions aloud to you. Figure 11-5 shows the main menu for TeleNav. (Note that there are network-branded versions of TeleNav; for example, Figure 11-5 shows an AT&T version. The functionalities from TeleNav are the same, regardless of network branding.)

The extensive features come at a price. Depending upon your network carrier, TeleNav costs about $10 per month. TeleNav does offer a 30-day free trial. Visit www.telenav.com/products/tn for more information. After the product is downloaded, an icon appears on your screen (refer to Figure 11-1).

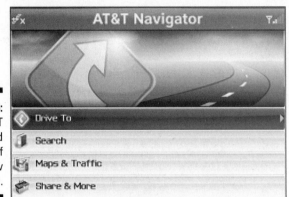

Figure 11-5:
AT&T
branded
version of
TeleNav
main menu.

Garmin Mobile

Like TeleNav, Garmin also offers a full-featured GPS solution. It costs a one-time fee of $99 (U.S. dollars) and is good for the life of the device. The features of Garmin Mobile are very similar to its GPS counterpart. If you have ever owned a Garmin GPS, the user interface is very similar and friendly. Figure 11-6 shows the main menu for Garmin Mobile.

Figure 11-6:
Garmin
Mobile's
main menu.

We like the simplicity of Garmin's user interface and its one-time cost.

To find out more, visit www.garmin.com/mobile/mobilext.

Part IV
Music, Pictures, and Movies on Your Bold

The 5th Wave   By Rich Tennant

©RICHTENNANT

Seven presentations in as many days, and <u>still</u> no investors.

Ready? Here they come...

TD RESEARCH INC.

Smert Phone Technology

○ DYNAMIC
○ INNOVATIVE
○ COST EFFICIEN

In this part . . .

Use your BlackBerry Bold as a video camera. Get entertained and have fun with Bold's multimedia capabilities. And manage your Media files.

Chapter 12

Taking Great Pictures and Videos

. . . .

In This Chapter

▶ Getting ready to say, "Cheese!"

▶ Saving and organizing your pictures

▶ Sharing your photos with other people

▶ Getting ready to say, "Action!"

▶ Configuring your video camera

. . . .

*O*h, shoot, you forgot your camera. Don't worry! Your BlackBerry is there when you need to capture the unbelievable: Grandma doing a handstand, Grandpa doing a cartwheel, or your roommate doing her laundry. And if pictures aren't enough, you can record your unbelievable scene in full motion.

Before you try taking pictures or get the BlackBerry camera rolling, read this chapter so you know what to expect and how to get the best shot. We walk you through the easy steps for capturing that funny pose, and tell you how to store those photos and videos. And don't miss reading how to share the joy with your buddies.

Saying "Cheese"

Snapping shots with your BlackBerry Bold couldn't be easier. Just turn on the Camera app, line up your shot, and snap away. Here's the bird's-eye view:

1. **Press the bottom key on the right side of your BlackBerry to bring up the Camera application. (See Figure 12-1.)**

   Alternatively, you can select the Camera icon from the Home screen.

   Make sure that your finger isn't blocking the lens on the back side of your device.

The camera button on the right side of your Bold is really a convenience key, which you can program to open your favorite application. By default, it's set to launch Camera. Chapter 3 shows how to change this setting.

2. **When you see the image onscreen, press the Camera key to take the picture.**

    You should hear a funky shutter-like sound. Neat and easy, isn't it?

That's the quick version. Keep reading to discover more about Camera's features.

Figure 12-1:
The camera screen ready to take pictures.

Screen

Number of pictures you can save

Zoom indicator

Zoom amount

Flash indicator

Camera key

Reading the screen indicators

When you open the Camera application, the first thing you see is the screen shown in Figure 12-1. The top portion of this screen shows you the image you're about to capture. Immediately beneath the preview are icons (starting from the left) that indicate

✔ Number of pictures you can capture

✔ Zoom

✔ Flash

Choosing the picture quality

Your Bold can capture images in as much as 2.0 megapixels (MP) of resolution. Saving images at this resolution requires considerable space, though. Just be mindful when shooting, and consider saving images at a lower quality to save some space on your BlackBerry.

Get a big microSD card. Nowadays, even a 32GB microSD card is inexpensive, and it holds thousands of pictures.

Here are the three resolutions you can choose:

✔ **Normal:** The default setting. This is the lowest quality but lets you save the most pictures. The trade-off is that Normal picture quality won't be as smooth or fine as the other resolution choices.

If you're just taking pictures of your friends' faces so you can attach them as Caller IDs, Normal is appropriate.

✔ **Fine:** A middle setting between Normal and SuperFine. This is a compromise if you are concerned about space and want to capture more pictures. Best use is only for any electronic viewer; it isn't so good for printing.

✔ **SuperFine:** The best quality that your Camera can capture. Choose this if you plan on printing the images.

Changing picture quality is a snap. Follow these steps:

1. **Open the Camera application.**

2. **Press the Menu key, and then select Options.**

3. **Highlight Picture Quality, and then press the Space key.**

   Pressing the Space key toggles the picture quality value among Normal, Fine, and SuperFine. You might have to press the Space key twice to select the setting you want.

4. **Press the Menu key, and then select Save.**

   The picture quality you chose is active.

Zooming and focusing

You need to be steady to get a good focus while taking your shots. Although it's convenient to use one hand while taking pictures, most of the time, you'll get a blurry image if you try that.

When taking pictures, hold your Bold with both hands, one holding the smartphone steady and the other pressing the trackball. If the right convenience button is set to Camera, you can press that instead of the trackball.

Holding the smartphone with both hands is even more important if you're zooming in. Yes, your camera is capable of up to 3x digital zoom. Here's what you need to do to focus and zoom:

   ✓ **To focus:** Your camera has autofocus. Just hold it steady.

   ✓ **To zoom in:** Slide the trackball up.

   ✓ **To zoom out:** Slide the trackball down.

While zooming, the value in the indicator changes from 1x to 2x to 3x and vice versa, depending on the direction you scroll.

When zooming, your thumb is already on the trackball. What a convenient way to take the picture — just press.

We don't recommend using the zoom. Digital zoom (which is what your camera has) gives poor results because it's done through software and degrades the quality of the picture. The higher the zoom factor, the more pixilated the picture becomes. To get a clearer picture, get closer to the object.

Setting the flash

The rightmost indicator on the Camera screen is the flash. The default is Automatic, which shows a lightning bolt with the letter _A_. Automatic means that the camera detects the amount of light you have at the moment you capture the image. Where it's dark, the flash fires; otherwise, it doesn't.

You can turn the flash on, off, or to automatic. The default setting is automatic. When set to off, the lightning bolt is encircled with a diagonal line, just like you see on No Smoking signs. You can toggle the settings on the camera's Options screen, which is accessible by pressing the Menu key.

Setting the white balance

In photography, filters are used to compensate for the dominant light. For instance, a fluorescent versus an incandescent light could affect how warm the picture appears. Instead of using filters, most digital cameras have a feature to correct or compensate for many types of light settings. This feature is *white balance.* Your Bold has this feature. You can choose from Sunny, Cloudy, Night, Incandescent, Fluorescent, and Automatic. *Automatic* means your camera determines what it thinks are the best settings to apply and it's the default setting.

You can change the white balance through the camera's Options screen.

The camera's Options screen is accessible by pressing the Menu key and selecting Options from the menu that appears.

Setting the picture size

Aside from picture quality, you can also adjust the actual size of the photo:

- ✔ **Large:** 1600 x 1200. This is the default setting.

  Large uses more memory.
- ✔ **Medium:** 1024 x 768
- ✔ **Small:** 640 x 480

Again, camera settings are accessible through the camera's Options screen by pressing the Menu key and selecting Options from the menu that appears.

Geotagging

Because your Bold has GPS capability, your location based on longitude and latitude can be determined easily. This information can be added to your media files, including the pictures taken from your camera. Adding geographic information is as *geotagging.* Photos taken on your Bold can have longitude and latitude information. Now, you don't have to wonder where you took that crazy pose.

Geotagging is disabled by default. Enable it from the camera's Options screen: Press the Menu key, and select Options to get to the Options screen.

If you have longitude and latitude information from one of your photos, you can use one of the free sites on the Web to locate where you were when you took the photo. One such site is `www.travelgis.com/geocode/default.aspx`.

Working with Pictures

You've taken a bunch of pictures, and you want to see them. And maybe delete the unflattering ones. Or perhaps organize them. No problem.

Viewing pictures

If you take a picture, you want to see it, right? You can see an image you just captured right then and there, as shown in Figure 12-2.

All the pictures you took on your Camera are filed directly to a folder in your system. The possible default folder location of pictures is based on whether you opted to save it in:

- **Device Memory:** /Device Memory/home/user/pictures
- **Media Card:** /Media Card/BlackBerry/pictures

Let your device file the pictures in the media card (microSD). The first time you use Camera, it prompts you whether to save pictures to the media card. If you aren't sure what the current setting is, simply close the Camera application, and then take out the microSD card and put it back in. The next time you open Camera, it displays the same prompt about letting you save pictures to the media card.

The format of the filename is based on current date and time and named as `IMG<counter>-<yyyymmdd>-<hhmm>.jpg`. So if you took the 21st picture at 9:30 a.m. on December 20, 2009, you end up with IMG00021-20091220-0930.jpg.

If you're browsing through your picture folders, view a picture by highlighting it and pressing the trackball.

Creating a slide show

To see your pictures in a slide show, follow these steps:

1. **From the Camera screen, press the Menu key, and then select View Pictures from the menu that appears.**
2. **Press the Menu key.**
3. **Select Slide Show.**

   Voilà! Your BlackBerry displays your pictures one at a time at a regular time interval. The default interval between each picture is two seconds; if you aren't happy with this interval, change it in the Options screen. (Press the Menu key and select Options to get to the Options screen.)

Figure 12-2:
The Camera screen after taking a picture.

Trashing pictures

If you don't like an image you captured, you can delete it. Follow these steps:

1. **Highlight the picture you want to trash.**
2. **Press the Menu key, and then select Delete from the menu that appears; alternatively, press the Del key.**

   A confirmation screen appears.
3. **Select Delete.**

You can also delete an image right after taking the picture; just select the trash can icon when viewing the photo. (Refer to Figure 12-2.)

Listing filenames versus thumbnails

When you open a folder packed with pictures, your BlackBerry automatically shows *thumbnails,* which are small previews of your pictures.

A preview is nice, but say you want to search for a picture by filename. Here's how:

1. **Go to a picture folder.**

2. **Press the Menu key.**

3. **Select View List.**

   That's exactly what you get: a list of all the pictures in the folder. What's neat is that the option also displays the file size, which can give you a clue about what settings you used to take the picture. For example, a photo taken at a SuperFine quality produces a much bigger file size compared with one taken at Normal.

Checking picture properties

Curious about the amount of memory your picture is using? Want to know the time you took the photo?

1. **Highlight the picture from a list.**

   On the Camera screen, view the list of your pictures by pressing the Menu key and selecting View Pictures.

2. **Press the Menu key.**

3. **Select Properties.**

   You see a screen similar to Figure 12-3, which displays the location of the file in your BlackBerry, size, and last modification. The arrow with Removable text indicates that it's filed in the media card. The hidden check box allows you to hide the file when navigating through your picture list. Once hidden, the file disappears from the list and the only way to see the file in your Bold again is to use Explore. Check Chapter 13 for details about Explore.

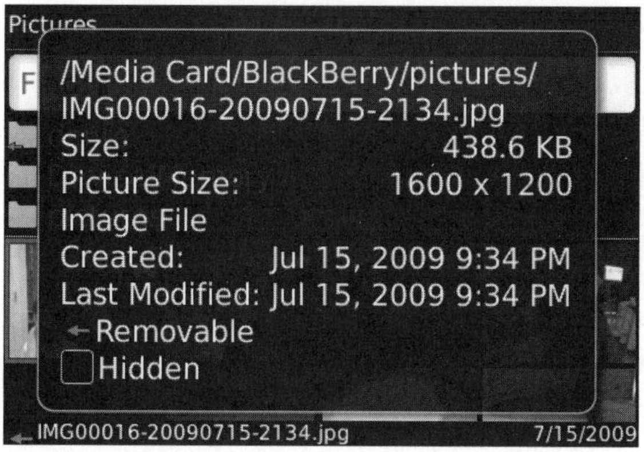

Figure 12-3:
Your
picture's
properties.

> Pictures
>
> /Media Card/BlackBerry/pictures/
> IMG00016-20090715-2134.jpg
> Size: 438.6 KB
> Picture Size: 1600 x 1200
> Image File
> Created: Jul 15, 2009 9:34 PM
> Last Modified: Jul 15, 2009 9:34 PM
>   ← Removable
>   ☐ Hidden
>
> IMG00016-20090715-2134.jpg   7/15/2009

Organizing your pictures

Organization is all about time and the best use of it. After all, you want to spend your time enjoying looking *at* your pictures — not looking *for* them. Your BlackBerry Bold enables you to rename and move pictures to different folders. Plus, you can create folders, too. With those capabilities, you should be on your way to organization nirvana.

Renaming a picture file

BlackBerry autonames a file when you capture a picture. However, the name of the picture is generic, something like IMG*xxxx-currentdate-time,* where *x* is a number. Not very helpful.

Make it a habit to rename a photo as soon as you capture it. Using a name like *Dean blows birthday candles* is much more helpful than *IMG0029-20081013-0029.*

Renaming a photo file is a snap. Here's how:

1. **Display the picture screen or highlight it in the list.**

   The list is displayed from Camera when you choose View Pictures through the Menu key.

2. **Press the Menu key and select Rename.**

   A Rename screen appears, as shown in Figure 12-4.

3. **Enter the name you want for this picture, and then select Save.**

   Your picture is renamed.

Figure 12-4:
Rename
your picture
here.

Creating a folder

Being the organized person you are, you must be wondering about folders. Don't fret; it's simple to create one. Here's how:

1. **From the Camera screen, press the Menu key, and then select View Pictures.**

   The screen displays the list of pictures in the folder where Camera saves the pictures.

   • If this is still the default pictures folder location, this will be the root of where you can create your subfolder.

   • Otherwise, you can select the Up icon to navigate up to the folder above this folder.

2. **Select the Up icon to navigate to the main folder where you want your new folder to be created.**

   You should be *within* the folder where you want your new folder to be created. If not, repeat this step to navigate to that folder.

3. **Press the Menu key, and then select New Folder.**

4. **Type the name of the folder, and then select OK.**

   Your folder is created.

Moving pictures

Here's how to move pictures to a different folder:

1. **From the Camera screen, press the Menu key, and then select View Pictures.**

The screen displays the list of pictures in the current folder. If the picture you want to move isn't in this folder, click the Up icon to navigate up to other folders.

2. **Highlight the picture you want to move, press the Menu key, and then select Move.**

   In the screen that opens, navigate to the folder where you want to move this picture.

3. **Click the Up icon and use the trackball to navigate to the folder where you want to move this picture.**

4. **Press the Menu key, and then select Move Here.**

   Your picture is moved.

You can easily transfer your pictures to your PC or copy pictures from PC to your Bold as well. See Chapter 13 for more details.

Sharing your pictures

Where's the joy in taking great pictures if you're the only one seeing them? Your BlackBerry has several options for sharing your bundle of joy:

1. **From the Camera screen, press the Menu key and select View Pictures.**

2. **Highlight a picture you want to share.**

3. **Press the Menu key.**

4. **Select from the choices listed here:**

   • *Send as E-mail:* This goes directly to the Message screen for composing e-mail, with the selected picture as an attachment.

   • *Send as MMS:* Similar to Send as Email, this opens a Compose MMS screen with the selected picture as an attachment. MMS first displays Contacts, though, letting you select the person's phone number to receive the MMS before going to the Compose screen. Another difference is that in MMS, it sends a tiny version of the picture.

   • *Send to Messenger Contact:* This option is available if you have BlackBerry Messenger installed. This function is similar to Send as MMS, but displays only those contacts you have in BlackBerry Messenger. It uses BlackBerry Messenger to send a tiny version of the picture file.

   • *Send Using Bluetooth:* Send the picture to any Bluetooth-capable device.

You might also see other ways to send a picture file if you have other IM clients installed. For example, if you have Google Talk installed, you will see Send as Google Talk.

Setting a picture as Caller ID

Wouldn't it be nice when your girlfriend calls if you also could see her beautiful face? Sure, you can. Start with a photo of her saved on your BlackBerry Bold. Then follow these steps:

1. **Select the Media icon from the Home screen and select Pictures.**

2. **Navigate to the location of the photo.**

3. **Highlight the photo you want to appear when the person calls.**

4. **Press the Menu key and select Set as Caller ID.**

   The photo is displayed onscreen, with a superimposed, portrait-size cropping rectangle. Inside the rectangle is a clear view of the photo; outside the rectangle, the photo is blurry. The clear view represents the portion of the photo that you want to show up as Caller ID. You can slide the trackball to move the rectangle to make sure that you crop to capture the face.

5. **Crop the photo by pressing the trackball and selecting Crop and Save.**

   Contacts appears.

6. **Select the contact you want this picture to appear for.**

   A message indicating a picture is set for that contact appears. You're set.

Adding a photo to your contacts can also be done through the Contacts application (refer to Chapter 4).

Setting a Home screen image

Suppose you have a stunning picture that you want to use as the background image for your BlackBerry. Follow these steps to set the image:

1. **Select the Media icon from the Home screen and select Pictures.**

2. **Navigate to the location of the picture you want to use.**

3. **Highlight the picture.**

4. **Press the Menu key and select Set as Wallpaper.**

   You can always reset or go back to the default Home screen image by going back to the Menu screen and selecting Reset Wallpaper.

Say Action: Capturing Video

Your BlackBerry Bold camera application can do more than take still photos. You can also use it to take videos.

Here are the quick and easy steps to use Video Camera mode:

1. **Open the Camera application.**

2. **Press the Menu key, and then select Video Camera (see Figure 12-5).**

   The screen displays like a viewfinder on a typical digital video camera, as shown in Figure 12-6. Use the trackball to start recording.

   The indicators from left to right, as shown in Figure 12-6:

   Available Memory: Video Light: Zoom: Recorded Time:

Figure 12-5: Toggle to Video Camera mode here.

The onscreen controls are all context related. When you first launch the video camera, all you see is the Record button with the big white dot at the bottom of the screen (shown in Figure 12-6). By using the trackball to select the Record button, the video camera starts taking video, and the only available control is a Pause button.

The indicators on your screen, as shown in Figure 12-6:

  ✔ **Available Memory:** The more squares you see, the more free space you have for saving videos to the device memory or the media card.

  ✔ **Video Light:** A circle around the lightning icon like you see in Figure 12-6 indicates that Video light is off, which is the default setting.

   The following section shows how to enable Video light.

  ✔ **Zoom:** Like your still camera, it's capable of giving you 3x digital zoom.

  ✔ **Recorded Time:** Tells you how long in seconds you've been recording.

Figure 12-6:
Your
BlackBerry
becomes a
digital video
camera.

Available Memory   Video Light   Recorded Time

Zoom

You can use the Escape key to stop recording and save the captured video, or press the trackball to pause recording. When you pause the recording, the screen updates to show the rest of the controls, as you see in Figure 12-7. The controls are the familiar buttons you see on a typical video recorder/player.

Figure 12-7:
The video
camera
controls.

From left to right, they are as follows:

✔ **Record:** Continue recording.

✔ **Stop:** End the current recording.

✔ **Play:** Play the current video you just recorded.

✔ **Rename:** Rename the video file.

✔ **Delete:** Get rid of the video file of the current recording.

✔ **Send:** Share your current video recording. You have the option to send it as e-mail, as MMS, or through Bluetooth. If you have IM clients installed, such as Google Talk or Yahoo! Messenger, the IM client will be listed as one of the options for sending the video file.

Customizing the Video Camera

Your BlackBerry has a few settings you can tweak to change the behavior of the video camera. And like every other BlackBerry application, to see what you can customize, don't look anywhere else but the application's Options screen — in this case, the Video Camera Options screen.

Follow these steps to get to the Video Camera Options screen:

1. **Open the Camera application.**

2. **Press the Menu key, and then select Video Camera (refer to Figure 12-5).**

3. **Press the Menu key and select Options.**

   The Video Camera Options screen displays, as shown in Figure 12-8.

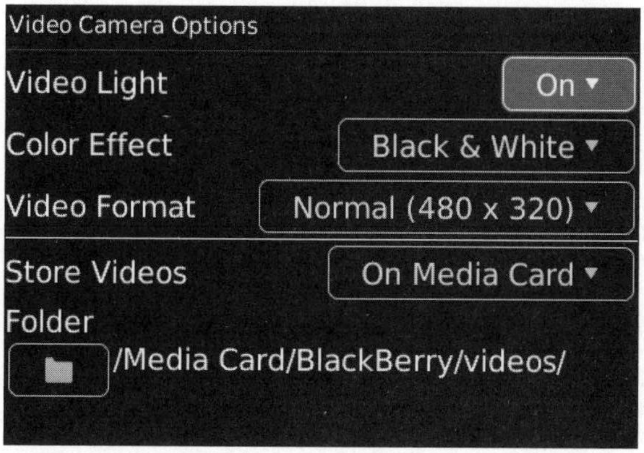

Figure 12-8:
Customize your video camera here.

Video Camera Options

Video Light   On ▾

Color Effect   Black & White ▾

Video Format   Normal (480 x 320) ▾

Store Videos   On Media Card ▾

Folder
■ /Media Card/BlackBerry/videos/

The available options are quite easy to digest, but in case you need a little help, here's what you can tweak:

✔ **Video Light:** In case it's a little dim, you can turn on the video camera's lights.

Dropped something on a dark alley? This video light is a good alternative to a flashlight if you really need one.

This is the flash that you used when taking still pictures. It will keep lit when you set the setting to On and when you open the Video Camera. The default is Off.

This is a drain on your battery.

- **Color Effect:** The default is Normal, which is standard color. If you're in the mood for effects, you can opt for Black & White or Sepia.

- **Video Format:** This is a screen resolution size. The default here is Normal, at 480 x 320. If you're planning to send your video to friends through MMS, you can choose MMS mode, which has the smaller size of 176 x 144 and is optimal for MMS.

- **Folder:** You can use this to change the default location where your BlackBerry saves the video file.

Chapter 13

Satisfy Your Senses with the Media Player

In This Chapter

▶ Listening to, recording, and viewing media

▶ Importing your PC media collection

▶ Downloading media

*I*f one word describes today's phone market trends, it's *convergence.* Your BlackBerry Bold is one of the latest participants in this convergence race. In addition to sending and receiving e-mail and being a phone, a camera, and a PDA, your BlackBerry Bold is also a portable media player.

In this small package, you can

✔ Listen to music.

✔ Record and watch video clips.

✔ Sample ring tones.

✔ Snap and view pictures.

These capabilities are bundled into an application with a name you'd recognize even after sipping a couple of pints of strong ale — Media.

Accessing Media

To run Media, simply select the Media icon from the Home screen. The Media icon is very easy to distinguish, bearing the image of a CD and a musical note.

Media is a collection of media applications:

- ✔ Music
- ✔ Video
- ✔ Ring tones
- ✔ Pictures
- ✔ Voice Notes

Upon opening Media, each app is represented with an icon, as shown in Figure 13-1. You don't need to be Einstein to figure out what each one of these media applications is used for. Ready to have some fun?

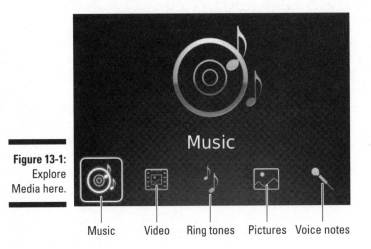

Figure 13-1: Explore Media here.

Music   Video   Ring tones   Pictures   Voice notes

Let the music play

You don't need a quarter to play music on your BlackBerry Bold. Just select Music from the Media screen. Several potential views of your music collection appear, as shown in Figure 13-2. *Music* is the screen heading. The views include the following:

- ✔ **All Songs:** Display all your music files in alphabetical order.
- ✔ **Artists:** List your music files by artist so that you can play your John Mayer songs in one go.
- ✔ **Albums:** View your music collection one album at a time.

✔ **Genres:** If you prefer not to mingle your country with your cutting-edge techno, navigate through this view.

✔ **Playlists:** Organize and play songs as you prefer — the perfect mix tape!

✔ **Sample Songs:** When you're dying to check the player but haven't yet put your collection into the BlackBerry, go here. Your smartphone comes with a couple of songs, and you can find them here.

✔ **Shuffle Songs:** Life is all about variety, and when you're tired of the song order in your playlist, select this.

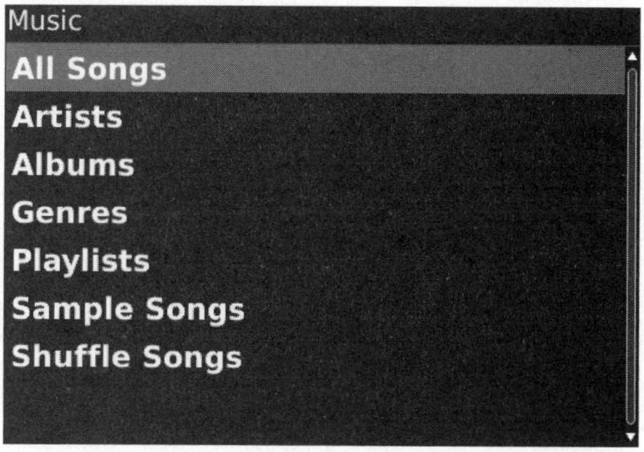

Music

All Songs

Artists

Albums

Genres

Figure 13-2: **Playlists**
Choose how
to view **Sample Songs**
your music
collection. **Shuffle Songs**

After you choose a view, select one of the songs to start playing it. After BlackBerry starts playing a song, it plays the rest of the music listed in the view you selected. The standard interface shown in Figure 13-3 doesn't require explanation.

Figure 13-3:
The music
plays here.

MusicDemo -World Traveller
Aeson

0:02   0:50

The two small icons on the bottom left indicate repeat and shuffle:

- ✔ If you want the songs to be played again after the last song in the list is played, just press the Menu key and select Repeat.
- ✔ Bored of hearing the same sequence of songs played? Hit the Menu key and select Shuffle. Your songs will be played randomly.

You can't fast-forward or rewind, but you can position where Bold is playing by dragging the progress slider. Use the trackball to select the progress slider, and then scroll the trackball to change the slider's position. Press the trackball again, and the music starts playing from that position.

BlackBerry supports many music formats. The following list shows the supported formats, along with the file extensions:

- ✔ **ACC:** Audio compression formats AAC, AAC+, and EAAC+ (`.aac` and `.m4a`)
- ✔ **AMR:** Adaptive Multi-Rate–Narrow Band (AMR-NB) speech coder standard (`.mmr` and `.3gp`)
- ✔ **MIDI:** Polyphonic MIDI (`.mid`, `.midi`, and `.smf`)
- ✔ **MP3:** MPEG Part 1 and Part 2 audio layer 3 (`.mp3` and `.mp4`)
- ✔ **WMA:** Windows Media Audio 9, Pro, and 10 (`.wma` and `.asf`)

The earpiece/mic combo that comes with your Bold is for one ear only. This is an issue when you're on a train. You may prefer using a stereo (two-ear) headset — or a Bluetooth headset is a good option.

Creating a Playlist

Sure you have favorites out of your song library. Having a playlist would be nice, right? On your Bold, you can create two types of playlists:

- ✔ **Standard:** A barebones playlist where you manually add the music you want.
- ✔ **Automatic:** You can specify a combination by Artists, by Album, and/or by Genres.

To create a playlist, follow these steps:

1. **Select Playlists from the Music screen.**

   Music Screen can be found by selecting Music in Media or from the home screen.

2. **Select [New Playlist].**

3. **Select Standard Playlist or Automatic Playlist.**

   The screen that follows allows you to enter the name of your playlist and either

   - Add songs you select (Standard).

   - Specify your playlist criteria (Automatic).

   Skip to Step 5 if you selected Automatic.

4. **If you select Standard Playlist, repeat these steps for each song:**

   a. *Press the Menu key and select Add Songs.*

   The listing of your music library shows up. All you need to do is select the songs you want.

   b. *Scroll to your music list and select the song you want added to your playlist.*

   You'll return to the preceding screen with the selected song added to your playlist.

   After you add all the songs you want in Standard Playlist, press the Menu key and select Save. You're done!

5. **If you select Automatic Playlist, select the + button to the right of the music type criteria and select from available combinations listed.**

   Again, you can choose from either by Artist, by Albums, by Genres, or a combination of any of the three options. If you choose by Artist, you'll be presented with the list of artists; the same is true for by Albums, where a list of albums will be shown for you to select.

   Repeat this step to add more values on your criteria. After you add all the criteria you want in Automatic Playlist, press the Menu key and select Save. You're done!

 From time to time, you may have played a song and happened to like it. Want to add it to your playlist? No problem. While you are playing the song, simply press the Menu key and select Add to Playlist. Then select the playlist you want that song added into from the screen that follows.

Playing from your playlist

Playing your playlist is a no-brainer:

1. **Select Playlists from the Music screen.**

   Music Screen can be found by selecting Music in Media or selecting Music from the Home screen.

2. **Scroll to highlight the playlist you want to start playing.**

3. **Press the Menu key and select Play.**

Now showing

Playing or recording a video is similar to playing music:

1. **Select Video from the Media screen.**

   The screen shows Video Camera, and a list of video files appears at the bottom. If you want to watch a video, skip to Step 5.

2. **To start video recording, select Video Camera.**

   A screen shows the image in front of the camera.

3. **Select the screen again to start recording.**

   Don't wait for "Cut!" You can pause the camera by pressing the Pause button. The familiar video/audio controls appear, from left to right, showing

   - Continue Recording
   - Stop
   - Play

   The functions of the other buttons are also obvious, including the following:

   - Rename (for the filename)
   - Delete
   - Send via E-Mail

4. **Press the Stop button when you're ready to wrap up your home video.**

   You wind up at the previous screen with the video clip file listed. We know you're itching to watch it.

5. **Select the file to play it onscreen.**

Lord of the ring tones

Ah, the proliferation of ring tones. Nothing beats hearing a loud funky ring tone while you're sleeping on a bus or a train. You can wake other passengers, too, whether you want to use the Top 40, old-fashioned digital beats, or something you recorded.

To hear ring tones that come with your BlackBerry, do the following:

1. **Select Ring Tones from the Media screen.**

   You see three views:

- All Ring Tones
- My Ring Tones
- Preloaded Ring Tones

2. **Select Preloaded Ring Tones.**

   The preloaded ring tones are displayed.

3. **Select any one of them and enjoy.**

   While playing a ring tone, select the right arrow to go to the next tone; select the left arrow to go the preceding one.

4. **Choose a ring tone you like.**

5. **Press the Menu key, and select Set as Ring Tone.**

   That ring tone is what plays when your phone rings.

A ring tone is similar to a music file and includes many of the same music formats:

- ✔ **ACC:** Advanced Auto Coding format used by iTunes.
- ✔ **M4A:** A subset of ACC for audio only.
- ✔ **MIDI:** Musical Instrument Digital Interface, a popular audio format for musical instruments.
- ✔ **AMR:** Adaptive Multi-Rate, a popular audio format for mobile transmission and mobile applications.
- ✔ **MP3:** MPEG Audio Layer 3, the most popular music format.
- ✔ **WMA:** Windows Media Audio, a Microsoft audio file format.

If you're familiar with any audio-editing software, you can make your own ring tones. Save the file in one of the formats in the preceding list and copy it to your Bold. (See the "Working with Media Files" section, later in this chapter.) You can also find many free ring tones on the Internet. The only possible harm from downloading one is being annoyed with how it sounds. The default home page on Browser (http://mobile.blackberry.com) has links to sources of ring tones as well. See Fun and Pages on the home page.

Picture this

If you upgraded from an older BlackBerry, you may already know about Pictures, which you use to view, zoom into, and rotate pictures:

1. **Select Pictures from the Media screen.**

   Your options are similar to those for other Media applications.

2. **Navigate to the view you want.**

3. **Find the picture you're looking for.**

4. **Select the file.**

   Pretty easy, right? At this point, your photo file will be displayed in the screen.

Check out Sample Pictures. Your BlackBerry comes with a collection of pictures that you can use as your Home screen background. Or, assign one of the cartoons to a contact as a Caller ID until you get a chance to take the person's picture and use that instead. (We describe how to do that in Chapter 12.)

Viewing in Pictures

When you are in Pictures and navigating on a folder, the default view is always showing thumbnails. This allows you to quickly view many pictures at the same time before deciding which one to open.

Want to view all of them? Run a slide show. Press the Menu key and select View Slide Show.

A convenient way to view pictures in OS 5.0 is to scroll the trackball sideways. Scrolling right transitions the view to the next picture and you'll see a smooth sideways movement of the picture in the screen. Of course, scrolling left is transitioning in the opposite direction until it displays the preceding picture.

Zoom to details

To zoom in a photo, open it, press the trackball, and then select Zoom. A tiny unobtrusive slider bar appears on the left side of the image. Now, use your trackball: Scrolling up zooms in, and scrolling down zooms out.

While scrolling, the slider bar indicates the degree of zoom. The exact center of this bar is the original image (no zooming applied). You can easily go back to the original zoom size by pressing the Menu key and selecting Zoom All.

An image normally defaults to fit the screen, but you can toggle it by pressing the Menu key and selecting one of these options:

   ✔ Fit to Screen

   ✔ View Actual Size

Pressing the trackball while a picture is displayed is equivalent to zooming in 5.0. Once zoomed in, you can zoom out by pressing the Escape key (the arrow key to the right of the trackball).

Recording your voice

A feature-packed smartphone like your Bold *should* come with a voice recorder, and it does. Within Media, you can find Voice Notes, a neat recording application. Now you can record your billion-dollar ideas:

1. **Select Voice Notes (that little microphone icon) from the Media screen. (Refer to Figure 13-1.)**

   The Voice Notes application launches, sporting the simple and clean screen shown in Figure 13-4. At the top of the screen is a Record button, and the bottom part lists your previous recordings.

2. **Select Record.**

3. **Press the trackball.**

   Your BlackBerry's microphone is designed to be close to your mouth, like any mobile phone should be.

   You can pause anytime you want by pressing the Pause button. A familiar video/audio control appears, from left to right:

   • Continue Recording

   • Stop

   • Play

   Other buttons include Rename (for renaming the file), Delete, and Send via E-Mail.

4. **Press the trackball, and then press the Stop button to wrap it up.**

   You return to the preceding screen. Your recent voice recording appears in the list.

5. **Select your voice recording to play it.**

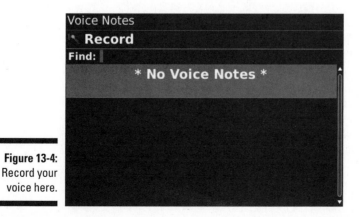

Figure 13-4:
Record your
voice here.

Rotating a photo

Want to view yourself upside down? Maybe not. But sometimes your pictures look better when viewed horizontally.

If your Bold runs OS 4.6, you can rotate an image on the screen while you view it in Pictures: Just press the trackball and select Rotate.

The image rotates 90 degrees clockwise.

By repeating the same steps, you can keep rotating it; each press is an additional 90-degree clockwise rotation.

The Rotate feature isn't available in OS 5.0.

Viewing and Controlling Media Files

The previous sections show what types of files you can record or play on your BlackBerry. The following sections give you the lowdown on controlling those files when you're playing or viewing them.

Turning it up (or down)

Whether you're listening to music or watching a video, adjusting the volume is easy.

Your Bold comes with dedicated volume buttons on the upper-right side of the device. The top button (with the plus sign) turns up the volume, and the second button below (with the minus sign) turns down the volume. The onscreen volume slider reflects anything you did with the volume buttons.

Navigating the menu

You can easily jump to the next item in the list. Press the Menu key while you are viewing an image, listening to songs, or watching a video clip. On the menu that appears, you see the following items:

- **Next:** Jumps to the next item in the list. This item appears only if there's an item after this media file in the current folder.

- **Previous:** Jumps to the preceding item. This item appears only if there's a previous item in the current folder.

- **Delete:** Deletes the media file.

- ✓ **Move:** Moves the file to a different folder.
- ✓ **Rename:** Renames the media file.
- ✓ **Properties:** Displays a screen that shows the location of the media file, its size, and the time it was last modified.

Using Explore

There are many ways you can navigate to your media file, but Explore is probably the quickest way for you find a file. Not only that it's easy to use because it has some similarities to Windows Explorer, it also has a search facility similar to Find in other BlackBerry applications like Contacts, MemoPad, or Tasks.

To launch Explore, simply select Media from the home screen, press the Menu key, and select Explore.

The Explore screen starts with the device root folders: Media Card, Device Memory, and System.

Folders are in a tree hierarchy; you can get into the child folders, or subfolders, by selecting from the parent folder, starting from one of the root folders.

If you've set a property of a picture to hidden, using Explore is the only place in your Bold through which you'll be able to locate the file again:

1. **Navigate to the folder where your picture file is located.**
2. **Press the Menu key and select Show Hidden.**

The default location for pictures taken by Camera is either

```
/Device Memory/home/user/pictures
```

```
/Media Card/BlackBerry/pictures
```

Changing the media flavor

Like the rest of your BlackBerry applications, you can customize Media.

1. **Press the Menu key while in Media.**
2. **Select Options.**

    The screen looks like the one shown in Figure 13-5. You can specifically customize the Pictures application and Media in general. Each is described in the following sections.

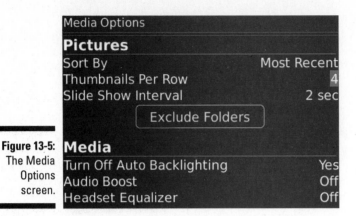

Figure 13-5:
The Media
Options
screen.

Customizing pictures

You can change the Pictures application in the following ways:

- ✔ **Sort By:** Toggle file sorting based on recent updates or name.

- ✔ **Thumbnails per Row:** When your files appear as a grid of *thumbnails* (small versions of your photos), this number of thumbnails is displayed per row. The higher the number, the smaller the thumbnails.

- ✔ **Slide Show Interval:** When viewing your files in a slide show, a picture appears for this many seconds before moving to the next picture.

- ✔ **Exclude Folders:** Use this option when you don't want to display any pictures inside a particular folder. This makes it faster to load the list of pictures. (The fewer the pictures you have, the faster the Pictures application can load the list.) This option isn't for your secret folders.

- ✔ **Set Convenience Keys:** A button available only in OS 5.0 which allows you to change the settings for the right and left side convenience keys. A convenience key is a shortcut key to an application. The default setting for the right-side key launches the Camera, and Voice Dialing for the left-side key.

Customizing media

You can finesse the rest of Media as follows:

- ✔ **Auto Stop Media Player When Idle:** The default is Off, but you can set it at 5, 10, 20, 30, or 45 minutes. This can save you battery life if you get distracted and leave your Bold on a table playing video.

✔ **Turn Off Auto Backlighting:** The *backlighting* feature provides additional screen lighting when Bold detects that you need it. You will notice it when you move your Bold from shade to direct sunlight. We find it bothersome when watching a movie. For that reason — and to extend battery life — toggle it off here.

✔ **Audio Boost:** Allows you to increase the volume beyond the normal level. The default setting is Off. If you set it On, it gives you a fair warning about possible ear discomfort when you're using headphones.

✔ **Headset Equalizer:** The default is Off, but if you want to have a different audio setting, you have several options, including Bass Boost, Bass Lower, Dance, Hip Hop, Jazz, Lounge, Loud, R&B, Rock, Treble Boost, Treble Lower, and Vocal Boost.

Media shortcuts

It's all about saving your valuable time. Taking the time to master these shortcuts now will pay you back in time later. Here are the must-know Media shortcuts:

✔ **Mute:** Toggle between pausing and playing music and video. (The key is located at the upper right of the device and has a muted-speaker label.)

✔ **6:** Move to the next item.

✔ **4:** Move to the preceding item.

✔ **3:** Zoom in on a picture.

✔ **9:** Zoom out on a picture.

✔ **5:** Zoom back to the original picture size.

✔ **, (comma):** Rotate a picture counterclockwise.

✔ **Space:** Toggle between pausing and resuming a slide show.

Chapter 14

Managing Media Files

• •

• •

*T*he ways that you can get your hands on media constantly evolve. Ten years ago, who would have thought that you could buy music from a tiny card, or download music from an "all you can eat" monthly subscription?

Someday, you'll wake up with a technology that doesn't require you to constantly copy media files to your handheld music player. But for now, enjoying music while on the move means managing these files.

Media, the BlackBerry application on your Bold, is a great music player, but without music files, it's as useless as a guitar without strings. And to satisfy your quest on mobile media satisfaction, this chapter gives you good information on ways to manage your media files.

This chapter is for PC users. If your computer is a Mac, Chapter 16 covers the PocketMac media application.

Working with Media Files

To acquire media files for your BlackBerry Bold, there are as many choices as there are ice-cream flavors. The succeeding sections describe the most common ways.

Using your Bold as a flash drive

The most common way of manipulating media files into and out of your Bold is to attach it to a PC and use Windows Explorer:

1. **Connect your BlackBerry to your PC, using the USB cable that came with your Bold.**

It's only the microSD that is going to be exposed to your PC as a flash drive. Make sure to have the microSD card in your BlackBerry Bold before you do this.

When connected, the Bold screen displays a prompt for enabling mass storage mode.

2. On the Bold screen, select Yes.

A screen appears on your Bold, asking for your password.

3. On the Bold screen, type your BlackBerry password.

The device is now ready to behave like an ordinary flash drive. And on your PC, the Removable Disk dialog box opens.

4. On your PC (the Removable Disk dialog box), click Open Folder to View Files, and then click OK.

This opens the familiar Windows Explorer screen. You can do anything you typically do with a normal Windows folder — you know, drag and drop, copy, and delete files.

5. Close Windows Explorer when you're done.

Meet and greet BlackBerry Desktop Media Manager

Roxio is known for its CD-ripping software. (*Ripping* converts music files in CD format to other popular compressed formats.) RIM licensed a portion of Roxio and packaged it with BlackBerry Desktop Software. Even though this version doesn't offer the whole Roxio software suite, you can still take advantage of fantastic features, such as

- ✔ Ripping CDs
- ✔ Converting files to get the best playback on your Bold
- ✔ Managing music files
- ✔ Syncing media files to your device

If you have an old version of Media Manager, just point your desktop Internet browser to http://na.blackberry.com/eng/services/desktop for directions on downloading the latest version for free and installing it on your PC.

In the following sections, we show you the Media Manager interface and how to copy a video file onto your Bold.

Accessing Media Manager

You can access Media Manager through BlackBerry Desktop Manager, which Chapter 15 describes in detail. Get to Desktop Manager this way:

1. On your PC, click the Windows Start button.

2. Choose All Programs⇨BlackBerry⇨Desktop Manager.

BlackBerry Desktop Manager appears, as shown in Figure 14-1.

3. Click the Media icon.

A screen displays showing Media Manager and BlackBerry Media Sync sections. Each section has a Start button.

4. Click the Start button in the Media Manager section.

The initial Media Manager screen is well organized and gives you the following options:

- Manage Pictures
- Manage Music
- Manage Videos
- View Connected Devices

5. Click one of the options.

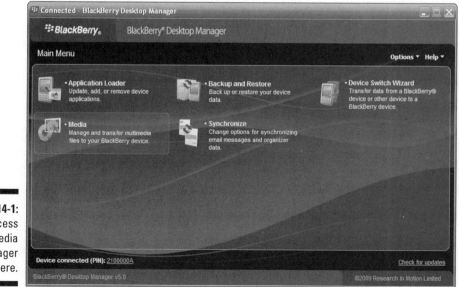

Figure 14-1: Access Media Manager here.

The Media Manager screen (shown in Figure 14-2) is really easy to use. Plus, it has the same interface as Windows Explorer:

✔ The left side is where you navigate to your folders and files.

✔ The right side displays the files in the folder you selected (from the left side).

Figure 14-2:
View your media files on this screen.

The top section looks the same as the bottom section. The top half — My Media — represents your desktop; the bottom — My Devices — represents your Bold. You can move or copy files easily. When you're copying, for example, one section can be the source, and the other section, the destination. By simply dragging the files between the two sections, you can copy on the same screen. Neat, right?

Importing media files to Media Manager

Here's a quick and easy way to import media files:

1. **Navigate Windows Explorer to find the media files you want.**

2. **Drag and drop the files into Media Manager.**

   You can drag and drop files to the folder in the left part of the screen (where the folder tree appears) or to the right part (where the files are listed). Just make sure that when you're doing the latter, the current folder in the tree view is the folder where you want the media files to be imported.

You can also use Media Manager to locate the files you want without going through Windows Explorer. The trick is to change the view to Folders. Check out the two tabs at the upper left. The first tab, My Media, is the default view. The Folders tab, just to the right of My Media, bears an icon of (go figure) a folder.

Click the Folders tab. You see a tree view, but this time, it looks exactly as you see it in Windows Explorer, as shown in Figure 14-3. The files can be on your local hard drive or in a network folder accessible by your desktop computer.

Not all media file types are directly compatible with your Bold. This is especially true for video files. But the Media Manager can convert most media files to a usable Bold format.

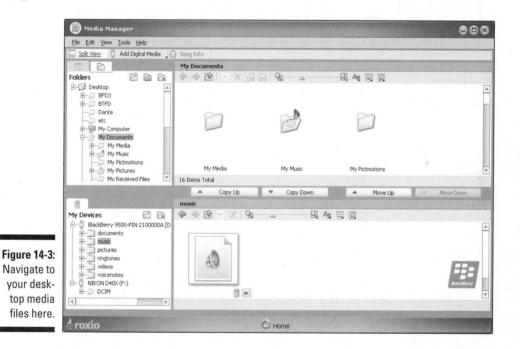

Figure 14-3: Navigate to your desktop media files here.

Adding a media file to your Bold

Time to copy files to your Bold. Here's the rundown:

1. **Connect your Bold to your PC, using the USB cable that came with your BlackBerry.**

2. **On the Media Manager screen, drag and drop your media files from the My Media view to any folder in My Devices.**

   You can drag and drop an entire album. After dropping a media file, you're prompted to convert the file into a format that's usable by your Bold, as shown in Figure 14-4.

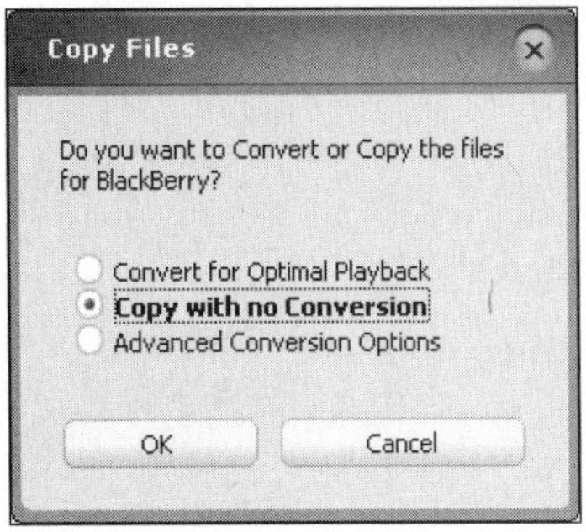

Figure 14-4:
Choose to convert your media files for optimum playback.

> **Copy Files** ✕
>
> Do you want to Convert or Copy the files for BlackBerry?
>
> ○ Convert for Optimal Playback
> ● Copy with no Conversion
> ○ Advanced Conversion Options
>
> OK   Cancel

3. **Select a conversion option:**

   • *Convert for Optimal Playback:* This is the safest bet and is the default. This is applicable to video files where the converter makes sure that the video fits perfectly with Bold's screen resolution.

   • *Copy with No Conversion:* Copies the file faster. The file is copied to your Bold as is, but it might not play on your Bold.

   • *Advanced Conversion Options:* From here, another screen lets you downgrade the quality to minimize the file size. It also allows you to crop video so that the entire screen is filled, instead of seeing dark margins.

4. **Click OK to begin the transfer.**

Other features of Media Manager

Spend some time exploring Media Manager. It has interesting features you may find useful. Here's a quick rundown of what you can do with Media Manager:

✔ Import media files.

✔ E-mail media files.

✔ Enhance photos and apply special effects to photos by using PhotoSuite.

✔ Set song info (such as title, artist, album, genre, year, or an image) to show as track art when playing a song.

✔ Record audio.

✔ Customize photo printing.

Synchronizing with iTunes using BlackBerry Media Sync

If you have an iPod, you're probably using iTunes and maintaining a play-list and perhaps a subscription to podcasts or videocasts. Podcast files are downloaded to iTunes using RSS. (RSS — really simple syndication — is a kind of digital file publish-subscribe mechanism. This is the mechanism iTunes uses to receive audio and video recordings, which most people refer to as podcasts and videocasts.)

To sync your Bold with iTunes, follow these quick and easy steps:

1. **Click the Windows Start button.**

2. **Choose All Programs⇨BlackBerry⇨Desktop Manager.**

3. **When BlackBerry Desktop Manager appears (refer to Figure 14-1), click the Media icon.**

   A screen displays showing Media Manager and BlackBerry Media Sync sections. Each section has a Start button.

4. **Click the Start button in the BlackBerry Media Sync section.**

   In the dialog box that appears (such as the one shown in Figure 14-5), click the double-chevron icon in the lower left of the window to bring up options for what part of iTunes you want to synchronize.

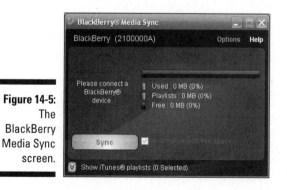

Figure 14-5: The BlackBerry Media Sync screen.

5. **Click the Show iTunes Playlist icon (lower left).**

   A selection of what you have in iTunes appears, as shown in Figure 14-6. This is the part of the screen where you choose iTunes media file types.

6. **Select the iTunes media you want copied to your Bold.**

7. **Click the Sync button.**

   There you go. You see a progress bar showing the synchronization of the media files from iTunes.

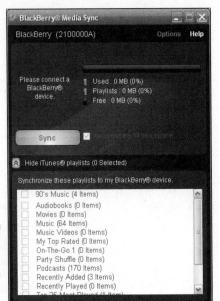

Figure 14-6:
Choose
your iTunes
media here.

Downloading sounds

RIM offer a Web site from which you can sample and download new ring tones, alarms, notifiers, and tunes. On your Bold, simply go to

```
http://mobile.blackberry.com
```

On this page, scroll down to the Personalize section and click on the Ringtones link. A list of available ring tones will be displayed. And did we mention that they're free?

Clicking on the ring tone link gives you an option to either play it or download to your Bold. Downloaded ring tones are filed in the My Ring Tones section when you open the Ring Tones inside the Media application.

RIM isn't the only site where you can find ring tones. The Web is a treasure trove, and ring tones and other media files are safe to download, so go hunting.

And the best place to find BlackBerry-related software — including ring tones — is to visit the ever growing BlackBerry community on the Web. Check out `http://crackberry.com`, `http://blackberrycool.com`, and `http://blackberryreview.com`, to name a few.

Part V

Working with Desktop Manager and PocketMac

The 5th Wave   By Rich Tennant

"Russell! Do you remember last month when I told you to order 150 SMART phones for the sales department?"

In this part . . .

Here you discover essential information about some behind-the-scenes-yet-integral processes. Read all about BlackBerry Desktop Manager, which you direct to monitor and control database. If you are a Mac user, you'll find details on PocketMac and how you could use it for database synchronization. You'll also find out how to leverage Switch Device Wizard to migrate your existing data to your new BlackBerry Bold. Find out how to back up your data. And discover the many ways of installing third-party applications.

Chapter 15

Syncing the Synchronize Way

What better way to keep your BlackBerry Bold updated than to synchronize it with your desktop application's data?

Arguably, most of the data you need to synchronize is from your personal information manager (PIM) applications: notes, appointments, addresses, and tasks. The crucial piece for data synchronization to and from your device and desktop computer is Synchronize. This software within BlackBerry Desktop Manager (BDM) allows you to synchronize your PIM data as well as upload and download media files between your PC and your Bold.

In this chapter, you explore Synchronize and see how to manually and automatically synchronize your Bold with your desktop computer. You find tips about which options you may want to use. Before delving into all that, however, is a section on BDM.

If you're a Mac user, skip this chapter. Chapter 16 covers PocketMac, which provides similar data synchronization functionality.

 If you're using a corporate BlackBerry Bold that's running under BlackBerry Enterprise Server (BES), you can skip this chapter. BlackBerry smartphones running under BES synchronize over the air (OTA) or wirelessly.

Meeting Your BlackBerry Desktop Manager

The centerpiece of your desktop activities on the BlackBerry is *BlackBerry Desktop Manager* (BDM), which is a suite of programs that includes the following:

✔ **Application Loader:** Installs BlackBerry applications and updates the BlackBerry OS.

✔ **Backup and Restore:** Backs up your Bold data and settings. Check out Chapter 18 for details.

✔ **Synchronize:** Synchronizes Bold data with your PC (um, the topic of this chapter).

✔ **Media Manager:** Uploads media files to your Bold from your PC and vice versa (another topic in this chapter).

✔ **Device Switch Wizard:** Helps you transfer data from your existing mobile device to your Bold. See Chapter 17 for details.

BDM is software loaded on the CD that comes with your Bold. Your Bold's packaging provides instructions on how to install BDM on your desktop computer. For corporate users, check with your BlackBerry system administrator for more details.

Installing BDM and Desktop Redirector

As we mention, use the CD that comes with your Bold to install BDM on your computer. At the same time, you can also install Desktop Redirector. (Read more about this in Chapter 8.) Desktop Redirector allows you to redirect e-mail that you receive in Outlook. This means that even if you get your e-mails through Outlook like your work e-mails, you can have those e-mails redirected to your Bold.

Only e-mails from mailboxes connected to your Outlook mailbox are redirected. Your PC and the redirector must run all the time to keep redirection active.

When you insert the CD, the installation wizard automatically runs. Follow the wizard. On one of the wizard screens, you choose whether this installation is for personal or for work e-mail. Choosing for work enables you to use Desktop Redirector for both personal and work.

If you aren't using a corporate BES and you want to redirect your Outlook e-mail to your Bold, when you're installing BDM, make sure that you select the Redirect Messages Using the BlackBerry Desktop Redirector radio button on the installation screen, as shown in Figure 15-1.

If your Bold is running under a corporate BES, your e-mail is already redirected to your smartphone wirelessly, and choosing the BlackBerry Desktop Redirector could really mess things up. So don't do it! Most companies are protective of corporate data, including your work e-mails. Make sure you aren't violating your company's policy before you decide to redirect your work e-mails to your personal BlackBerry.

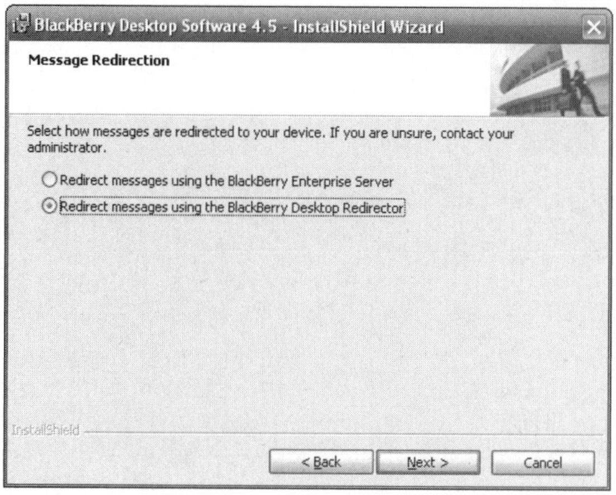

Figure 15-1: Configure the BDM installation to include Desktop Redirector.

(screenshot: BlackBerry Desktop Software 4.5 - InstallShield Wizard — Message Redirection)

Select how messages are redirected to your device. If you are unsure, contact your administrator.

○ Redirect messages using the BlackBerry Enterprise Server
◉ Redirect messages using the BlackBerry Desktop Redirector

InstallShield

< Back   Next >   Cancel

Launching BDM

In most Windows installations, you find the shortcut to launch BDM through your computer's Start menu. Follow these steps to launch BDM:

1. **Choose Start⇨All Programs⇨BlackBerry⇨Desktop Manager.**

2. **Connect your Bold to your computer using the USB cable that came with your device.**

   With the microSD card in your Bold, upon connecting to your PC, your Bold screen displays a prompt for enabling mass storage mode. It also asks for your Bold's password when you answer Yes to the prompt. Upon answering Yes and entering your password, your Bold will behave like a flash drive. A drive letter will be added to My Computer (or just plain Computer in Microsoft Vista) in Windows Explorer, allowing you to treat the microSD card as a normal flash drive.

3. **Launch BDM.**

   The BDM opening screen appears; see Figure 15-2.

BDM installation can vary from phone provider to provider. You should see at least the following four icons, or applications.

✔ Application Loader (see Chapter 19)

✔ Backup and Restore (see Chapter 18)

✔ Media (see Chapter 13)

✔ Synchronize

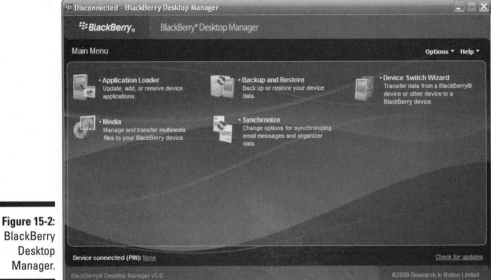

Figure 15-2:
BlackBerry
Desktop
Manager.

Connecting BDM to your Bold

You establish a connection between your Bold and BDM through the USB cable. Plug in your device to your desktop. After BDM is running, it tries to find a BlackBerry (your Bold) on the type of connection specified. The default connection is USB, so you shouldn't need to configure anything.

Follow these steps to connect your Bold to BDM:

1. **Plug in your device to your desktop.**

   Keep your device on.

2. **Launch BDM.**

   BDM tries to find a BlackBerry (your Bold) on a USB connection.

3. **If your device has a password, BDM prompts you for the password.**

4. Enter the password.

You see `Connected` as the screen heading. If for some reason, you
see `Disconnected` and no password prompt, one of the following is
happening:

- BDM can't find the device being connected via the USB cable. Make
  sure that the USB cable is properly attached at both ends.

- The connection setting isn't set to use USB. To check this connectivity setting, go to Step 5.

**5. Choose Options⇨Connection Options at the right side of the BDM
screen.**

The screen shown in Figure 15-3 appears. Make sure that the connection
setting uses USB.

**6. In the Connection Type drop-down list, select the USB connection with
your Bold's PIN.**

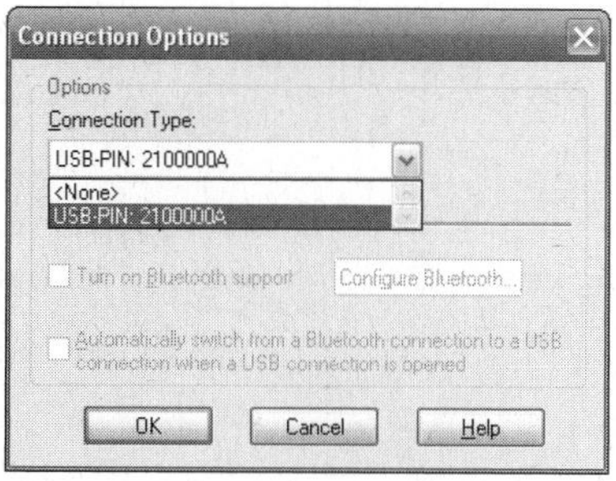

Figure 15-3:
Possible
connec-
tion types
to your
BlackBerry
Bold.

Running BDM for the first time

If you're running BDM for the first time, the program does these things:

✔ Tries to make the initial configuration on your machine, which includes
security encryption setup. It asks you to randomly move your mouse to
generate security encryption keys.

✔ Checks what applications are on your device and what required applications need to be installed. If it can't find a required application on your
device, it prompts you to install it. Of course, you have the option to
cancel and install later.

✔ Looks at the settings you have for your Synchronize software. If autosynchronization is turned on, BDM attempts to run synchronization for your
PIM. This is discussed in the section "Automatic synchronization," later
in this chapter.

Setting Up Synchronize

Synchronize is the part of BDM that allows you to synchronize your data between your desktop computer and your Bold. (If your Bold is running on BES, your data is already synced wirelessly, so you don't need your desktop for synchronization.) Synchronize is an icon on the BDM screen with two opposing arrows on top of two paper images. To launch Synchronize, simply double-click its icon. A screen like the one shown in Figure 15-4 appears.

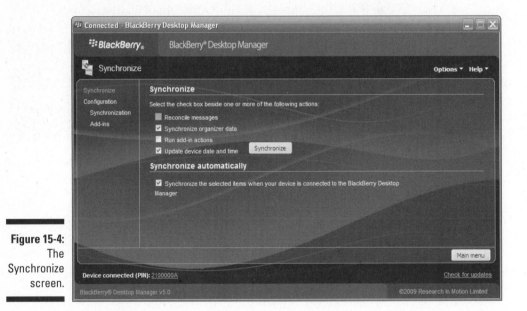

Figure 15-4:
The
Synchronize
screen.

The Synchronize screen is divided into two sections. You can navigate through the links on the left:

- ✔ **Synchronize,** the default view, allows you to manually trigger synchronization. See Figure 15-4. See the "Using on-demand synchronization" and "Automatic synchronization" sections, later in this chapter, for more details and for when you use this screen.

- ✔ **Configuration** is where you can set up configuration and rules for reconciling data. Under the Configuration link are two subsections, Synchronization and Add-ins. These further help you organize the interface. See Figure 15-5. The first thing you need to work with is the Synchronization Configuration screen. The following section helps you do that.

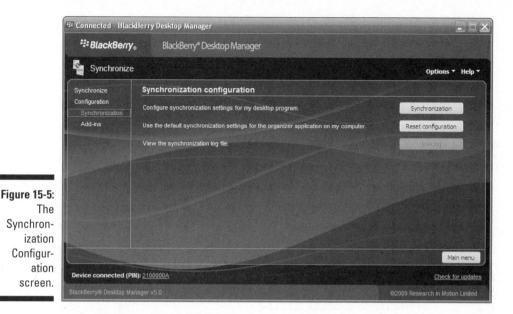

Figure 15-5:
The
Synchron-
ization
Configur-
ation
screen.

Configuring PIM synchronization

The important item in the Synchronization Configuration subsection, as shown in Figure 15-5, is the Synchronization button. You use that button to configure PIM synchronization.

Clicking the Synchronization button displays the screen shown in Figure 15-6. You can see that names correspond to the BlackBerry Bold applications except for Contacts, which goes by Address Book. This is the entry point of the entire synchronization configuration for PIM applications. Selecting the application on this screen allows you to pair the PIM handheld application to a desktop application (most likely Outlook).

From the PIM configuration screen, select which application data you want to sync with your Bold. The following popular PIM applications can be synced to your Bold: ACT!, ASCII Text File Converter, Lotus Notes, Lotus Organizer, Microsoft Outlook, Microsoft Outlook Express, and Microsoft Schedule.

The types of application data that can be synchronized to your Bold are

- **Calendar:** Synchronize your appointments and events stored in your favorite PIM application.

- **MemoPad:** Synchronize any notes or text that you have been storing in your PIM application.

✔ **Address Book:** Synchronize any contact information with your Bold.

✔ **Tasks:** Synchronize your to-do list.

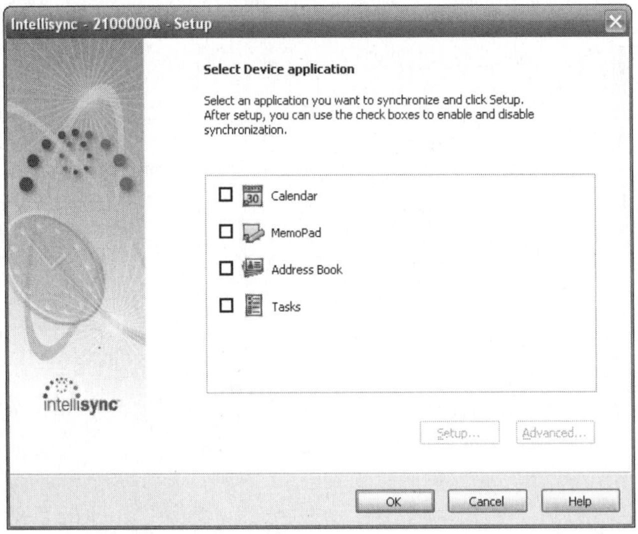

Figure 15-6:
The PIM
configura-
tion screen.

Follow these steps to set up your device's synchronization:

1. **Connect your Bold to BDM.**

2. **Click the Synchronize icon.**

3. **Click the Synchronization link. (It's under the Configuration link on the left side of the screen. Refer to Figure 15-5.)**

   In the Synchronization Configuration section is the Configure Synchronization Settings for My Desktop Program label. Click the Synchronization button beside this label, and the PIM configuration screen is displayed.

4. **Select the check box next to an application data type (such as Calendar, MemoPad, Address Book, or Tasks) that you want to synchronize.**

   For example, we select the Calendar application data type

5. **Click the Setup button.**

   This opens Calendar Setup screen.

6. **Select a PIM application to retrieve application data from by highlighting your desired application.**

BDM pulls your selected application data from the application selected from this screen. (In Figure 15-7, we select Microsoft Outlook.) This means that when you synchronize your Bold, BDM retrieves Calendar data from Microsoft Outlook.

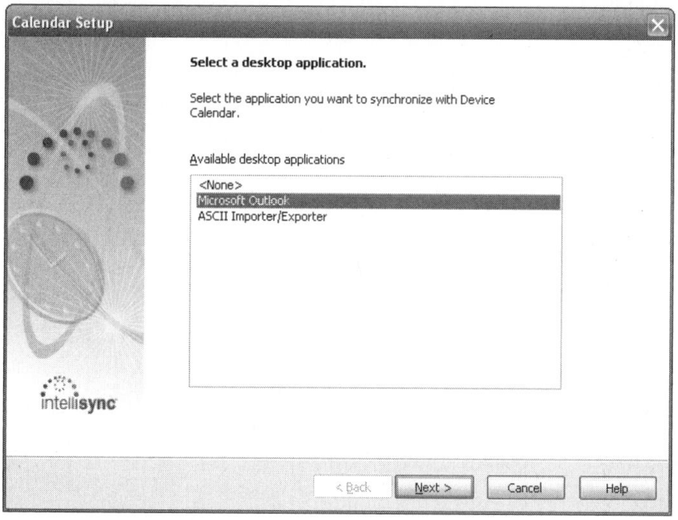

Figure 15-7:
Choose the desktop application here.

7. **Click Next.**

8. **On the Synchronization Options screen that opens, select which direction the synchronization will follow (see Figure 15-8).**

   Here are the three available synchronization options:

   - *Two Way Sync* allows you to synchronize changes in both your Bold and in your desktop application.

   - *One Way Sync from Device* synchronizes only the changes made to your Bold. Changes to your desktop application aren't reflected in your Bold.

   - *One Way Sync to Device* synchronizes changes made in your desktop application with your Bold. Any changes made in your Bold aren't reflected in your desktop application.

9. **Click Next.**

   The Options screen opens for the PIM application you selected in Step 6. Figure 15-9 shows the Microsoft Outlook Options screen.

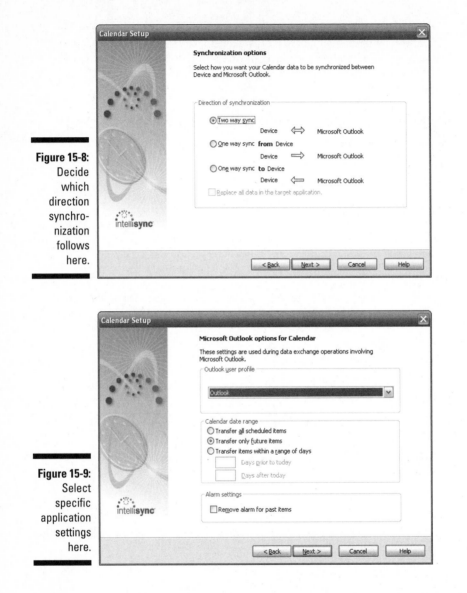

Figure 15-8: Decide which direction synchronization follows here.

Figure 15-9: Select specific application settings here.

For synchronization to Microsoft Outlook, make sure that you select the correct user profile in the Outlook User Profile drop-down list. This is particularly pertinent in cases in which you have multiple user profiles in your computer. Choosing the wrong one may result in putting the wrong data into your Bold.

The amount of data that is reconciled or synchronized in a given application can also be controlled. For example, as shown in Figure 15-9, the center portion of the configuration allows you to specify whether to transfer all Calendar items, transfer just a set of appointments in the future, or transfer items within a range of dates you enter.

Select the Remove Alarm for Past Items check box if you don't want to keep the alarm setting for events that have already occurred.

10. Click Next and then click Finish.

Clicking the Next button brings you to the Calendar Setup Finish screen. Clicking the Finish button completes configuring the Calendar synchronization you selected.

Mapping fields for synchronization

For all four PIM applications, Synchronize is intelligent enough to know what information — such as names, phone numbers, and addresses in Contacts — corresponds to Outlook. This specific bit of information, or attribute, is a *field.* For instance, the value of a home phone number field in Contacts needs to be mapped to the corresponding field in Outlook so that information is transferred correctly.

But not all fields on the desktop side exist on the handheld (and vice versa). For example, a Nick Name field doesn't exist in the Bold Contacts but is available in Exchange (Outlook) Address Book. In some instances, Synchronize provides an alternate field and lets you decide whether to map it.

If you ever need to change the default mapping, you can. The interface is the same for all PIM applications. To illustrate how to map and unmap fields, we use Contacts. The following steps lead you to the screen where you can map the fields for Contacts:

1. From BDM, click the Synchronize link.

The Synchronize screen appears.

2. Click the Synchronization link.

3. Click the Synchronize button.

The PIM configuration screen appears; refer to Figure 15-6.

4. Select the Address Book check box.

The Advanced button is enabled.

5. Click the Advanced button.

The Advanced screen opens, as shown in Figure 15-10.

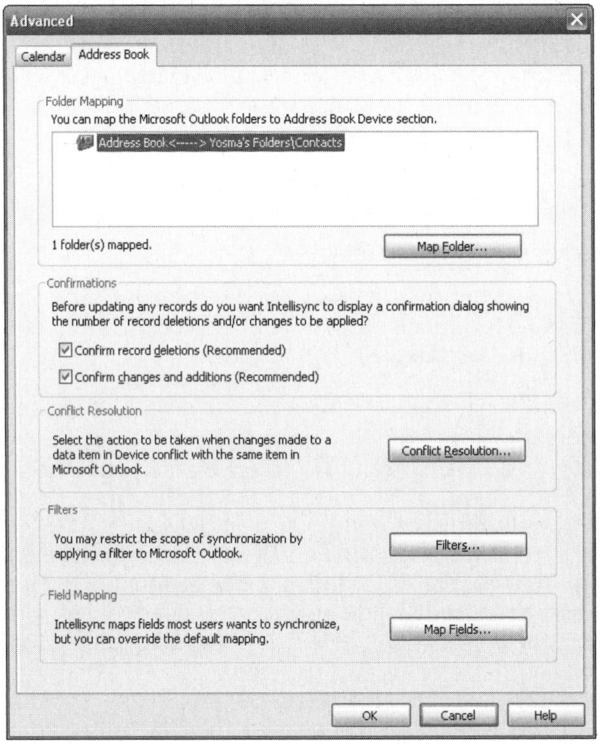

Figure 15-10:
The
Advanced
screen for
Address
Book.

6. Click the Map Fields button.

The Map Fields screen for the Address Book/Contacts application appears; see Figure 15-11. To map or unmap, click the arrow icons.

Figure 15-11:
The Map
Fields
screen for
Address
Book.

If you aren't careful, you can inadvertently unclick a mapping (such as Job Title), and suddenly, your titles aren't in sync. Double-check your mapping before you click OK. If you think you made a mistake, click Cancel to save yourself from having to restore settings.

7. Click OK to save your changes.

Confirming record changes

Face facts: Doing a desktop synchronization isn't a very interesting task, and few people perform it on a regular basis.

You can tell Synchronize to prompt you for any changes it's trying to make (or perhaps undo) on either side of the fence. The Advanced screen comes into picture here. To get to this view, follow these steps:

1. From BDM, click the Synchronize link.

The Synchronize screen appears.

2. Click the Synchronization link.

3. Click the Synchronize button.

The PIM configuration screen appears; refer to Figure 15-6.

4. Select the Address Book check box.

If you want a PIM application other than Address Book, select that application from the list.

5. Click the Advanced button.

The Advanced screen for Address Book screen appears; refer to Figure 15-10. This screen has a Confirmations section and gives you two options:

- Confirm Record Deletions (Recommended)
- Confirm Changes and Additions (Recommended)

Regardless of whether you select the first option, Synchronize displays a prompt if it detects that it's about to delete *all* records.

Resolving update conflicts

Synchronize needs to know how you want to handle any conflicts between your Bold and your desktop application. A conflict normally happens when the same record is updated on your Bold and also in Outlook. For instance, you change Jane Doe's mobile number on both your Bold and PC in Outlook. Where you resolve these conflicts is the same for all PIM applications. Again, for illustration, we use Address Book as an example.

1. **From BDM, click the Synchronize link.**

   The Synchronize screen appears.

2. **Click the Synchronization link.**

3. **Click the Synchronize button.**

   The PIM configuration screen appears; refer to Figure 15-6.

4. **Select the Address Book check box.**

   If you want a PIM application other than Address Book, select that application from the list.

5. **Click the Advanced button.**

   The Advanced screen for Address Book appears; refer to Figure 15-10. This screen has five sections, and the third section is Conflict Resolution.

6. **Click the Conflict Resolution button.**

   The Conflict Resolution screen is shown in Figure 15-12.

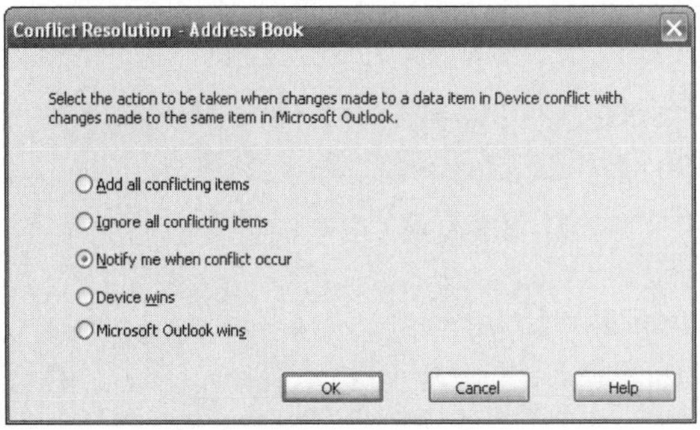

Figure 15-12: Manage conflicts here.

From the Conflict Resolution screen (Figure 15-12) that appears, you can tell Synchronize to handle conflicts in a few ways. Here are the options:

- *Add All Conflicting Items:* When a conflict happens, add a new record to the Bold for the changes on the desktop and add a new record to the desktop for the changes on the Bold.

- *Ignore All Conflicting Items:* Ignores the change and keeps the data the same on both sides.

- *Notify Me When Conflicts Occur:* This option is the safest. Synchronize displays the details of the conflict and lets you resolve it.

- *Device Wins:* Unless you're sure this is the case, you shouldn't choose this option. It tells Synchronize to disregard the changes in the desktop and use handheld changes every time it encounters a conflict.

- *Microsoft Outlook Wins:* If you aren't using MS Outlook, this option is based on your application. This option tells Synchronize to always discard changes on the handheld and use the desktop application change when it encounters a conflict.

   We don't recommend this option because there's no telling on which side you made the good update.

7. **Select the option you want.**

8. **Click OK to save the settings.**

Ready, Set, Synchronize!

Are you ready to synchronize? Earlier in this chapter, we show you ways to define synchronization filters and rules for your e-mail and PIM data. Now it's time to be brave and push the button. You can synchronize one of two ways:

- ✔ **Manually:** Click the Synchronize Now icon.
- ✔ **Automatically:** Choose How Often on the calendar.

Using on-demand synchronization

This portion of Synchronize is a feature that lets you run synchronization manually. Remember that even if you set up automatic synchronization, actual synchronization doesn't happen right away. So, if you make updates to your appointments in Outlook while your Bold is connected to your PC, this feature allows you to be sure that your updates make it to your Bold before heading out the door.

Without delay, here are the steps:

1. **From BDM, click the Synchronize link.**

   The Synchronize screen appears; refer to Figure 15-4. The following four check boxes let you be selective:

   - *Reconcile Messages:* Synchronize your e-mails between Outlook and your Bold.

- *Synchronize Organizer Data:* Include notes, appointments, addresses, and tasks.

- *Run Add-in Actions:* You have third-party applications that require data synchronization between your PC and your Bold.

- *Update Device Date and Time:* You want both the PC and Bold to have the same time. This ensures that you're reminded of your appointments at the same time for both Outlook and your Bold.

 2. **Select the check boxes for the data you want to synchronize.**

 3. **Click the Synchronize button.**

    Synchronize starts running the synchronization, and you see a progress screen. If you set up prompts for conflicts and Synchronize encounters one, a screen appears so that you can resolve that conflict. When finished, the progress screen disappears and the Synchronize screen reappears.

    If you turned on automatic synchronization (see the next section), the items you select in Step 2 automatically sync every time you connect your Bold to your PC.

 4. **Click the Close button.**

Automatic synchronization

How many times do you think you reconfigure your Synchronize setup? Rarely, right? After you have it configured, that's it. And if you're like me, the reason you open BDM is because you want to run Synchronize. So, opening Synchronize and clicking the Synchronize button is somewhat annoying.

To make Synchronize run automatically every time you connect your Bold to your PC, simply make sure that you select the last check box on the Synchronize screen (refer to Figure 15-4) — Synchronize the Selected Items When Your Device Is Connected to the BlackBerry Desktop Manager.

You may be asking, "What items will autosynchronization sync?" Good question. Synchronize automatically syncs the items you selected in the top portion of the Synchronize screen (refer to Figure 15-4). Note that if you make a change, selecting or deselecting an item on the Synchronize screen, only the selected items will be automatically synced the next time you connect your Bold to your PC.

Chapter 16

Syncing the PocketMac Way

· ·

· ·

*I*n Chapter 15, you can find a way of synchronizing your BlackBerry Bold to Windows PC. But what if you're a Mac user?

There are a couple of solutions to synchronizing your Bold data with your Mac. Some are free and others not, but the most obvious one is using PocketMac, which is software you can download from the RIM Web site. And yes, PocketMac is free. This chapter explores PocketMac and how you can synchronize your Mac PIM data into your BlackBerry.

If you're using a corporate BlackBerry Bold that's running under BlackBerry Enterprise Server (BES), some or most of the feature of PocketMac might not work because BlackBerry smartphones running under BES synchronize over the air (OTA) or wirelessly. Too, BES administrators have the ability to disable features of your device, like the microSD.

Meet and Greet PocketMac

PocketMac is almost the equivalent of Desktop Manager in the Windows world. It's used for data synchronization, but you can also use PocketMac for installing software. Because you can install software easily by downloading it directly to your Bold, it's very likely that you're not going to use any other features of the PocketMac other than data synchronization. And that's what I discuss in the rest of this chapter.

In terms of what type of information you can synchronize between your Mac and Bold, here's a quick rundown:

- ✔ **Contacts:** This is defaulted to sync to the Mac Address Book. However, you have the option to choose other applications if you have it on your Mac, such as Entourage or Lotus Notes.

- ✔ **Calendar:** The default setting is to sync to the Mac iCal calendar. However, you have the option to also sync to other applications, such as Entourage, Lotus Notes, Meeting Maker, or Now Calendar.

- ✔ **Tasks:** This defaults to Mac's iCal. Available options are Lotus Notes, Meeting Maker, and Now Tasks.

- ✔ **Notes:** No default is set. You can choose from Entourage, Stickies Notes, OSXMailNotes, and PocketMac Secure Notes.

- ✔ **Bookmarks:** This is not set by default, but you have the option to copy Safari Bookmarks into your BlackBerry Bold's Browser Bookmarks. This option requires software to be installed in your Bold. The software is already available in PocketMac; you only need to click the Install button on the Bookmarks tab. (See Figure 16-3 later this chapter.)

- ✔ **Email:** This allows you to copy messages from your Bold to Mac Mail. Most likely, you don't need this because you can set up Mac's Mail to receive the same e-mail you get on your BlackBerry Bold.

- ✔ **iTunes:** This helps you transfer music from iTunes files to your Bold.

- ✔ **iPhoto:** This helps you transfer photos from iPhoto to your Bold and also import photos from your Bold to iPhoto.

Installing PocketMac

Installing PocketMac is no big deal. Here's what you need to do:

1. **Via your Mac Safari browser, navigate to**

   `http://na.blackberry.com/eng/services/desktop/mac.jsp`

   The preceding link is RIM's download page for PocketMac as of this writing.

   You can easily locate this page by searching for "blackberry pocketmac download" in as search engine. The first hit is most likely the download site.

2. **Download PocketMac and PocketMac Drivers Installation Files.**

The download page should look like Figure 16-1 with two steps linking to downloading PocketMac and its latest drivers.

3. Double-click the installation files.

Both installation files have a .dmg extension. Double-clicking the file will install the application to your Mac. And you should see a PocketMac icon on your Mac's Dock or on the Desktop. (The Dock is the bar of application icons at the bottom of the screen.)

Launching and connecting PocketMac to your Bold

After PocketMac is installed, you should see the launcher icon on the Dock. You establish a connection between your Bold and PocketMac through the USB cable.

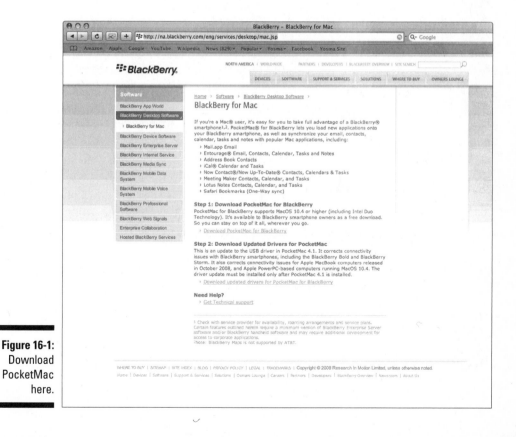

Figure 16-1:
Download
PocketMac
here.

1. **Connect your Bold to your Mac using the USB cable.**

   With the microSD in Bold upon connecting to your Mac, your Bold screen displays a prompt for enabling mass storage mode. It's important that you select Yes to this prompt. iTunes synchronization will not work if you choose No.

2. **On your Bold, select Yes on enabling mass storage prompt.**

3. **Click PocketMac on the Dock.**

   The PocketMac opening screen appears; see Figure 16-2. If you don't see PocketMac on the Dock and you're sure you installed it, try looking at your Desktop. If it's not there, use Finder to look for the application.

Figure 16-2:
PocketMac
Sync
Manager.

   You should see three icons:

   - *.mac:* If you subscribed and have an online .Mac account, you can explore this button. This section is not covered on this book but feel free to navigate this link if you have a .Mac account.

   - *BlackBerry:* Choose this link to specify how you want the synchronization to behave. You'll see sample configuration on the succeeding steps.

   - *Sync:* Click this button to start the data synchronization.

4. **On your Mac, click the BlackBerry icon.**

   The screen shown in Figure 16-3 appears. This is where you specify configuration for the sync. The connection tab is also the place to enter your Bold password if you have one. You can skip Step 5 if you don't have a password on your Bold.

5. **Click the Connection tab and enter your Bold password.**

   Your Bold and PocketMac can now fully communicate with each other.

After your PocketMac can communicate to your Bold, your next step is to make sure the setting for synchronization is how you want it to happen.

Setting Up Synchronization Options

PocketMac does not automatically sync without you telling it to do so. But before you get those trigger happy fingers of yours to click the Sync, though, take a minute to go over how you want the sync to happen.

Click the BlackBerry button, and PocketMac SyncManager displays a screen like the one shown in Figure 16-3. As you can see on this screen, all the goodies you want to sync are displayed on each tab.

Setting up direction of Sync

The first thing that you probably want to know is what direction of sync each of the data behaves. Each tab has simple settings, telling you where the data should come and where it is going. For instance, look at iTunes tab. It should read `Pushing iTunes Music to the BlackBerry from Mac`. If you don't see any description about the direction, that means that you have the ability to control it. And that's where the Advanced Preferences screen comes in.

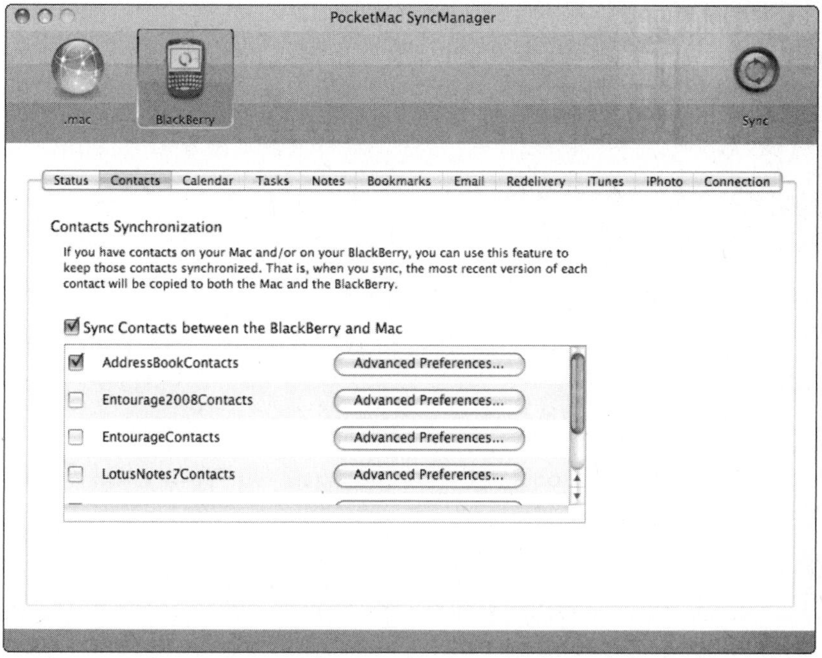

Figure 16-3: Navigate through the tabs to configure data sync here.

As an example, here's how you can change the direction of Contacts synchronization:

1. **Launch PocketMac and connect your Bold to your Mac.**

   The PocketMac SyncManager screen shows up (refer to Figure 16-2). If you need a quick review on how to do this, see the previous section.

2. **On the PocketMac SyncManager screen, click the BlackBerry button.**

   The PocketMac SyncManager screen displays with data tabs. Refer to Figure 16-3.

3. **Click the Contacts tab.**

4. **Click Advanced Preferences button next to AddressBookContacts.**

   The Address Book Advanced Preference screen, as shown in Figure 16-4, appears.

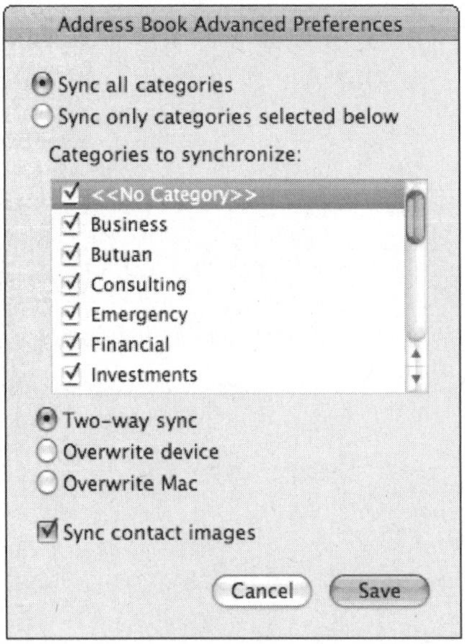

Figure 16-4:
Configure
Advanced
Sync
options
here.

> **Address Book Advanced Preferences**
>
> ⦿ Sync all categories
> ◯ Sync only categories selected below
> Categories to synchronize:
>
> ☑ <<No Category>>
> ✓ Business
> ✓ Butuan
> ✓ Consulting
> ✓ Emergency
> ✓ Financial
> ✓ Investments
>
> ⦿ Two-way sync
> ◯ Overwrite device
> ◯ Overwrite Mac
>
> ☑ Sync contact images
>
> (Cancel)   (Save)

The Advanced Preference button is where to go for all the nitty-gritty details of synchronization for that particular data type. For example, you'll see in Figure 16-4 the ability to pick and choose the contacts you want to sync based on the categories. You could also opt to not include photo images on synching.

Going back to setting the direction of sync, you'll see on the Advanced Preferences screen (refer to Figure 16-4) three radio buttons for such a purpose:

- ✔ **Two-way sync:** This is the default setting. Any updates you made on both Mac and Bold is sync to the other side.

- ✔ **Overwrite device:** This indicates a one-way direction sync from Mac to your Bold.

- ✔ **Overwrite Mac:** This indicates a one-way direction sync from your Bold to your Mac.

Synchronizing iTunes

For a Mac user like you, no need to tell you about iTunes. The app comes with the territory and is probably something you'd be happy to also sync into your Bold, right?

While you're in the PocketMac SyncManager, clicking the iTunes tab gives you a screen similar to Figure 16-5.

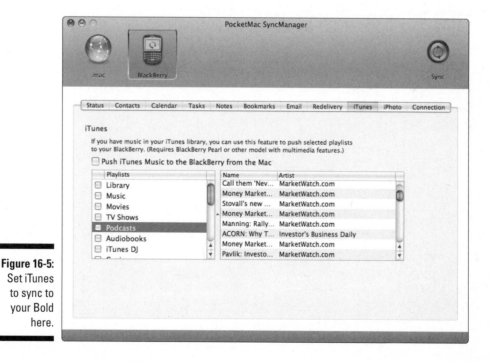

Figure 16-5: Set iTunes to sync to your Bold here.

Select the check boxes you want to be synched to your Bold. Make sure you to select the first check box (Push iTunes Music to the BlackBerry from Mac).

PocketMac copies your iTunes files to the Bold's microSD. If you see that the first check box is disabled, that means that PocketMac didn't see the microSD. Make sure that you have the microSD in your Bold; the reconnect the device and select Yes on the prompt in the device for enabling mass-storage mode.

Ready, Set, Sync

Are you ready to synchronize? Upon clicking the Sync button, you'll see a screen similar to Figure 16-6. Again, nothing complicated lurks here: just a simple status bar indicating the progress of the synch.

Figure 16-6:
Synch is
in-progress
here.

Do not unplug the device in the middle of a synch! You take a serious risk of messing up your data on both your Mac and your Bold. Have a little patience because the synch could take a couple of minutes.

Chapter 17

Switching Devices

· ·

· ·

*W*ouldn't it be nice if you could just make one device's data available to another? That's the future. But right now, RIM (Research In Motion) wants to make switching devices as painless as possible. That's why the Device Switch Wizard is part of the suite of applications in BlackBerry Desktop Manager.

Switching to a New BlackBerry

Switching from an older BlackBerry to your new Bold is no big deal. When you want to transfer application data (e-mails and contacts, for example) to your new Bold, the BlackBerry Desktop Manager (BDM) Device Switch Wizard backs up your old BlackBerry and loads that backup to your new device.

The following steps help you transition from your old device to your new BlackBerry Bold:

1. **On your PC, choose Start➪All Programs➪BlackBerry➪Desktop Manager.**

   The Desktop Manager screen opens, where you can find Device Switch Wizard, as shown in Figure 17-1.

2. **Click the Device Switch Wizard icon.**

   The Device Switch Wizard screen lets you choose whether to switch from BlackBerry to BlackBerry Bold or from non-BlackBerry to BlackBerry Bold. The BlackBerry-to-BlackBerry section tells you to connect your current (old) BlackBerry to your PC.

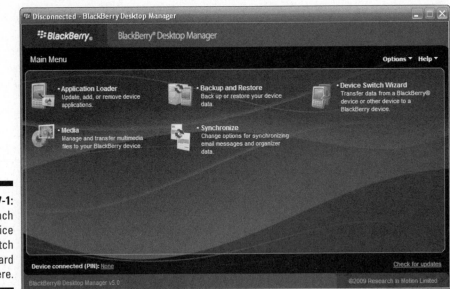

Figure 17-1:
Launch
Device
Switch
Wizard
here.

3. **Connect your old BlackBerry to your PC with the USB cable.**

   Keep your Bold on when connecting.

4. **Click the Start button below Switch BlackBerry Devices.**

   The next screen lets you verify the PINs for both devices — the old BlackBerry on the left and your new Bold on the right, as shown in Figure 17-2. Because you connected only your old BlackBerry, it should be preselected.

   Your BlackBerry PIN isn't a password — it's your BlackBerry smartphone identifier. You can find the PIN by going to Options⇨Status on your BlackBerry.

5. **Decide whether to include user data and third-party applications, and then click Next.**

   If you want all the data, leave the screen untouched; this backs up everything. *Third-party applications* are all the programs you installed — the ones that didn't come with the device originally.

   A status screen appears, showing the progress of the backup operation. When the backup is finished, the next screen prompts you for the PIN of your new BlackBerry Bold.

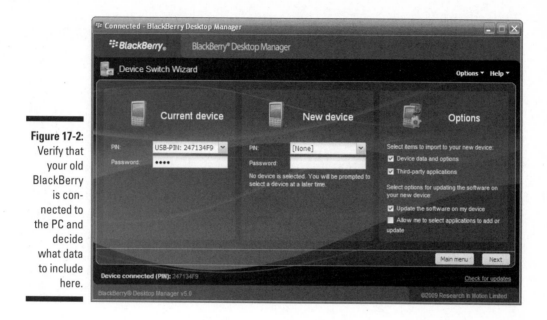

Figure 17-2:
Verify that
your old
BlackBerry
is con-
nected to
the PC and
decide
what data
to include
here.

6. Connect your BlackBerry Bold to your PC with the USB cable.

The next screen, as shown in Figure 17-3, lets you verify that your Bold is connected properly with the PIN displayed. It also asks you for the password. Since data is already backed up from the old BlackBerry, the old device is no longer needed on succeeding steps, and it doesn't matter whether you keep the old one connected.

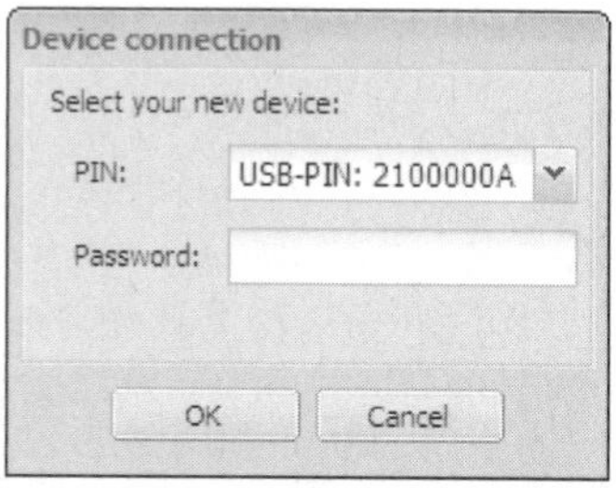

Figure 17-3:
Type your
device
password
here.

7. Enter the password of your Bold, and then click OK.

A screen similar to Figure 17-4 tells you what will be restored to the new device. Nothing has been done to your new BlackBerry Bold yet, and this is your last chance to cancel the process.

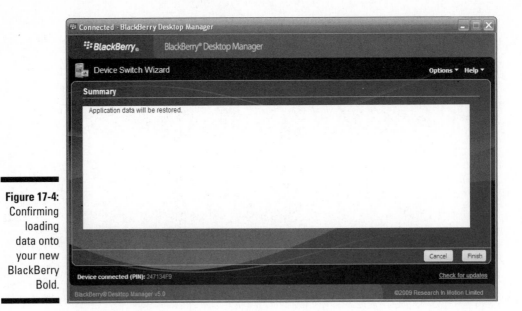

Figure 17-4:
Confirming
loading
data onto
your new
BlackBerry
Bold.

8. **Click Finish.**

   A progress screen shows you the loading process.

9. **When the Success screen appears, click the Close button.**

Switching from a Non-BlackBerry Device

Device Switch Wizard supports two types of non-BlackBerry devices:

- ✔ Palm
- ✔ Microsoft Windows Mobile

This doesn't mean that you can't import your old data if you have another device. The Device Switch Wizard just makes it simpler for these two types of devices. Check out Chapter 15 for synchronization options to your Desktop PIM application if your old device is neither a Palm nor Microsoft Windows Mobile.

Palm device requirements

Your equipment has to meet three prerequisites for Device Switch Wizard to import data from Palm to your BlackBerry Bold:

✔ Your PC must be running Windows 2000 or later.

✔ One of the following Palm Desktop Software versions must be installed on your desktop:

- 4.0.1

- 4.1

- 4.1.4

- 6.0.1

✔ The Palm Desktop Software installed is synchronizing properly with the Palm device.

You can check your Palm user guide for more details about your Palm device and on synchronizing it to your PC. You can also download the user guide from www.palm.com/us/support/index.hml. Navigate to this page by selecting the Palm model you have and the wireless network provider on which it runs.

Windows Mobile device requirements

You need the following things for the wizard to work properly with a Windows Mobile device:

✔ Your PC must be running Windows 2000 or later.

✔ Microsoft ActiveSync versions must be installed on your PC.

✔ The mobile device must run one of the following operating systems:

- Microsoft Windows Mobile 2000, 2002, 2003, 2003SE, or 2005/5.0 for Pocket PC

- Microsoft Windows Mobile SmartPhone software 2002, 2003, or 2003 SE

Running the wizard

Before you run the wizard, make sure that all the requirements for your device are in place.

We recommend hot-syncing or synchronizing your Palm or Windows Mobile device; this ensures that the data you're sending to your Bold is current. Palm Desktop Software, as well as Microsoft ActiveSync, should come with help information on how to hot-sync.

Although the following steps migrate Windows Mobile data into the Bold, the steps are similar for Palm as well. We indicate at what point the steps vary. Do the following to get your other device's data migrated to your new Bold:

1. **Connect both the Windows Mobile device and BlackBerry Bold to your desktop computer.**

2. **On your PC, choose Start⇨All Programs⇨BlackBerry⇨Desktop Manager.**

   The Desktop Manager screen appears; refer to Figure 17-1.

3. **Click the Device Switch Wizard icon.**

4. **When Device Switch Wizard appears, click the image next to Switch from Another Device to BlackBerry Device.**

   The Welcome screen, as shown in Figure 17-5, describes what the tool can do.

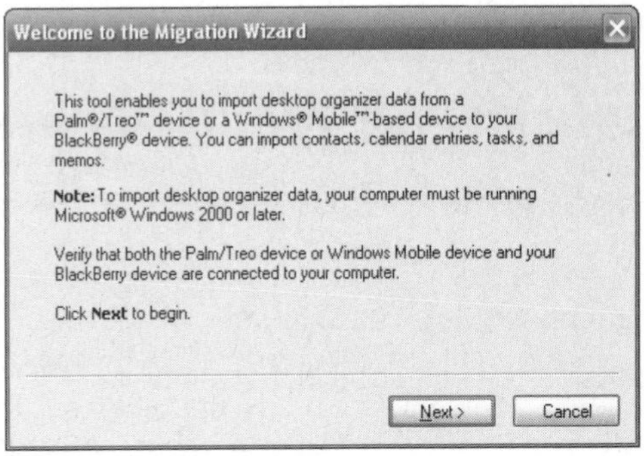

Figure 17-5: Migrating data from a non-BlackBerry device.

> **Welcome to the Migration Wizard**
>
> This tool enables you to import desktop organizer data from a Palm®/Treo™ device or a Windows® Mobile™-based device to your BlackBerry® device. You can import contacts, calendar entries, tasks, and memos.
>
> **Note:** To import desktop organizer data, your computer must be running Microsoft® Windows 2000 or later.
>
> Verify that both the Palm/Treo device or Windows Mobile device and your BlackBerry device are connected to your computer.
>
> Click **Next** to begin.
>
> [Next >] [Cancel]

5. **Click Next.**

   A screen prompts you to decide whether you're migrating from Palm or Windows Mobile, as shown in Figure 17-6. The wizard is intelligent enough to enable the option associated to the connected device, which (in this figure) is a Windows Mobile device.

6. **Click Next.**

   Hot-syncing the Windows Mobile device kicks in at this point. You see a series of screens that appear for each of the application's data, such as Calendar, Contacts, and MemoPad. A sample for the Calendar data is shown in Figure 17-7. The screen indicates what to sync and will be empty if you already performed a hot-sync prior to running the wizard. Otherwise, it will take some time, depending on how much data there is to sync between the device and the desktop software.

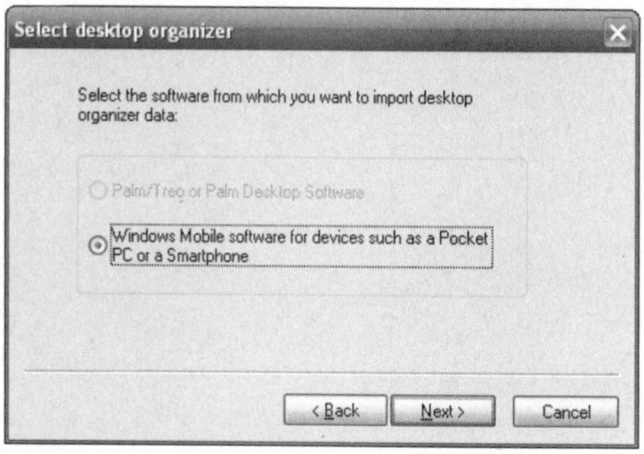

Figure 17-6:
The wizard
has already
selected
which
device to
port.

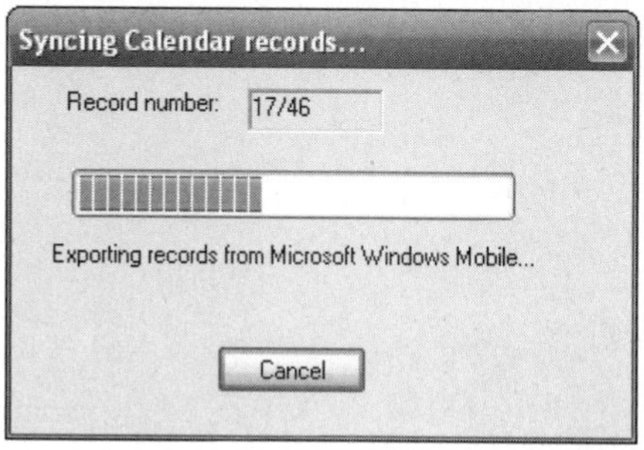

Figure 17-7:
A message
showing
hot-syncing
on your
device.

7. Click OK.

A progress screen appears. Before the data is applied to your Bold, the
wizard prompts you about the change, as shown in Figure 17-8. Click the
following buttons on this screen to either confirm or reject the change:

- *Details:* You want to know the records the wizard is trying to apply.

- *Accept:* You just want the data migrated.

- *Reject:* Ignore this data and continue.

- *Cancel:* Change your mind and cancel the whole operation.

**8. Click the Accept or the Reject button on any confirmation screens that
appear.**

The wizard migrates all the data you accepted. Obviously, the wizard
skips everything you rejected. When the migration process is finished, a
success screen appears.

9. Click Finish.

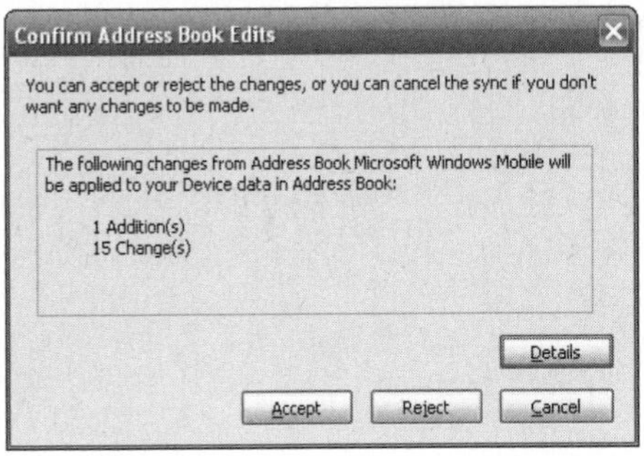

Figure 17-8:
Confirm the
importing of
data here.

Chapter 18

Protecting Your Information

· ·

In This Chapter

▶ Performing a full backup of your BlackBerry Bold data

▶ Restoring from backups

▶ Selecting what data to back up

▶ Backing up and restoring wirelessly

· ·

*I*magine that you left your beautiful Bold in the back of a cab. You lost your Bold for good! Okay, not so good. What happens to all your information? How will you replace all those contacts? What about security?

Take a deep breath and relax a bit. One thing you don't need to worry about is information security — *if* you set up a security password on your Bold, that is. With security password protection enabled, anyone who finds your Bold has only ten chances to enter the correct password; after those ten chances are up, it's self-destruction time. Although the conclusion isn't as smoky as those self-destructing tapes from *Mission Impossible,* your Bold does erase all its information, thwarting your would-be data thief. Sad but safe.

If you haven't set up a password for your Bold, do it *now!* For information on how to do so, see Chapter 3.

Hmm. But how do you get back all the information that was on your Bold? That's what this chapter is all about. Vital information — clients' and friends' contact information; notes from phone calls with clients; and, of course, those precious e-mail messages — shouldn't be taken lightly. Backing up this information is a reliable way to protect it from being lost forever.

If your Bold isn't on a BlackBerry Enterprise Server (BES), BlackBerry Desktop Manager (BDM) is the only way to back up and restore information to and from your desktop PC. And SmrtGuard (pronounced *smart guard*) offers a wireless backup and restore service if you who don't have the habit of plugging your Bold into your PC. If that sounds like you, go to the end of this chapter to find an introduction to SmrtGuard backup and restore solution that can give you peace of mind when it comes to protecting your data.

Accessing Backup and Restore

Backup and Restore — a BDM application — allows you to back up all the sensitive data on your Bold, including contacts, e-mails, memos, to-do's, all personal preferences and options, and more.

For most users, your e-mails are already stored in accounts, such as Gmail or Yahoo! Mail. But you can still back up e-mails just in case.

To back up information on your Bold, follow these steps:

1. **Open BDM on your PC by choosing Start➪All Programs➪BlackBerry➪ Desktop Manager.**

   If you haven't already installed BDM on your PC, see Chapter 15.

2. **Connect your Bold to your PC with the USB cable that came with your Bold.**

   If everything is set up right, a pop-up window on your PC asks you to type your BlackBerry security password. Make sure your Bold is turned on.

3. **Type your password.**

   The Bold connects to the PC.

4. **Double-click the Backup and Restore icon on the BlackBerry Desktop Manager screen.**

   The Backup and Restore screen opens; see Figure 18-1. You're ready to back up data from or restore information to your Bold.

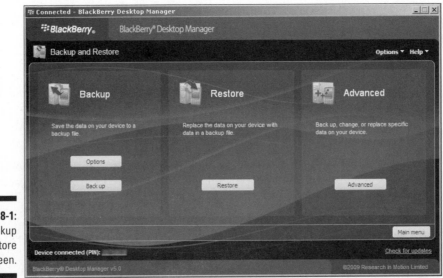

Figure 18-1: The Backup and Restore screen.

Backing Up, BlackBerry Style

Everyone knows that backing up data provides tremendous peace of mind. So do the folks at RIM, which is why backing up your information is quite easy. You can back up your Bold manually or by autopilot.

Backing up your Bold manually

To back up your Bold on demand, follow these steps:

1. **From the BDM screen, double-click the Backup and Restore icon.**

   The Backup and Restore screen appears; refer to Figure 18-1.

2. **Click the Backup button.**

   The dialog box shown in Figure 18-2 appears, where you can name the backup file and figure out where on your PC you want to save it.

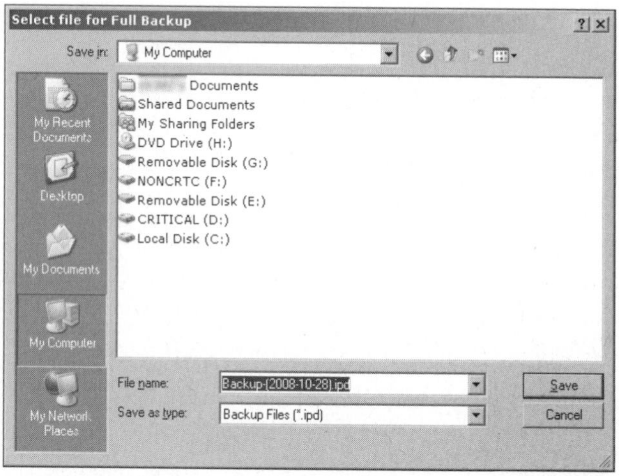

Figure 18-2:
Name and find a home for your backup file.

Select file for Full Backup	? X

Save in: My Computer

- Documents
- Shared Documents
- My Sharing Folders
- DVD Drive (H:)
- Removable Disk (G:)
- NONCRTC (F:)
- Removable Disk (E:)
- CRITICAL (D:)
- Local Disk (C:)

File name: Backup-(2008-10-28).ipd   Save

Save as type: Backup Files (*.ipd)   Cancel

3. **Name your backup file and choose a place to save it.**

4. **Click Save.**

   BDM starts backing up your Bold information to your PC. Figure 18-3 shows the backup progress in the Transfer in Progress window.

   Don't unplug your Bold from the PC until the backup is finished!

   Depending on how much information you have on your Bold, the backup might take ten minutes to finish.

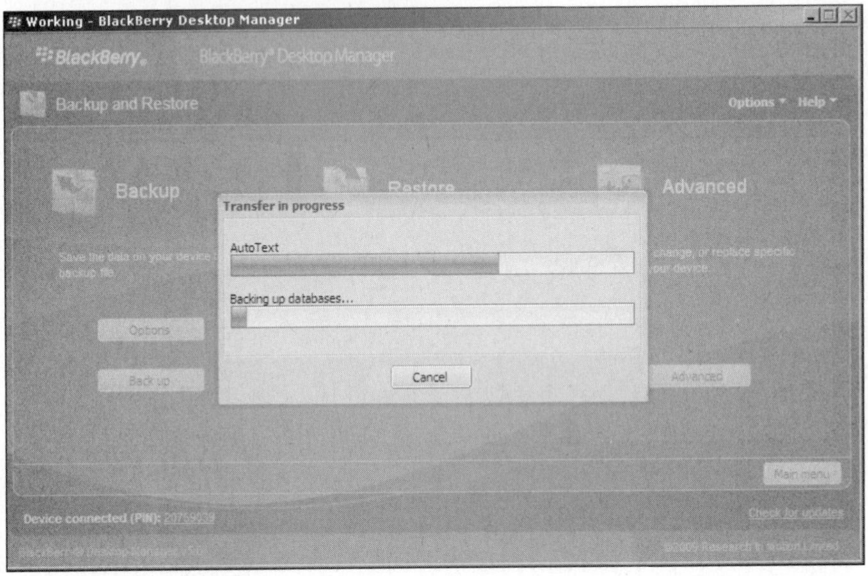

Figure 18-3:
A backup is
in progress.

5. **When the Transfer in Progress window disappears, unplug the Bold from the PC.**

Setting up automatic backups

What's better than backing up your information once? Remembering to back up regularly! And what's better than backing up regularly? You guessed it — running backups automatically. After you schedule automated BlackBerry backups, you can really have peace of mind when it comes to preventing information loss.

Follow these steps to set up an automatic backup:

1. **From the BDM screen, double-click the Backup and Restore icon.**

2. **In the Backup and Restore screen, click the Options button.**

   The Backup Options screen appears, where you can schedule automatic backups. See Figure 18-4.

3. **Select the Back Up My Device Automatically Every *xx* Days check box.**

   Choosing this option allows you to make more decisions (check boxes and options become active), such as how often you want BDM to back up your Bold.

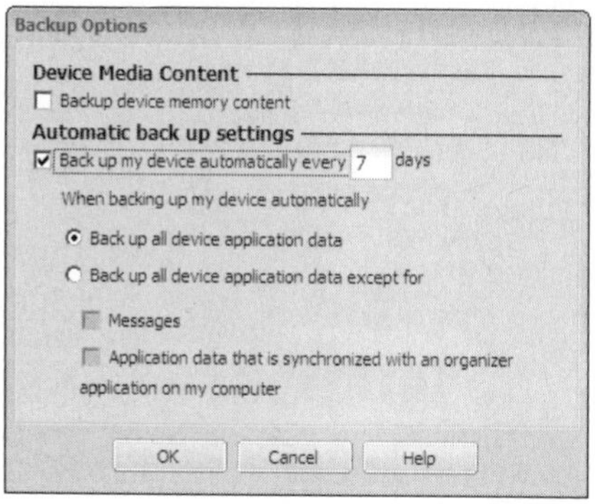

Backup Options

Device Media Content —————————
☐ Backup device memory content

Automatic back up settings —————————
☑ Back up my device automatically every 7   days

When backing up my device automatically

◉ Back up all device application data

○ Back up all device application data except for

☐ Messages

☐ Application data that is synchronized with an organizer
application on my computer

OK   Cancel   Help

Figure 18-4: Set automatic backups here.

4. **In the Days field, enter a number of days between 1 and 99.**

   This interval sets how often your Bold is backed up. For example, if you enter 14, your Bold is backed up every 14 days. Go figure.

5. **Select the Back Up All Device Application Data radio button.**

   This option backs up all the data on your Bold each time autobackup runs.

   Although you can exclude e-mail messages and information (such as from Contacts, to-do's, and memos), we recommend that you back up *everything* each time. That way, when it's time to restore to a new BlackBerry, you get everything where you left off, including e-mail.

6. **Click OK.**

   Now you can go on with your life without worrying when to back up.

   To run a backup, your Bold must be connected to your PC. Make sure that you plug your Bold into your PC once in a while so that autobackup has a chance to back up your information.

Restoring Your Data from Backup Information

We hope that you never have to read this section more than once. A *full restore* means bringing back all your BlackBerry information from a previous backup stored on your PC.

The steps to fully restoring your backup information are simple.

1. **From BDM, double-click the Backup and Restore icon.**

2. **In the Backup and Restore screen, click the Restore button.**

   An Open File dialog box asks where the backup file is on your PC.

3. **Choose a backup file and click Open.**

   A Warning window appears when you're about to do a full restore (see Figure 18-5), alerting you that you're about to overwrite existing information.

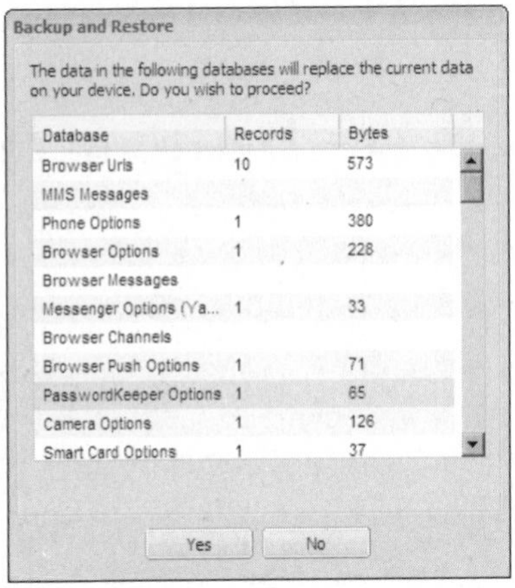

Backup and Restore

The data in the following databases will replace the current data on your device. Do you wish to proceed?

Database	Records	Bytes
Browser Urls	10	573
MMS Messages		
Phone Options	1	380
Browser Options	1	228
Browser Messages		
Messenger Options (Ya...	1	33
Browser Channels		
Browser Push Options	1	71
PasswordKeeper Options	1	65
Camera Options	1	126
Smart Card Options	1	37

Yes   No

Figure 18-5:
Be careful
when
overwriting
existing info.

4. **Click Yes to go ahead with the full restore.**

   A progress bar appears. It might take a while for the full restore to finish.

   Don't unplug your BlackBerry from your PC during this time!

5. **When the progress bar disappears, unplug the device from the PC.**

Protecting Your Data, Your Way

A certain burger joint and BlackBerry both say that you can have it *your way* with their products. Just like you can get your burger with or without all the toppings and condiments, you can choose to not back up and restore things that you know you won't need.

For example, say you accidentally deleted all your Internet bookmarks and now you want them back. *Don't* restore all the information from your last backup. That could be more than 90 days ago (depending upon how often your autobackup runs, if at all). You may unintentionally overwrite other information, such as e-mail or new contacts. You want to restore bookmarks only.

If you lose something in particular, or want something specific restored on your Bold, use the *selective* backup and restore function in BDM to restore only what you need. The same goes with backing up. If you're a big e-mail user, back up just your e-mails but nothing else.

In the following sections, we use the term *databases.* Don't worry; this isn't as technical as you think. Just think of a database as an information category on your Bold. For example, saying, "backing up your Browser bookmarks database" is just a fancy way of saying, "backing up all your Browser bookmarks on your Bold."

Backing up, your way

To back up specific information — selectively — follow these steps:

1. **From BDM, double-click the Backup and Restore icon.**

2. **In the Backup and Restore screen, click the Advanced button.**

   The advanced Backup/Restore screen appears, as shown in Figure 18-6. The right side of the screen shows different information categories, or *databases.*

3. **In the Device Databases list on the right, Ctrl-click the databases you want to back up.**

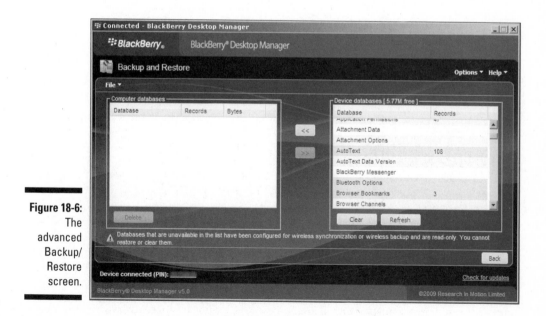

Figure 18-6: The advanced Backup/ Restore screen.

4. **Click the left-pointing (backup) double arrow.**

   This step merely transfers the databases onto your PC; it doesn't save them. That's next.

   A progress bar moves while your Bold is backed up. When the backup transfer is finished, you can see the databases on the left side of the window.

5. **Choose File➪Save As.**

   A file chooser appears.

6. **Name your file and specify where you want to save it on your PC.**

   Make sure to name it something specific so that you know exactly what is in the backup.

You need to manually save the backup file on your PC even after you choose a location for the file in Step 6. Remember that a selective backup doesn't automatically save your backup on your PC.

Restoring, your way

When you're restoring selectively, you must already have a backup file to restore from. Although this may sound obvious, the point here is that you can selectively restore from any backup — auto or manual.

For example, say you have autobackup running every other day and you want to restore only your e-mail messages from two days ago. You don't need to do a full restore; that would overwrite that new contact you put in Contacts only yesterday. Rather, you can use the selective restore method and get back only your e-mail messages.

Looking at backup BlackBerry files

Whether you use the one-button backup method or you manually back up your files, backup files are saved on your PC as IPD files. Are you asking, "Can I read these backup files without a BlackBerry?" The answer is yes! With the third-party product ABC Amber BlackBerry Converter, you can view any IPD file. What's the point? Suppose you lost your BlackBerry but need to read an old e-mail or get contacts from your backup files. This tool allows you to convert anything in your backup file (e-mails, SMS messages, PIM messages, and contacts) into PDF or Word documents. For more information and to try ABC Amber BlackBerry Converter for free, go to www.processtext.com/abcblackberry.html.

To restore your way, follow these steps:

1. **From BDM, double-click the Backup and Restore icon.**

2. **In the Backup and Restore screen, click the Advanced button.**

   The advanced Backup/Restore screen appears; refer to Figure 18-6. The right side of the screen shows your different information categories, or *databases.*

3. **Choose File⇨Open.**

   A window opens so that you can choose which backup file you want to restore from.

   A BlackBerry backup file has an `.ipd` extension.

4. **Select a backup file.**

5. **Click Open.**

   The different information categories, or databases, appear on the left side of the screen. You are now ready for a selective restore.

6. **Select the database(s) you want to restore.**

   You can select multiple databases by Ctrl-clicking the databases you want.

7. **Click the right-pointing (Restore) double arrow.**

   You see a warning window asking whether you want to replace all the information with the data you're restoring. Refer to Figure 18-5.

   If your Bold has the same categories as the ones you're restoring (which is likely), you'll overwrite *any* information you have on your Bold.

   You can confidently move on to Step 8 (clicking the Yes button) if you know the database you're restoring has the information you're looking for.

8. **Click Yes.**

   A progress bar appears while the selected databases are being restored. When the progress bar window disappears, the information categories that you selected are restored on your BlackBerry.

Clearing Bold information, your way

You can also selectively delete information on your Bold from BDM. Suppose you want to clear only your phone logs from your Bold. One way is to tediously select one phone log at a time and press Delete, repeating until all phone logs are gone. However, you could instead delete a database from the advanced Backup/Restore screen by using the Backup and Restore function.

To selectively delete databases on your Bold, follow these steps:

1. **From BDM on your PC, double-click the Backup and Restore icon.**

   The Backup and Restore screen appears.

2. **In the Backup and Restore screen, click the Advanced button.**

   The advanced Backup/Restore screen appears; refer to Figure 18-6. The right side of the screen shows your Bold's databases.

3. **Ctrl-click the database(s) you want to delete.**

   The database is highlighted.

4. **Click the Clear button on the right side of the screen.**

   A warning window asks you to confirm your deletion.

5. **Click Yes.**

   A progress bar shows the deletion. When the progress bar disappears, the information categories you selected are cleared from your Bold.

Backup and Restore Wirelessly

You can even backup and restore wirelessly without being on the BES or going through the trouble of plugging your Bold to your PC via BDM. However, you do have to pay a little bit for this service.

SmrtGuard (www.smrtguard.com/smrtguard.jsp) offers software that you can install on your BlackBerry that can wirelessly back up your data. Currently, SmrtGuard supports backing up contacts, memos, calendar items, call logs, to-do's, SMS, and e-mails.

In addition to its backup and restore capabilities, SmrtGuard also has features to help you locate, recover, and destroy data on your device. SmrtGuard has a BlackBerry tracking feature (a similar concept to LoJack for cars), which helps you determine whether you simply misplaced your device or your device was stolen. If you determine your device was stolen, you can send a signal to have your data destroyed via the SmrtGuard Dashboard on its Web site.

SmrtGuard has three pricing plans:

- Monthly Plan: $3.99 a month
- 6-Month Plan: $22.99 for 6 months
- 12-Month Plan: $44.99 for 12 months

Chapter 19

Installing and Managing Third-Party Applications

. . . .

In This Chapter

▶ Getting started with Application Loader

▶ Installing a BlackBerry Bold application

▶ Uninstalling an application

▶ Upgrading your operating system

. . . .

*T*hink of your Bold as a mini-laptop where you can run preinstalled applications as well as install new applications. You can even upgrade the operating system. (Yup, that's right — your Bold has an OS.)

This chapter starts by introducing Application Loader, which you use to load applications (who'd have guessed?) onto your Bold. Then you'll find ways to install and uninstall apps to and from your Bold. Finally, we explore the portion of Application Loader that allows you to upgrade the OS.

In the Part of Tens, you'll find a few great applications that make your BlackBerry Bold that much more productive.

Accessing Application Loader

In this chapter, as you work closely with your PC and your Bold. On your PC, you use the BlackBerry Desktop Manager (BDM) application, which comes on a CD along with your Bold. You can find Application Loader in BDM.

For an introduction to BlackBerry Desktop Manager, see Chapter 15.

After installing BDM on your PC, do the following to access Application Loader:

1. **On your PC, choose Start➪All Programs➪BlackBerry➪Desktop Manager.**

2. **In BDM, connect your Bold to your PC via your USB cable.**

   If the connection is successful, you see the password dialog box, as shown in Figure 19-1.

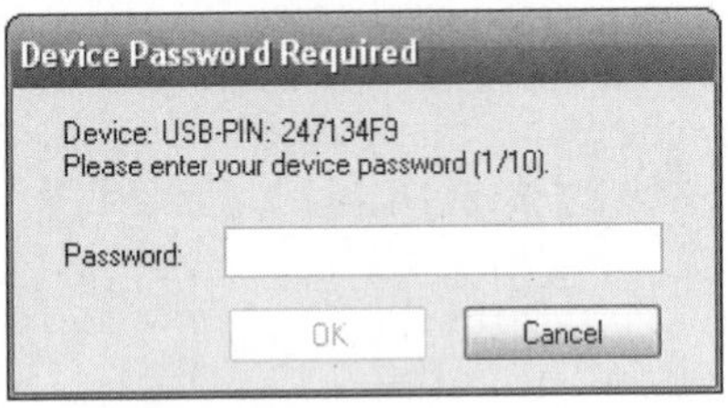

Figure 19-1:
The
password
dialog box
on your PC.

Device Password Required

Device: USB-PIN: 247134F9
Please enter your device password (1/10).

Password: [   ]

[OK]   [Cancel]

   If the connection isn't successful, see whether the USB cable is connected properly to both your PC and your Bold, and then try again. If all else fails, contact the technical support of your service provider.

3. **Enter your password.**

   Your Bold-to-PC connection is complete.

4. **On your PC, double-click the Application Loader icon in BDM.**

   The Application Loader screen opens, as shown in Figure 19-2. At this point, you're ready to use the Application Loader.

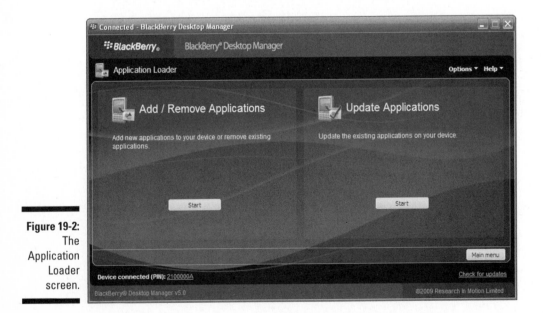

Figure 19-2:
The
Application
Loader
screen.

Installing an Application

In this chapter, we show you how to install iSkoot for Skype for BlackBerry. *iSkoot* is a free application that connects to the Web directly and allows you to use Skype. You can download this application at

```
www.download.com/iSkoot-for-Skype-BlackBerry-/3000-7242_4-10797721.html
```

No matter what application you're installing from your PC to your Bold, the steps are the same. Use the following steps as a guide to installing the application of your choice:

1. **Install the application on your PC.**

   The installation onto your PC varies, depending on the application, so refer to its manual.

2. **Locate the application's ALX file.**

   You can usually find a file with the `.alx` extension in the folder where you installed the application on your PC.

   The ALX file doesn't get installed on your Bold. It tells Application Loader where the actual application file is located on your PC.

3. **Double-click the Application Loader icon in BDM.**

   The Application Loader screen shows. Refer to Figure 19-2.

4. **Connect your Bold to your PC using the USB cable.**

   A screen appears, prompting you to enter your Bold password.

5. **Enter your password (refer to Figure 19-1).**

   After entering your password, the Application Loader screen indicates that your device is connected.

6. **Click the Start button below Add/Remove Applications.**

   The screen listing of what applications to install appears.

7. **Click the Browse button and locate and select the ALX file you want to install.**

   You return to the Application Loader screen, where iSkoot is one of the applications in the list, as shown in Figure 19-3.

8. **Select the application you want to install (for this example, select iSkoot Skype for BlackBerry) and then click Next.**

   A summary screen appears, listing only the applications that will be installed or upgraded.

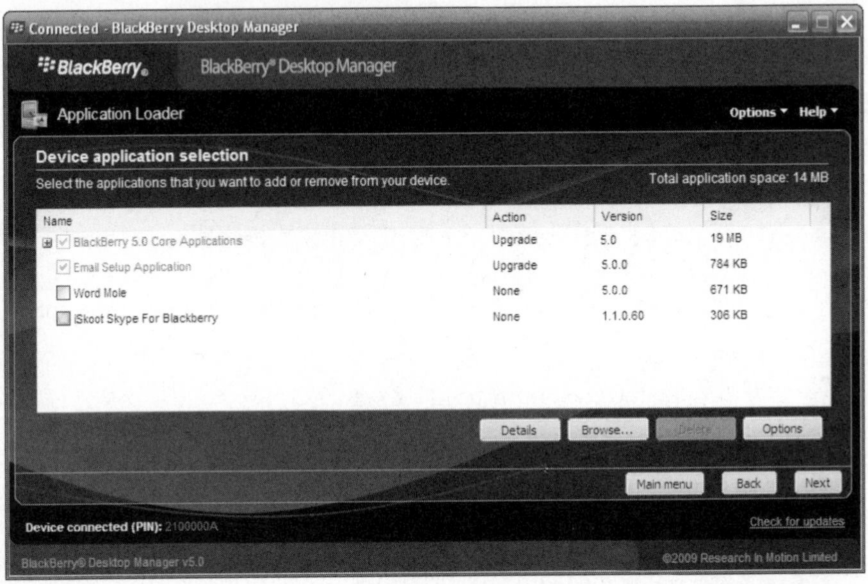

Figure 19-3:
Your
application
is added
to the list
of installed
applications
and can be
installed on
your Bold.

9. Click Finish.

The installation process starts, and a progress window appears. When the progress window disappears — and if all went well — the application is on your Bold. The application should be in the Applications folder of your Bold.

If you get an invalid signature error after clicking the Finish button, the solution depends on how you received your Bold:

✔ **You didn't get your Bold from your employer:** Something is probably wrong with the application. You need to contact the software vendor.

✔ **You got your Bold from your employer:** You don't have permission to install applications on your Bold. The IT department rules the school.

You don't have to use Application Loader to get the goods onto your Bold, though. You can install applications other ways as well:

✔ **Wirelessly, through an *over-the-air (OTA)* download:** See Chapter 10 for more on wireless installations.

✔ **BlackBerry Enterprise Server (BES) wireless install (if your Bold is employer-provided):** In this case, you have no control over the installation process. Your company's BlackBerry system administrator controls which applications are on your Bold.

✓ **Through the PC via Microsoft Installer:** Some application installations automate the preceding steps. All you need to do is connect your Bold to the PC and then double-click the installation file. Applications installation using the Microsoft Installer bear an `.msi` file extension.

Uninstalling an Application

You can uninstall an application in two ways:

✓ Using Application Loader
✓ Using your Bold

We use iSkoot as an example here and assume that you already installed the iSkoot application. You can follow the same steps for uninstalling other applications.

Uninstalling with Application Loader

To uninstall a BlackBerry application, follow these steps:

1. **On your PC, double-click the Application Loader icon in BDM.**

2. **Connect your Bold to your PC using the USB cable.**

   A screen prompting you to enter your Bold password appears.

3. **Enter your password (refer to Figure 19-1).**

   If your handheld isn't connected properly, the PIN of your device won't show up in the Application Loader screen. Connect your Bold to the USB cable and then connect the USB cable to the PC.

   After entering your password, the Application Loader screen indicates that your device is connected.

4. **Click the Start button below Add/Remove Applications.**

   The screen listing of applications appears, similar to Figure 19-3.

5. **Scroll to the application you want to delete and then deselect its check box.**

   For example, when we deselect the iSkoot Skype for BlackBerry check box, the Action column for iSkoot indicates Remove.

6. **Click Next.**

A summary screen that lists the action of the Application Loader shows up. It indicates that iSkoot is to be removed from your Bold.

7. **Click Finish.**

The uninstall process starts, and a progress window appears. When the progress window disappears, you have uninstalled the application from your Bold.

Uninstalling with your Bold

When you don't have access to your PC, you can uninstall an application directly from your Bold. Follow these steps:

1. **Locate the application icon from the BlackBerry Home screen.**

By default, any applications you installed into your Bold are filed in Applications folder of the Home screen. However, you always have the option to move it.

2. **Highlight the application icon and then press the Menu key.**

3. **From the menu that appears, Select Delete.**

4. **In the confirmation dialog box that appears, select Delete to confirm the deletion.**

You're given a choice to restart now or at a later time. After restarting, the deleted application is uninstalled.

Upgrading Your BlackBerry Bold OS

The OS used by Bold has gone through a few revisions. When it comes down to upgrade, the BlackBerry OS update comes from BlackBerry Handheld Software, which is available from three sources:

- ✔ Your network service provider
- ✔ The Research In Motion Web site
- ✔ Your BlackBerry system administrator

Because the handheld software might differ from provider to provider, we recommend getting it from the service provider's Web site. RIM has a download site for different service providers at

http://na.blackberry.com/eng/support/downloads/download_sites.jsp

In this section, we assume that the latest BlackBerry Handheld Software for Bold is already installed on your PC. For help with installing BlackBerry Handheld Software, refer to the instructions that come with it.

If you plan to upgrade your BlackBerry OS and you've installed many third-party applications, check whether those applications support the new OS revision. Most of the time, third-party applications work as-is, but there is always a possibility of losing third-party application data.

Start the upgrade process by doing the following:

1. **Enter your Bold password (if you have set one) into BDM on your PC.**

2. **Double-click the Application Loader icon on the Desktop Manager screen.**

   The Application Loader screen appears, as shown earlier in Figure 19-2.

3. **Click the Start button below Add/Remove Applications.**

   A list of software appears, as shown in Figure 19-4.

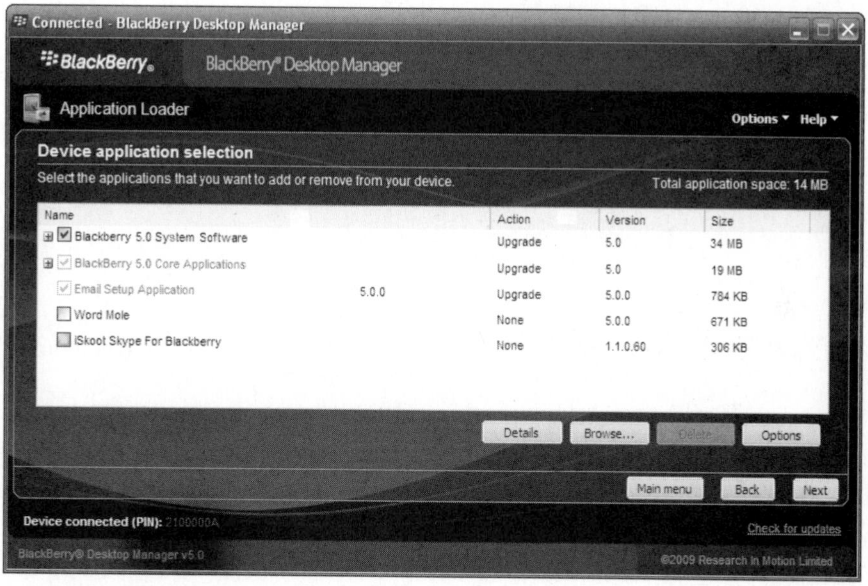

Figure 19-4: Application updates that are available.

> **Connected - BlackBerry Desktop Manager**
>
> **☷ BlackBerry.**   BlackBerry® Desktop Manager
>
> 🖳 Application Loader   Options ▾ Help ▾
>
> **Device application selection**
>
> Select the applications that you want to add or remove from your device.   Total application space: 14 MB
>
> | Name | | Action | Version | Size |
> |---|---|---|---|---|
> | ☑ Blackberry 5.0 System Software | | Upgrade | 5.0 | 34 MB |
> | ☑ BlackBerry 5.0 Core Applications | | Upgrade | 5.0 | 19 MB |
> | ☑ Email Setup Application | 5.0.0 | Upgrade | 5.0.0 | 784 KB |
> | ☐ Word Mole | | None | 5.0.0 | 671 KB |
> | ☐ iSkoot Skype For Blackberry | | None | 1.1.0.60 | 306 KB |
>
> Details   Browse...   Delete   Options
>
> Main menu   Back   Next
>
> Device connected (PIN): 2100000A   Check for updates
>
> BlackBerry® Desktop Manager v5.0   ©2009 Research In Motion Limited

4. **With your mouse, you can opt out of the upgrade by deselecting the OS portion.**

   This appears as BlackBerry 5.0 System Software in Figure 19-4.

The OS is listed only if you need an upgrade — meaning that your BlackBerry OS is out of date. If the OS doesn't appear in the list, the handheld software you installed on the desktop machine is the same as the one installed on your device, or a prior version compared with the one installed on your device.

You also need to back up your device in case something goes wrong with the upgrade. Backup options can be accessed through the Options button.

5. Click Options.

The Options screen appears, as shown in Figure 19-5. This is where you decide whether you want to back up your Bold content before upgrading your OS. We suggest that you do.

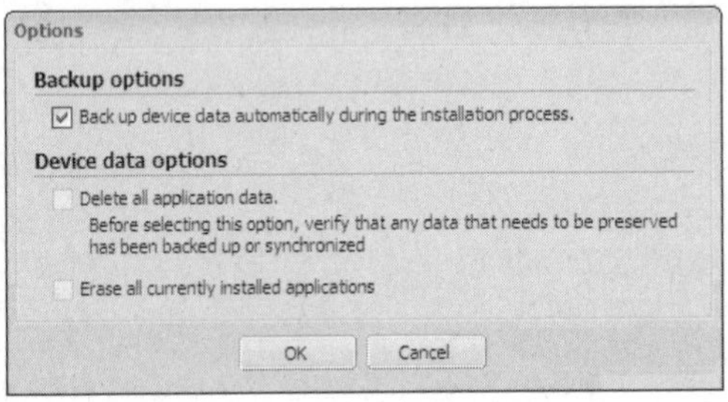

Figure 19-5:
Choose
whether
to back
up before
upgrading.

> **Options**
>
> **Backup options**
>
> ☑ Back up device data automatically during the installation process.
>
> **Device data options**
>
> ☐ Delete all application data.
>   Before selecting this option, verify that any data that needs to be preserved has been backed up or synchronized
>
> ☐ Erase all currently installed applications
>
> [OK]   [Cancel]

6. Select the Back Up Device Automatically During the Installation Process check box and then click OK.

You return to the screen shown in Figure 19-4.

7. Click Next.

A summary page confirms your actions — a final chance for you to either proceed with the OS upgrade or not.

8. Click Finish.

The BlackBerry OS upgrade starts, complete with a progress window that shows a series of steps and a progress bar. The entire process takes about ten minutes, depending on your PC model and the OS version you're upgrading to.

At times during the BlackBerry OS upgrade, your Bold's display goes on and off. Don't worry; this is normal.

When the progress window disappears, the OS upgrade is complete.

Finding and Installing Applications from App Stores

With the success of the iPhone App Store, several copycats sprouted up for other platforms, including the BlackBerry. Broadly, an "app store" is an application that showcases storefronts for applications that you can download directly to your device. Applications can be either free or fee-based:

- **Handango** (www.handango.com): Handango is one of the oldest storefronts that sell applications for mobile devices. It started selling apps through the Web but now has an app store that you can download from its Web site.

- **CrackBerry On-Device App Store** (http://crackberryappstore.com): Partnering with MobiHand, CrackBerry also provides an app store where you can find great applications to download.

- **BlackBerry Application Center:** This is software built by RIM, but the carrier has controls on what shows up on the Application Center.

- **BlackBerry App World:** In contrast with BlackBerry Application Center, with the BlackBerry App World, RIM has full control on what applications are available instead of the carrier.

If you don't have the App World on your Bold, you can download it from the RIM Web site:

```
http://na.blackberry.com/eng/services/appworld
```

Part VI

The Part of Tens

The 5th Wave   By Rich Tennant

In this part . . .

If the earlier parts of this book are the ice cream and hot fudge, this part is the whipped cream and cherry on top. Delve into these three short but sweet chapters to find out how to accessorize your BlackBerry, boost your productivity, and max your BlackBerry experience with useful sites.

Chapter 20

Ten Great Accessories

*T*he BlackBerry retail box contains a few essentials: a battery, a charger, a micro USB cable, a belt clip, and possibly a 1GB microSD card. If you're like most of us, though, you're not satisfied with what is included in the box. In this chapter, you'll find accessories that supplement your Bold well — and the site to get them.

Check out our companion Web site, www.blackberryfordummies.com, for an updated accessories list.

Unify AV Solution

Unify AV Solution is an innovative product of Unify4Life, making smartphones (including your BlackBerry) a universal remote control.

You can find a whole suite of features on the Unify4Life Web site, but a sample includes complete TV listings available in your BlackBerry for informative channel switching. You can purchase it directly from `http://unify4life.com/products.html`.

microSD Card

Your new BlackBerry normally comes with external memory: a *microSD card*. But if you are not satisfied with its capacity, then go hunt for a much bigger one. After all, you want to carry with you a boatload of music and video files, right? Many electronic gadgets use microSD cards, so they're easy to find.

A normal price range at the time of this writing is $30 for an 8GB capacity and $60 for 16GB capacity. Your best bet of finding a good deal is on the Internet. Special promotions come and go, but you can always find a good deal somewhere. So, shop around. And for any Internet purchase, take into consideration the shipping and handling costs plus the vendor's return policy (or lack thereof).

Any brand will do, as long as you make sure that you're buying a microSD card.

Bluetooth Keyboards

As netbooks becomes more popular, people forget that the BlackBerry that they already carry is a "mini netbook." Internet? Check! E-mail? Check! Word docs and Excel? Check! Sure, the screen is a bit smaller and the keyboard is small, but with a little help from a Bluetooth keyboard, your BlackBerry will save you the cost of a netbook and still get it done.

We recommend the Freedom Universal Bluetooth Keyboard, which you can find under Bluetooth keyboards at `shop.crackberry.com` or `Amazon.com`.

Stereo Headsets

Although your new BlackBerry is a stereo music player, it doesn't come with stereo headphones. You will definitely yearn for stereo sound the moment you listen to music or watch video clips. A quick search on the Internet for *BlackBerry + stereo headphones* yields many results. But you want to be able to talk, too.

You could spend $30 to $200. Several good headsets are:

- ✔ BlackBerry stereo headset with noise-isolating ear gels
- ✔ V-MODA Vibe duo in-ear headphones with mic
- ✔ Motorola S9 stereo Bluetooth headset

The best place to get stereo headphones for your BlackBerry is good ol' Amazon: www.amazon.com.

Case and Belt Clip

You have plenty of cases to choose from, with looks ranging from sporty to professional. These cases can set you back anywhere from $20 to $40, which isn't too bad for looking hip.

Here's where you can buy a new case or belt clip:

- ✔ http://shop.crackberry.com
- ✔ www.bberry.com
- ✔ www.blackberryden.com
- ✔ www.blackberrysource.com
- ✔ www.amazon.com

When you buy a new belt case or clip, buy one made specifically for your BlackBerry model. Also, it's important that the case/clip comes with a small magnet. BlackBerry is holster-aware and conserves battery juice. And this magnet is the key for the BlackBerry to know that it is inside a holster.

Screen Protector and Skins

If the protector case described in the preceding section is a bit stressful for your wallet, try the Blackberry Pro high-definition screen protector with mirror effect. That's a mouthful, but for about $10, it protects your screen from scratches. Go to www.accessorygeeks.com.

Other popular bestsellers are skin cases. It comes with many colors and keeps your BlackBerry looking new. The price is usually between $9 and $12. Go to http://shop.crackberry.com or www.accessorygeeks.com.

Extra Battery, Charger, and Charging Pod

An extra battery for your BlackBerry will come in handy if you're a daily user.

Buy your battery only from Research In Motion, at `www.shopblackberry.com`, or an authorized RIM reseller, and not from some unknown vendor. A faulty battery can damage your BlackBerry beyond repair.

Make sure that the battery you buy is for your BlackBerry model. You'll spend around $50 for the extra battery.

If you watch video on your BlackBerry, you know that the battery needs to be charged every couple of hours. And if you're always on the go, you better have a portable charger on hand. The charger included with your BlackBerry is great to carry around town (and the world) because it has multiple adapters for different countries' electric plugs.

If you're a road warrior, get the BlackBerry car charger. It will set you back around $30. To top it off, you can also get a power station or charging pod. It's an accessory that connects to a power supply for charging and at the same time holds your BlackBerry firmly in place in your desk or nightstand. On your nightstand, you can take advantage of the sleep mode which sets the device to not disturb you, such as dimming the light and turning off the LED. The charging pod costs from $12 to $30, depending on how fancy it is.

Make sure that the charger and the charging pod you buy is for your BlackBerry model.

You can get a BlackBerry car charger and charging pod from the following sites:

- `http://shop.crackberry.com`
- `www.blackberrysource.com`
- `www.amazon.com`
- `www.shopblackberry.com` (RIM's official store)

Full Keyboard

If you write long e-mails or draft long proposals on your BlackBerry, a full-sized keyboard is perfect for you. You'll save time and your thumbs.

You have the choice of Bluetooth and non-Bluetooth connection options. We recommend Bluetooth to minimize the clutter. A Bluetooth keyboard is the most convenient option for the obvious reasons: You don't have to carry cables, and you can position your BlackBerry any way you want.

For less than $100, you can own the cool iGo Stowaway Ultra-Slim Bluetooth keyboard, available at `www.amazon.com`. Or you can buy the ThinkOutside Stowaway Shasta Bluetooth keyboard for BlackBerry, available at `http://yahooshopping.com` for $45.

External Speaker

BlackBerry comes with a speaker, but if the sound quality just isn't good enough for your listening taste, an external Bluetooth speaker can bring your outdoor listening to the next level. We recommend the following:

- Blueant M1 Bluetooth stereo speakers
- Motorola EQ5 wireless travel stereo speaker

For about $110, you can get either of them from `http://shop.crackberry.com`.

Car Mount

To complete your BlackBerry car experience, mount your BlackBerry in your car. The market offers many products that range from $15 to $30. You can search from major sites. You can also get a car mount from these BlackBerry sites:

- `http://shop.crackberry.com`
- `www.blackberrysource.com`
- `www.amazon.com`

Make sure that the product you're choosing supports your BlackBerry model.

The latest wireless speakerphone from RIM is BlackBerry Visor Mount SpeakerPhone VM-605. It's a Bluetooth speakerphone that you attach to your car's visor, just like you attach your garage door opener. For $99, you can get it at `www.shopblackberry.com`.

If you like to accessorize your Bold, or purchase Bold, check out site promotions. Every now and then, a site like CrackBerry.com runs promotions and gives out big discounts. Also look at RIM's website at `www.shopblackberry.com`. They usually have accessory bundles for your Blackberry model.

Chapter 21

Ten Must-Have Applications

The industry of BlackBerry software is growing at a dizzying rate. In this chapter, we introduce ten must-have applications that make your BlackBerry Bold experience that much better.

There will be no specific reviews to quote here, but these choices are the results of our quest to find programs that people use, discerned from discussions with BlackBerry users, postings on message boards, and commentaries in the public domain. The applications featured here are just the tip of the iceberg. By all means, feel free to surf the Internet because by the time this book is published, more software will likely be available. And don't forget to visit our Web site at www.blackberryfordummies.com.

SmrtGuard, Your BlackBerry Guardian

Have you ever wondered what would happen to your data if you lost your BlackBerry? Data such as your sensitive e-mails, your phone call histories, your contacts, and all your appointments? It's scary to think of a stranger getting to know you through your e-mails and knowing what you're going to do next. These same thoughts haunt us as well. Thankfully there's SmrtGuard (formerly known as BerryFinder.com), which provides the following tools:

- ✔ **Locate and "LoJack" your BlackBerry:** With no GPS signal required, you can track your Bold's approximate location to determine whether you simply misplaced it or someone actually stole it.

- ✔ **Wireless data backup:** This is another must-have feature that SmrtGuard provides. If you self-destroyed your data and don't have a backup, the scheduled wireless backup of your PIM data will come in handy. From the SmrtGuard Web site (www.smrtguard.com), you can even see and browse through your backed up data and export it to a file (an Excel file or text file).

- ✔ **Sound the homing beacon:** If you simply misplaced your BlackBerry but can't find it by calling because you muted it, don't worry. Just send a homing beacon, and your BlackBerry will emit a loud sound regardless of your Profile setting. We wish our remote controls had this feature!

- ✔ **Self-destroy in five seconds:** Okay, perhaps not in five seconds, but you can decide when to destroy all your BlackBerry data. That includes e-mails, contacts, appointments, to-dos, memos, phone logs, text messages, and even all the files on your microSD card.

Always protect your BlackBerry Bold with a password. That way, if your Bold gets into the wrong hands, your data will be self-erased after ten unsuccessful password entries. However, it doesn't delete the files on your microSD card. This is why SmrtGuard is so helpful.

With SmrtGuard by your side, you can concentrate on your business instead of worrying about your BlackBerry data being stolen. You can get it for $3.99 a month, or $49.99 for a whole year's subscription. There is also a 10-day free trial. You can check it at www.smrtguard.com.

TetherBerry

Subscribing to a mobile broadband for your laptop is quite expensive. TetherBerry provides an inexpensive solution for you by using your BlackBerry Bold. You can check for details at www.tetherberry.com.

On their Web site, you can order the application for a one-time fee of $49.95. That's spare change considering that you get yourself a 3G connectivity using your Bold down to your laptop. There's a 30-day money back guarantee if you are not satisfied.

VibAndRing

Don't like the fact that you can't get your BlackBerry to alert you the way you want? Do you need custom vibration when a phone call comes in?

Time to get your hands on VibAndRing. With it, you can customize how many vibrate "bursts" you get before it starts ringing and how long each vibration lasts.

To download a free trial, go to www.mobihand.com and search for *vibandring*.

Viigo for BlackBerry

If there's an application that gets used on a daily basis, it's Viigo. Viigo is an RSS reader. The application is really a one-stop shop for almost all information you need. Whether you want news, blogs, podcasts, weather info, entertainment, finance, flight info and many, many more.

Download Viigo for free from your BlackBerry at http://www.viigo.com.

PeeKaWho — Email/SMS Alerts

Ever find yourself in the middle of browsing or composing an e-mail and all of a sudden, a new e-mail finds its way to your inbox? Instead of stopping what you are doing and heading to the inbox, with PeeKaWho, you can get a preview of the e-mail or SMS message that has just arrived, and you can dismiss, mark as read, go to your inbox, or delete the message — all right from the alert pop-up.

To find out more, go to www.smrtguard.com/peek.jsp.

Digby

For those online shoppers who need to shop all the time, Digby is the program for you. You can download it for free to start browsing its growing selections. What we don't like is that you have to enter your personal information on the BlackBerry instead of having the option to enter it on the PC first. To try it, point your BlackBerry browser to www.digby.com/download.

Google Talk Mobile and Yahoo! Messenger Mobile

If you currently use Google Talk or Yahoo! Messenger on your PC, both mobile versions are a must-download to keep up with your buddies no matter where you are. To download, point your BlackBerry browser to

- ✔ **Google Talk Mobile:** www.blackberry.com/GoogleTalk
- ✔ **Yahoo! Messenger Mobile:** www.blackberry.com/YahooDownload

iSkoot Skype Client

If you are a big fan of Skype, now you don't have to be at your computer to use the service. The folks at iSkoot make it possible for you to fully utilize Skype from your BlackBerry. Calling a Skype buddy? No problem. Chatting with your Skype friends? That's what this program is for. Plus, it's free! To download it from your PC, go to www.iskoot.com.

Nobex Radio Companion

FM radio on your BlackBerry? That's right. With Nobex, you can get streaming radio on your BlackBerry for free (for now)!

Over a hundred stations are available for streaming, and it works best if you have a 3G or EVDO network (the faster the network, the better your experience with Nobex).

To find out more, go to www.nobexrc.com.

Ascendo Money

Ascendo Money is one of the best-selling, best-rated, and most comprehensive personal finance managers for BlackBerry. You can manage your checkbook, track your expenses, sync with your PC, and integrate with popular finance PC applications such as Quicken and MS Money. It costs $29.95, but you can also get a free trial. You can download Ascendo Money from your PC by going to www.handango.com.

Index

Business/Accounting & Bookkeeping

Bookkeeping For Dummies
978-0-7645-9848-7

eBay Business
All-in-One For Dummies,
2nd Edition
978-0-470-38536-4

Job Interviews
For Dummies,
3rd Edition
978-0-470-17748-8

Resumes For Dummies,
5th Edition
978-0-470-08037-5

Stock Investing
For Dummies,
3rd Edition
978-0-470-40114-9

Successful Time
Management
For Dummies
978-0-470-29034-7

Computer Hardware

BlackBerry For Dummies,
3rd Edition
978-0-470-45762-7

Computers For Seniors
For Dummies
978-0-470-24055-7

iPhone For Dummies,
2nd Edition
978-0-470-42342-4

Laptops For Dummies,
3rd Edition
978-0-470-27759-1

Macs For Dummies,
10th Edition
978-0-470-27817-8

Cooking & Entertaining

Cooking Basics
For Dummies,
3rd Edition
978-0-7645-7206-7

Wine For Dummies,
4th Edition
978-0-470-04579-4

Diet & Nutrition

Dieting For Dummies,
2nd Edition
978-0-7645-4149-0

Nutrition For Dummies,
4th Edition
978-0-471-79868-2

Weight Training
For Dummies,
3rd Edition
978-0-471-76845-6

Digital Photography

Digital Photography
For Dummies,
6th Edition
978-0-470-25074-7

Photoshop Elements 7
For Dummies
978-0-470-39700-8

Gardening

Gardening Basics
For Dummies
978-0-470-03749-2

Organic Gardening
For Dummies,
2nd Edition
978-0-470-43067-5

Green/Sustainable

Green Building
& Remodeling
For Dummies
978-0-4710-17559-0

Green Cleaning
For Dummies
978-0-470-39106-8

Green IT For Dummies
978-0-470-38688-0

Health

Diabetes For Dummies,
3rd Edition
978-0-470-27086-8

Food Allergies
For Dummies
978-0-470-09584-3

Living Gluten-Free
For Dummies
978-0-471-77383-2

Hobbies/General

Chess For Dummies,
2nd Edition
978-0-7645-8404-6

Drawing For Dummies
978-0-7645-5476-6

Knitting For Dummies,
2nd Edition
978-0-470-28747-7

Organizing For Dummies
978-0-7645-5300-4

SuDoku For Dummies
978-0-470-01892-7

Home Improvement

Energy Efficient Homes
For Dummies
978-0-470-37602-7

Home Theater
For Dummies,
3rd Edition
978-0-470-41189-6

Living the Country Lifestyle
All-in-One For Dummies
978-0-470-43061-3

Solar Power Your Home
For Dummies
978-0-470-17569-9

Available wherever books are sold. For more information or to order direct: U.S. customers visit www.dummies.com or call 1-877-762-2974.
U.K. customers visit www.wileyeurope.com or call (0) 1243 843291. Canadian customers visit www.wiley.ca or call 1-800-567-4797.